Free-Wheeling Easy

in ^ Western Pennsylvania
and around

Motor-Free Trails for Cyclists, Walkers, and Cross-Country Skiers

Third Edition

Rail-trails, greenways, towpaths, and other motor-free bicycle touring routes in western Pennsylvania and nearby areas

Mary Shaw
Roy Weil

A portion of the purchase price of this guide supports trail development

Shaw-Weil Associates

Administrative Stuff

We are pleased to provide selected highlights on the World-Wide Web. Point your web browser at URL http://spoke.compose.cs.cmu.edu/fwe/fwe.htm

Table of Contents

On Safty, Judgment, and Personal Responsibility

We compiled this guide to support both individual trail users and the development of the trail systems. We have made a serious effort to present accurate descriptions and to confirm trail status. However, we are human, trails change with time, and we occasionally receive incorrect information. Weather, wear, construction, vandalism, changes in land status, and other forces can alter conditions, erode trail surfaces, create obstacles, or even close trails. Therefore we cannot be responsible for discrepancies between these descriptions and actual trail conditions. If you do encounter any discrepancies, please let us know.

Under no circumstances do we recommend that you trespass on private land or violate any laws. Nor do we recommend that you do anything dangerous: some trail activities have intrinsic risks, for which you must assume responsibility. Additional risks are inherent in the mix of activities that take place on the trails. Everyone who sets out on a trip assumes personal responsibility, not only for his or her own safety, but also for the safety of others on the trip. Ultimately the quality of your experience depends mostly on your own common sense and good judgment.

Acknowledgments

This guide would not be possible without the trails. Most of these trails exist only because of the dedication of many volunteers. These volunteers do everything from identifying possible routes, through negotiating land acquisition and public relations, to trail clearing, trash removal, ongoing maintenance, sign-making, and landscaping. We thank them all. Your favorite trail has something for you to do, too—give them a call.

We appreciate the support we've received from trail managers and other trail developers. Many have been generous with time and information. In particular, we thank the following for discussions, explanations, advice, and comments on the revised trail descriptions in this edition: Bob McKinley of the Regional Trail Council (Yough River North), Larry Ridenour of Steel Valley Trail, Hank Parke of Somerset County Rails to Trails (Allegheny Highlands in PA), Darla Cravotta of the City of Pittsburgh, Dave Wright, Dick Quasey, and Marshall Fausold of the Montour Trail Council, Larry Brock and Gerry Hebner of Allegheny Highlands Trail in Maryland, Malcolm Sias and Jack Paulik of the Five Star Trail Chapter of RTC, Tim Banfield of Mon Yough Trail Council, Doug Hoehn of Ohiopyle State Park (Yough River South), John Stephen of Friends of the Riverfront (Three Rivers), Linda Boxx, Bill Metzger, Sandra Finley, and George Tkach of the Allegheny Trail Alliance, Laurie Lafontaine of C&I Trail Council (Ghost Town), Michael Kuzemchak of Indiana County Parks (Ghost Town), Dee Columbus of CCCRA (Ghost Town), George Burns of PA DCNR, David Love of the Clarion-Little Toby Trail, Tim Kelly of the Allegheny Valley Land Trust (Armstrong Trail), Barry A Beere of PennDOT, Ron Bennett of the Butler-Freeport Community Trail Council, John Wallach of French Creek Recreational Trails (Ernst), Keith D. Shy of Metro Parks Serving Summit County (OH), Stephen D. Coles of Cleveland Metroparks, Brenda Adams-Weyant of Allegheny National Forest (Buzzard Swamp), Frederic Ammerman of the Clearfield to Grampian Trail, Rodney G. Daum of the Corps of Engineers (Kellettville to Nebraska Trace), Mark Abbott of the North Bend Trail Foundation, Tom Grote of the Loyalhanna Watershed Association (PW&S), Matthew A. Marcinek of Presque Isle State Park, John Houghton of Pymatuning State Park, JoAnne McBride of Lawrence County Tourism Bureau (Stavich), Dan Glotz of Warren County Planning, Nancy Brown of C&O Canal National Historical Park, Dave Moore of Fort Frederick State Park (Western MD RR), Megan Hess-Kalp of Salt Lick Township (Indian Creek), John Gardner (Greene County), and staff at Moraine, Oil Creek, and Ohiopyle State Parks and Forbes State Forest, District 4.

Dick Wilson suggested some valuable phrasing, Catherine Copetas give valuable advice on production, and J.W. Schoyer explained marketing. Jean Weil checked the text for internal consistency. Naturally, all these folks are responsible for corrections but not for any remaining misinformation.

Collecting information for a guide isn't quite the same thing as going out for a ride. We spent extra time driving around finding access points, we chased rumors about trails that sometimes led to unexpected riding conditions, and we rode a lot of unfinished ballast and side trails looking for trail routes. Thanks to Katherine Lynch, Don Bowman, Gordon and Jan Bugby, Weimard and Virginia McQuon, Dave and Ann Marschik, Millard and Julie Underwood, Barney Collins, George Schnakenberg, Paul Gleichauf, Frank and Laurie Bruns, and Kathy Ezar for putting up with all this on multiple occasions.

Freewheeling Easy

If you like to bicycle but you don't like to ride in automobile traffic or on rough, steep, undeveloped trails, this guide is for you. You will find trails for short family outings and trails for multi-day touring. If you like to walk or skate on wide smooth gentle paths, or if you're looking for easy cross-country skiing, you will also find this useful. The book provides information about trails and routes that are

- easy to ride or walk,
- off-limits to automobile traffic
- reasonably level

Depending on their history, these routes are variously called rail-trails, bike paths, greenways, towpaths, and linear parks. Some are paved, some dirt or crushed stone; a few have short excursions onto roads with very little (and very slow) traffic. Most are suitable for touring bikes with medium to wide tires and for hybrid or mountain bikes. We do include a few areas that are more challenging; they will take you to more intimate places, but they require a higher level of technical bike handling skill.

When we talk to people about these trails, their most common questions are "Is there a trail near where I live?", "How do I find that trail?", "What's the trail like?", "What facilities are there?", and "Can I buy lunch/rent bikes/swim nearby?". We emphasize this kind of information in the trail descriptions. That's why this guide is different.

Within western Pennsylvania or an easy drive into nearby regions, you will find dozens of trails that are closed to motor vehicles and that are graded and surfaced for easy bicycling, walking, and similar activities. Some are short, suitable for a morning, an evening, or a short day with the family. Some are longer, good for a full day's sport touring or several days of camping.

We personally rode or walked virtually all the sections of trails that we report as developed (and many that are not). We checked almost all the trails in this edition during 1998. Trail conditions change with time, though, so what you find may differ. On the one hand, the trail developers may have extended the trail. On the other hand, trails deteriorate over time because of weather and use; they need periodic maintenance; and occasionally they are closed. Trails along rivers are especially susceptible to flood damage. Although we also mention some mountain bike areas for your convenience, we have only ridden some of these.

Several trail organizations are very active now, and they need continuing support. When you find a trail you like, consider supporting its association; they need volunteer time and materials as well as money. The trail descriptions tell you how to find these organizations. You'll find something useful and fun to do with them. Give them a call.

Finding the Way

This guide covers western Pennsylvania and nearby areas. We include most of the trails longer than 2-3 miles that are west of US219 in Pennsylvania. We also include several longer trails outside that area but still within a two-and-a-half hour drive of Pittsburgh.

We group the trails in five clusters. The first covers the Pittsburgh area, the second covers trails to the south and east, primarily the Laurel Highlands, the third covers trails to the north in the upper Allegheny River valley, the fourth includes trails to the west and northwest at the edge of Pennsylvania and in northeastern Ohio, and the fifth covers the upper Monongahela valley and nearby areas of northern West Virginia.

We have tried to write directions so that you can find the trailheads with this book plus a state highway map. We usually begin with directions to some obvious location in the vicinity, such as a major intersection, then give detailed directions from there to each trailhead. On the trails themselves, the route is usually obvious. Bicycle routes that use roads often have extensive directions or cue sheets so you don't go astray at intersections. You won't need such instructions for these trails, because the motor-free trails have few intersections or decision points.

For extending trips, exploring nearby, or finding short-cuts to trailheads, you need more detail. We like the *Pennsylvania Atlas and Gazetteer* by DeLorme Mapping Co. It covers the entire state with topographic maps at 2.4 miles to the inch, it includes most roads, and it is good about both road names and numbers. For Pittsburgh, Allegheny County, and surrounding areas, *The Complete Atlas of Southwestern Pennsylvania and Metropolitan Pittsburgh* by Marshal Penn-York is good. Either is about $15 at many bookstores. For computer users, DeLorme also produces a CD-ROM called *Street Atlas USA* for both Macintosh and Windows, about $40. With this you can print maps of selected areas at the scale of your choice, though labeling and page segmentation are awkward.

For detailed information about the terrain, get the US Geological Service topographic maps for the area of interest, specifically the 7.5 minute series printed at a scale of 1:24,000 or about 1" to 0.4 miles. Many outfitters and sporting goods stores now stock these maps. DeLorme also offers topo maps in the four CD-ROM set TopoUSA, about $90, though the contour interval of 50' is a bit large for this area.

The Pennsylvania Chapter of the Rails-to-Trails Conservancy publishes *Pennsylvania's Great Rail-Trails*, which gives a very brief description and sketch map for each of the rail-trails in Pennsylvania. You can find it for $12.95 at many bike shops and bookstores. You can order it from Rails-to-Trails Conservancy, PA Chapter, 105 Locust St, Harrisburg PA, 17101 (add sales tax and $1.25 for shipping). The Rails-to-Trails Conservancy publishes other guides, as well.

In addition to the standard free highway map, PennDOT publishes a free road biking map that covers the whole state. They also have detailed quadrant maps for $1.25 each or $4.50 for the set of four, plus sales tax (specify northeast, southeast, northwest, or southwest quadrant). Most of the routes on these maps are through routes on high-ways—sometimes busy highways. We don't find these useful, but if you want them, write PennDOT Distribution Services Unit, PO Box 2028, Harrisburg PA 17105, with check or money order made out to PennDOT Sales Store.

For information on ordering copies of this guide by mail, see page 249.

Trail Rules and Etiquette

Trail rules are mostly based on common sense. They typically include points such as:
- Non-motorized uses only. Motorized wheelchairs are permitted on many trails, and snowmobiles are permitted on only a few trails.
- Keep to right, allowing room for faster people to pass. If you stop, move off the trail; don't park bikes on the trail surface.
- When there's snow on the ground, don't walk in cross-country ski tracks and don't ski where hikers have broken the trail.
- Pass on the left after giving audible signal. Bicycles yield to other users; every-one yields to horses.
- Don't litter, dump, or otherwise misuse trail land. Carry out any litter you find.
- As guests in the neighborhood, respect the rights and privacy of landowners.
- Keep pets on leash no longer than 6'. Clean up after your pet.
- Assume horses are prohibited unless explicitly allowed.
- Trails open from sunrise to sunset only; no overnight camping, open fires, or alcoholic beverages.

If rules for a trail differ significantly from these, we note the special rules.

Pennsylvania law requires children under the age of 12 to wear approved helmets when operating or riding on a bicycle, tricycle, or similar vehicle. This law applies on motor-free trails as well as roads. Helmets are a good idea for adults, too.

Many trails have rugged, remote sections. Be prepared for mechanical and medical problems. Go with a friend. Carry tools and a first-aid kit, and know how to use them.

Horseback riding is permitted on some trails. If horseback riding is permitted, it's usu-ally *beside* the finished surface, not *on* it. Horses are usually excluded from picnic areas and campgrounds, except those established specifically for equestrian use.

Many trails pass close to or through private land. In some cases the relations between the trail and the neighbors are delicate. Respect the privacy and property of all nearby landowners and residents.

Trail	Finish Dist	Unfin Dist	Surface	Rest Rooms	Food	Bike Rental	Horses OK	Pg #
Trails In and Around Pittsburgh								**15**
Three Rivers Heritage Trails		10.0						19
North Shore	3.4		paved/packed crushed stone					22
Eliza Furnace	2.5		paved	y	y			25
Washington Landing	1.4		packed crushed stone		y			19
Pittsburgh Cultural District	0.5		paved		y			19
South side	0.8		packed crushed stone		y			19
Ft Duquesne/Point Park	0.5		paved					20
Steel Valley	0	12.5		y	y	y		27
Montour		12.9						29
Robinson-Moon-Findlay-N Fayette	11.4		packed crushed stone	y	y	y	y	31
Quicksilver-McDonald	3.0	3.0	packed crushed stone	y	y			37
Cecil	5.9		packed crushed stone	y	y		y	39
Arrowhead	3.2	2.5	paved	y	y	y		44
Bethel Park Spur	0.9	1.7	packed crushed stone		y			48
South Park-Jefferson-Clairton	1.5	8.5	packed crushed stone	y	y			50
Shorter Trails and Bike Lanes								52
Schenley Park	1.9		packed crushed stone	y				52
Beechwood Blvd	4.0		bike lane	y	y			53
Lawrenceville	0.7		packed crushed stone					54
Riverview Park	2.1		bike lane	y				54
North Park	5.0		bike lane	y				55
South Park	2.2		bike lane	y		y		55
Trails East and South: Laurel Highlands								**57**
Youghiogheny River Trail North	42	1	packed crushed stone/shared road	y	y	y	y	60
Youghiogheny River Trail South	28		packed crushed stone	y	y	y		75
Allegheny Highlands Trail								83
Maryland		20.2						84
Upper Pa		11.0						86
Meyersdale-Pinkerton	21.3		packed crushed stone/gravel	y	y	y		88
Pinkerton-Confluence		7.7						91
Chesapeake & Ohio Towpath	181.5	3.0	dirt	y	y	y	y	94
Western Maryland	10.0	10.3	paved	y	y	y		99
Five Star Trail	6.1	7.0	packed crushed stone/shared road	y	y	y		101

Trail	Finish Dist	Unfin Dist	Surface	Rest Rooms	Food	Bike Rental	Horses OK	Pg #
Sheepskin		33.0						106
Indian Creek Valley Trail	6.0		packed crushed stone/shared road	y	y			107
Mountain Streams II System	10.0		dirt/gravel				y	110
PW&S Railroad Bike Trail	34.3		dirt/gravel	y		y		114
Trails North: Upper Allegheny Valley								**119**
Ghost Town Trail	15.5	4.0	packed crushed stone	y	y	y	y	121
Lower Trail	11.0		packed crushed stone	y	y		y	130
Roaring Run Trail	2.0	3.1	packed crushed stone					134
Armstrong Trail	2.7	49.8	paved/packed cr stone/gravel		y		y	138
Great Shamokin Path	4.0		dirt		y		y	148
Butler-Freeport Community Trail	12.7	8.3	packed crushed stone/tar & chips				y	152
Oil Creek State Park Trail	9.7		paved	y	y	y		158
Samuel Justus Recreational Trail	5.8		paved	y	y	y	y	163
Allegheny River Trail	10.0		paved	y	y	y	y	167
Tidioute Riverside Rec Trek Trl	3.5	1.5	dirt/ single-track					172
Kellettville to Nebraska Trace	12.2		dirt/single-track	y				175
Buzzard Swamp	9.6		dirt/gravel	y				178
Clarion-Little Toby Trail	15.3	2.7	packed crushed stone/cinders	y	y	y		181
Warren/North Warren Trail	1.7	1.3	paved		y			187
Clearfield to Grampian Trail	10.5		packed crushed stone		y	y		190
Trails North and West: Lake Erie and the Western Border								**193**
Moraine State Pk (Lake Arthur)	7.2		paved	y	y	y		194
Stavich Bicycle Trail	9.8		paved	y	y			198
Pymatuning State Park Trail	5.4		dirt	y	y			204
Ernst Trail	4.0	1.0	dirt	y				209
Presque Isle State Park Bikepath	9.5	3.1	paved	y	y	y		212
Ohio and Erie Canal Towpath	19.5		packed crushed stone/tar&chips	y	y	y	y	216
Metro Parks Bike and Hike Trail	29.0		paved/packed cr stone/shr road	y	y			224
Stow, Kelsey, Old Carriage Trls	4.6		paved/packed crushed stone					225
Emerald Necklace	47.0		paved	y	y	y		231
Trails South and West: Upper West Virginia								**234**
Wheeling Heritage Trails	11.9	1.3	paved	y	y	y		236
West Fork River Trail	13.3	2.7	packed crushed stone	y	y	y	y	241
North Bend Rail-Trail	60.1	10.0	packed crushed stone/ballast		y	y	y	244

Multi-Use Trails

We usually bicycle these trails, so this guide is written through cyclists' eyes. The trails, however, are designed for multiple uses. Because of the very different speeds of the trail users, all must be aware of other users and provide space for them.

The trail surfaces described here range from road-quality asphalt to rough gravel. Some trails and some unfinished sections of trails still have the original ballast from the railroads that formerly ran there. The trail descriptions describe the predominant trail surface. Each rider must decide what range of surfaces you enjoy riding.

Generally speaking, if you have a racing bike with 1-inch tires, stick to the dozen or so paved trails. If you want to go far and fast, stick with ordinary roads and ride in traffic. We swapped the tires on our old 10-speed road bikes for 1 3/8-inch touring tires with a bit more tread than the original tires. With this setup, we ride most of these trails quite happily, except for some that are still original ballast or rough dirt and stones. If you have a mountain bike or a hybrid with fat tires, you'll be able to enjoy all these trails. In some cases we mention nearby mountain biking areas for your convenience.

All these trails are suitable for walking, hiking, and jogging as well as cycling. They provide river access for fisherfolk, and many offer excellent opportunities for birding and wildlife viewing. Indeed, many copies of our first two editions serve walkers.

Most of the paved trails are suitable for in-line skaters. These include parts of the Three Rivers Heritage Trails, Arrowhead, Western Maryland, Armstrong, Oil Creek, Samuel Justus, Allegheny River, Warren-North Warren, Moraine, Stavich, Presque Isle, Metro Parks Bike and Hike, the Emerald Necklace, and Wheeling Heritage Trails.

Horses are permitted on some trails. Sometimes they require special permits. Our information is incomplete, but it indicates that horses are permitted on portions of Montour, Youghiogheny River North, C&O Canal, Mountain Streams II, Ghost Town, Lower, Armstrong, Great Shamokin Path, Butler-Freeport, Samuel Justus, Allegheny River, Ohio & Erie Canal, West Fork River Trail, and North Bend. Usually horses are not permitted on paved surfaces or fine packed crushed stone. Please treat this information as a preliminary hint and check with each trail on specific restrictions.

All the trails are suitable for cross-country skiers when there's enough snow. Many trail managers ask skiers and walkers to use different sides of the trail. It takes several skiers to "set" a good ski track; footprints in these tracks make skiing much harder. Parts of some trails are open to snowmobiles. Cross-country skiers should decide for themselves whether they like to ski in snowmobile tracks.

When it's possible to swim near the trail, we provide that information, as simply getting wet can make a big difference on a summer afternoon. Most of the swimming areas are unsupervised locations in rivers. They do not have lifeguards, there are rarely guarantees about water quality, and you use them at your own risk. We are not making a recommendation that you swim there.

How to Use this Guide

We have tried to make the descriptions easy to use. By reader request, we've kept the print size big enough for mature eyes. The typical format for descriptions includes:

- **Location map**: Approximate location of the trail on a miniature state map. The tiny bicycle shows approximately where the trail is located.
- **Description**: Narrative about the scenery and the character of the trail. Describes points of particular interest. Most of the trails are easy to follow, so you don't need detailed cue sheets.
- **Summary**: Basic information about trail, set off for reference in a special box. More details are in the text, especially about the amenities. Where we know the status of horses and snowmobiles we say what it is; if we don't have information, assume they're not permitted.
- **Detailed map**: Trail route and trailheads (access points) on a map that shows significant roads, towns, and rivers. Most of the maps in the book use the same scale, shown on the key below and on each map. These maps do not show all the roads, so don't just count intersections to find turns. A few sketch maps at larger scales show general location information for more distant trails.
- **Trailheads**: First, a starting point in the *vicinity*, usually a major intersection that you should be able to find easily on a standard state road map. Then *detailed directions* to each trailhead from the starting point. The GPS coordinates (latitude and longitude) for trailheads are provided in the table of trailhead locations on p. 252.
- **Amenities**: Brief information on services nearby, including rest rooms, water, bike shops, food, camping or other lodging, swimming, fishing, and winter sports, and wheelchair access.
- **Trail organization:** Trail development organization or manager.
- **Maps and guides** that tell you more about the trail or the area.

For some trails, we also describe **local history**, **attractions**, **extensions** of the route (often on roads), or **development** plans. For the major trails, the overall information appears at the beginning and separate descriptions give details about the major segments.

We use the following categories to describe trail surfaces, in more-or-less increasing order of roughness:

- **Paved:** asphalt or concrete, suitable for all bikes
- **Bike lane** or **shared road:** route is on a road, with or without a separate lane

- **Tar & chip:** coarse pavement, similar to a road before final asphalt layer is laid
- **Packed crushed stone:** fine crushed stone such as limestone, packed and rolled for a firm surface; the most common surface for finished trails
- **Dirt:** packed base, often with grass, rough spots, some ruts, or scattered gravel
- **Gravel:** substantial amounts of loose material (from pea-size to walnut-size)on surface
- **Ballast:** very rough, with loose stones up to fist-size
- **Single-track:** narrow, usually too narrow to pass; often rough and technical

Map Key

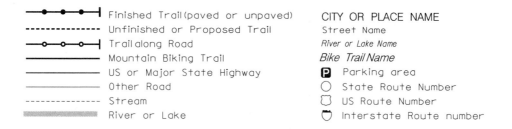

Trails in and Around Pittsburgh

The Pittsburgh area will eventually be served by an outer system (Montour Trail), an inner system (Three Rivers Heritage and Steel Valley Trails), and numerous local trails and bikeways. The trail system will put some part of the system within walking distance of practically every county resident. In addition, plans call for connections to the major cross-country trails that will lead north, southeast, and west from Pittsburgh.

Pittsburgh's 1998 Riverfront Development Plan inventoried over 40 miles of potential trail in the city, including the shores of the three rivers and spur trails along Nine Mile Run, Panther Hollow, and Chartiers Ck. Of these potential trail segments, about 10 miles are complete or actively under construction, and another 10 miles are identified as priorities for early development.

An engineering firm has proposed routes for the Steel Valley Trail and the North Hills Bikeway. The Steel Valley Trail will connect the Three Rivers Heritage Trail at Sandcastle, the Youghiogheny River Trail at McKeesport, and the Montour Trail at Clairton. It will pass through a number of landmark sites of Pittsburgh's industrial heritage. The proposed route includes 8.8 miles of separate trail, a bit less than 3 miles adjacent to roads, and a little more than 3 miles of bike lanes on roads. The North Hills Bikeway, including the Harmony Trail planned for the former interurban trolley line, will stitch together many communities of the North Hills. The proposed route for the North Hills/Harmony Trail includes 9.7 miles of separate trail, 6.3 miles adjacent to roads, and 3.9 miles of bike lanes along roads.

A trail-and-road loop ride in the city

One of our favorite in-town Sunday rides is a loop from Oakland to the North Side and Downtown, covering about 18-20 miles. It's a Sunday ride because of the 8-block stretch on Commonwealth Pl and the Blvd of the Allies in downtown, which has too much traffic for our taste the rest of the week. About half of this trip is on trails, about half on low-traffic neighborhood streets, and about 1 mile on busy city streets.

Begin at your favorite location in Oakland and work your way over to Melwood Av, between Craig St and Neville St. Go north on Melwood, crossing Centre Av and Baum Blvd. Just past Pittsburgh Filmmakers, turn left for one block up a short steep hill, then right on Gold Way. Follow Gold Way under the Bloomfield Bridge; it turns into Melwood somewhere along here. At Herron Av, turn right, then immediately left on Dobson St. Follow Dobson until it ends at Immaculate Heart of Mary Church. Turn right on Brereton and follow it until you can turn right to cross the busway. Cross the busway, emerging on 28th St at Penn Av. Cross Penn Av and turn right at the next alley

(Spring Way). Follow the alley to 31st St and turn left onto the 31st St Bridge. At the stoplight just before the end of the bridge, turn left on the ramp down to River Av.

At the end of the ramp, the North Shore trail is just across the railroad tracks, between the tracks and the river. A bike/pedestrian bridge offers an easy connection for a side trip around Washington Landing. Just past this bridge, cross the tracks from the road to the trail (there's a good crossing a block or two farther along River Av) and continue down the trail to the Vietnam Veteran's Memorial. Just before the Memorial, turn right into the underpass to Three Rivers Stadium. Enter the stadium at the right side of Gate C (the nearest one to the river) and bear right on the ramp to the Ft Duquesne Bridge. Cross the bridge and follow the marked bike path through Point State Park, emerging on Commonwealth Pl in front of the Hilton Hotel. (While the baseball station is being built in 1999-2000, you'll have to detour around the construction site: when you reach the construction fence, backtrack a few yards, take the ramp up to 6th St, follow 6th St for a block, turn left on General Robinson to stadium parking, then go left at Three Rivers Stadium to Gate C.)

Crossing the Allegheny

At the Hilton, turn right and follow Commonwealth Pl to Blvd of the Allies. Turn left on the Boulevard and go about six blocks to Grant St. Cross Grant St, jogging right on Court St (which runs adjacent to the Blvd, but stays level when the Blvd climbs). Take the first right (on Ross St), then the next left (on 1st Av), then the next right (into the parking lot). Go across the parking lot, then left toward the jail. Early in 1999 this will be signed as the official bike route through town.

Enter the Eliza Furnace Trail to the right of the driveway that leads past the jail. Follow the Eliza Furnace Trail to its end in the Swinburne St parking lot. Leave the parking lot via Swinburne St and turn left between the retaining wall and the Jersey barrier that separates the bike path from 2nd Av. Follow the protected bike path left under the railroad tracks, then turn left on Saline St and take the second left on Boundary St (the other side of Big Jim's). The city is building an off-road alternative in this area. At the end of Boundary St, climb the steep switchbacked trail to Locust Trail in Schenley Park. Turn left on Locust Trail and follow it until you see the Schenley Park swimming pool. Go under the Boulevard of the Allies using the underpass near the swimming pool and enter Anderson Playground. Return to your starting point in Oakland via the Boulevard of the Allies (to the left) or Panther Hollow Rd (across the playground). When the more level Neville St connection opens in summer 1999, you may prefer to continue off the end of Boundary St into Junction Hollow (popularly called Panther Hollow), emerging on Boundary St. Continue as straight as possible to Neville St, which will take you into Oakland near Fifth Av and Craig St.

Trail Managers in Allegheny County

Rails to Trails and Greenways Program

Allegheny County Planning Dept
441 Smithfield St
Pittsburgh PA 15222-2219
(412) 350-5960

(412) 350-5372 (fax)

Steel Valley Trail

Steel Valley Trail Council
Steel Industry Heritage Corporation
338 E 9th Av, 1st Floor
Homestead PA 15120

(412) 464-4418

web: trfn.clpgh.org/sihc/

City of Pittsburgh

City of Pittsburgh
Office of the Mayor
414 Grant St, Room 51
Pittsburgh PA 15219

web: www.city.pittsburgh.pa.us

Friends of the Riverfront

PO Box 42434
Pittsburgh PA 15203

(412) 488-0212

web: trfn.clpgh.org/fotr/

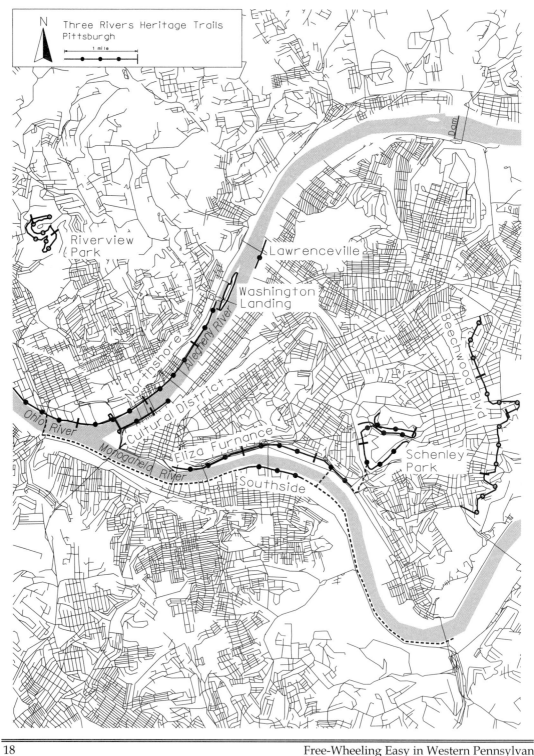

Three Rivers Heritage Trails
Pittsburgh

1 mile

Riverview Park

Lawrenceville

Washington Landing

Northshore

Allegheny River

Cultural District

Beechwood Blvd

Ohio River

Monogahela River

Eliza Furnance

Schenley Park

Southside

Dam

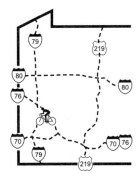

Three Rivers Heritage Trails

Along Pittsburgh's riverfronts with connections into neighborhoods

The Three Rivers Heritage Trails provide a network of trails inside the Pittsburgh city limits. They are developed and maintained by the City of Pittsburgh in cooperation with the Friends of the Riverfront. This is one of seven trails in the Allegheny Trail Alliance, which is coordinating the effort to establish the trail system connecting Pittsburgh with Washington DC via rail-trails and the C&O Canal Towpath.

Six segments are currently open: The North Shore Trail (3.4 miles), the Eliza Furnace Trail (2.5 miles), the Washington's Landing Trail (1.4 miles), the Pittsburgh Cultural District Trail (0.5 mile), the South Side Trail (0.8 miles), and the Ft Duquesne Bridge connection through Point State Park (0.5 mile). The first two of these are popular and long enough to describe separately. Here's how to find the others:

Washington's Landing: A beautifully landscaped crushed limestone trail follows the perimeter of Washington's Landing (formerly known as Herr's Island). This trail is only about 3' wide, so it's better suited for walking than riding. Including cross-trails, the Washington Landing trail offers 1.4 miles of pleasant strolling with views of barge traffic in the main channel, rowing in the back channel, and boats stored in the marinas. At the south end of the island, a bike/pedestrian bridge crosses the back channel and connects with the North Shore Trail. To get to Washington's Landing from PA28 (East Ohio St), turn onto the 31st St bridge, then immediately right at the traffic light onto a ramp, then immediately left at the next traffic light onto the 30th St bridge, which takes you onto Washington Landing. Turn left when the road does, and park any legal place. At this point you're inside the trail loop, which runs around the perimeter of the island. If you continue to the northeastern end of the road, watch out for the strategically hidden stop sign under the railroad bridge.

Pittsburgh Cultural District Trail: The former Allegheny Wharf has been completely remodeled into a pedestrian/bike path for half a mile along the river's edge. Despite the busy road 20 feet above you, the redevelopment has added natural touches such as trees and boulders. Check out the bollards for tying up boats, which have been sculpted to resemble tree branches.

South Side Trail: On the South Side, the completed asphalt trail runs 0.8 mile from 18th St to a quarter-mile upstream from the Birmingham Bridge. An additional 3/4 mile of heavy gravel that runs from the 10th St Bridge to 18th St is scheduled for improvement, and the trail will be extended upstream as well. The trailhead is under the Birmingham

Bridge at Southside Riverfront Park. This is also a public boat launch; note that they do ticket trailerless cars parked in trailer spaces.

Ft Duquesne Bridge Pedestrian Walkway and Point State Park: You can reach Point State Park via the Ft Duquesne Bridge pedestrian walkway by entering Gate C of the stadium (through the underpass from the North Shore Trail), and staying right for the ramp before entering the stadium proper. If a game is in progress, approach Gate C to the right of the turnstiles, and an usher will let you through (procedure in late 1998). The ramp takes you across the Ft Duquesne Bridge on the pedestrian walkway. On the other side, one marked route through Point State Park emerges in front of the Hilton Hotel, and another loops around under the bridge to connect with the Cultural District Trail. Bicycling and rollerblading are forbidden in Point State Park except for the marked through-routes. The distance from the Three Rivers Trail to the Hilton is about 0.5 mile.

Although these shorter segments don't yet provide enough trail for a full-day bike trip, they offer excellent close-to-town walking opportunities or short family excursions.

Three Rivers Heritage Trail	
Location	Along Allegheny, Ohio, Monongahela Rivers in Pittsburgh, Allegheny County
Trailheads	Washington's Landing, various points on North Side, Southside Riverfront Park
Length, Surface	Three completed sections: 3.4 miles, 2.5 miles 1.4 mile, 0.5 mile, 0.8 mile, 0.5 mile; paved and packed crushed stone
Character	sometimes busy, urban, sunny, mostly flat
Usage restrictions	No motorized vehicles; no snowmobiles; no horses
Amenities	Rest rooms, water, food, lodging, fishing
Driving time from Pittsburgh	Surrounds downtown Pittsburgh

Development plans

The Three Rivers Heritage Trail will eventually anchor a much-anticipated trail link between Pittsburgh and Washington DC. The Steel Valley Trail will connect the Sandcastle end of the Three Rivers Heritage Trail to the Youghiogheny River Trail at McKeesport and the Montour Trail near Clairton. A link between the West End Bridge and the Coraopolis trailhead of the Montour Trail has also been proposed.

Friends of the Riverfront maintains and improves the existing rail through monthly volunteer activities. This group and the City of Pittsburgh are working on connections to complete the trail from Washington's Landing down the Allegheny River, across the West End Bridge, and up the Monongahela River to Sandcastle.

Engineering design for expansion on the South Side is underway. The conversion of the Hot Metal Bridge near 29th St for automobile use will provide a connection from the South Side to 2nd Av near the east end of the Eliza Furnace Trail.

Trail organization

City of Pittsburgh, Office of the Mayor
414 Grant St, Room 51
Pittsburgh PA 15219
(412) 255-2626

web: www.city.pittsburgh.pa.us/ed/html/eliza_furnace_trail.html

Friends of the Riverfront
PO Box 42434
 Pittsburgh PA 15203
(412) 488-0212
e-mail: fotr@trfn.clpgh.org

web: trfn.clpgh.org/fotr/

Membership, $25 individual, $40 family

Maps, guides, other references

There are many guides to the city of Pittsburgh. A good street map will help.

Barringer Fifield, *Seeing Pittsburgh* narrates walking tours in and around the city. Many of them overlap the bike routes. University of Pittsburgh Press, 1996.

City of Pittsburgh Bicycling Plan:
www.city.pittsburgh.pa.us/cp/html/bicycling_plan.html

USGS Topographic Maps: Pittsburgh East, Pittsburgh West.

North Shore Trail

North Shore Trail

Along north side of Allegheny River in Pittsburgh

The North Shore Trail provides a close-at-hand urban outdoor experience in the form of a continuous walking path and bicycle commuting route just across the rivers from downtown Pittsburgh. Someday the trail will connect with other trails to provide a long route along the north side of the Allegheny River from Washington's Landing, past the stadiums, across the West End Bridge, then along the south side of the Monongahela River through Station Square to Sandcastle. At Sandcastle it will connect with other trails of the Allegheny Trail Alliance that will take you as far as Washington DC.

At present, this trail runs for 3.4 miles from near Washington's Landing to almost a mile west of the Carnegie Science Center. This trail, more than any other we know, breathes with the strength and vibrancy of the city. It offers vistas up and down the rivers, one of the finest views of downtown available, and close-ups of the contrast between old industry and new development on the North Side.

The northeast end of this section is beside River Rd close to where River Rd starts up the ramp to the 30th St (Washington's Landing) and 31st St (Allegheny River) Bridges. As you head toward the Point on the crushed limestone surface, for a tenth of a mile the trail is between River Rd and the river channel where rowing crews train. You can sometimes glimpse the rowers through the trees and hear the coaches calling out advice. At the end of the island, an unused railroad bridge crosses the road, trail and channel. Note the iron ring on the downstream end of the bridge pier for tying up boats during high water. In 1999, this bridge re-opened to link this trail to the trail on Washington's Landing. The next three-quarter mile, to the 16th St Bridge, lies between a railroad track and the Allegheny River. You'll see industrial buildings, including the Heinz plant, on the land side. Small piers, docks, and occasional benches dot the river side of the trail. Another tenth of a mile brings you to a park and overlook just upstream from Veteran's Bridge, then another tenth-mile takes you under the bridge.

Now downtown Pittsburgh towers across the river. A third of a mile beyond Veteran's Bridge you go under the 9th St Bridge, the first of the three identical prize-winning bridges from Downtown to the North Side. At the bridge the trail becomes paved, and the adjacent industrial area gives way to redevelopment. The new condominiums and ALCOA headquarters designed their riverfronts to further enhance the trail. At the ALCOA building several levels of ramps allow stair-free access to 7th St. Soon after the 7th St Bridge, you enter the modern sculpture garden at North Shore Center. Now you join an extensive esplanade, often quite wide with seating and extensive landscaping. Pause to watch commercial traffic on the river and downtown Pittsburgh on the opposite side. Soon you cross under the 6th St Bridge to the Pittsburgh river safety building. You'll recognize it from the city seal worked out in brick on the upper façade and more iron rings provide anchorage in (very!) high water. This is the beginning of Roberto Clemente Park. From here it's a quarter-mile to the future Korean Veteran's Memorial and another tenth-mile or so to the Vietnam Veteran's Memorial. Just before the latter, a pedestrian underpass to the right goes to Three Rivers Stadium and the ramp to Ft Duquesne ridge and downtown.

Ballpark construction may disrupt the trail between the 6th St and Ft Duquesne bridges during 1999 and 2000. To stay on the North Shore, detour via 6th St, General Robinson St, and stadium parking. To detour on the city side, use the Ft Duquesne Bridge walkway, Point Park, the Cultural District Park, and the 6th St bridge.

North Shore Trail	
Location	Along Allegheny River in Pittsburgh, Allegheny County
Trailheads	Washington's Landing, various points on North Side
Length, Surface	3.4 miles, paved and packed crushed stone
Character	Sometimes busy, urban, sunny, mostly flat
Usage restrictions	No motorized vehicles; no snowmobiles; no horses
Amenities	Water, food, lodging, fishing
Driving time from Pittsburgh	Surrounds downtown Pittsburgh

The trail jogs left around the Korean Veteran's Memorial to stay along the river. Here, you're across the river from Point State Park. You can look across the Point to see the Monongahela River joining the Allegheny to form the Ohio River. About a quarter-mile past the Three Rivers underpass, some benches allow you to enjoy the view of Point State Park and up both the Allegheny and Monongahela Rivers. Look the other way to watch the Duquesne Incline on the other side of the Ohio River carry passengers up and down Mt Washington. From here it's a tenth of a mile to the submarine USS Requin (that's French for "shark"), which is part of the Carnegie Science Center. The main part of the Science Center is just to your right. We wish the Science Center would install *secure* bicycle parking so we could combine a bike trip with some time at the exhibits.

After the Science Center, the trail passes alongside a commercial parking lot, following the edge of the lot next to the river for 500 feet. In the next two-thirds of a mile it passes three marinas before the pavement ends. The City of Pittsburgh owns the right-of-way from here to the West End Bridge and beyond. Eventually the City hopes to construct ramps for handicap and bicycle access to the West End Bridge.

Access point

North Side: For the eastern end, use legal street parking in the neighborhood on weekends. During business hours, Washington Landing is preferred. For the western end, use parking for Three Rivers Stadium or Carnegie Science Center.

Amenities

Rest rooms, water: Occasional water fountains. No public rest rooms, but there may be chemical toilets in the parking lots near the stadium.

Bike shop, rental: Many bike shops in the area, but none adjacent to the trail.

Restaurant, groceries: Off the trail on the North Side or in Pittsburgh. Troll's at the marina on Washington's Landing, alongside the trail. The Strip District, just across the 16th St bridge, is a mecca for both buying and eating food.

Camping, simple lodging: No camping. Hotels in town. The Priory B&B nearby.

Swimming, fishing: This section of the Allegheny has a lot of powerboat traffic, both commercial and recreational. The water is unappealing for swimming, and the currents can be treacherous. There are lots of fishing spots between the trail and the river.

Winter sports: There's probably too much foot traffic for XC skiing. No snowmobiles.

Wheelchair access: Generally good; no gates.

Downtown from Eliza Furnace Trail

Eliza Furnace Trail

Along north side of Monongahela River in Pittsburgh

When finished, this off-road commuter trail will connect Allegheny County's two largest employment centers, the offices of downtown Pittsburgh and the universities and hospitals of Oakland. The trail starts at the east edge of downtown, in the parking lot near the new jail, then goes behind the jail for a clean run of over two miles to Hazelwood. It now ends at a parking lot on an orphaned block of Swinburne St just west of Hazelwood. Eventually the trail will turn away from the river and connect to Schenley Park and Oakland.

The trail is named for the Eliza blast furnace that once produced steel where the Pittsburgh High Technology Center now reflects Pittsburgh's industrial shift from steel to high technology. It's often called the "Jail-Trail".

Currently, 2.5 miles of trail connect the 1st Av parking lot near the new Jail near Grant St downtown with the west end of Hazelwood, where 2nd Av jogs under the railroad track into Hazelwood. The center of the trail is paved for cyclists and rollerbladers, and a packed crushed stone strip along each side provides a more congenial surface for walkers and joggers. No cross streets interrupt this stretch. A short side trail provides access from Bates St.

Definitely an urban trail, it runs for most of its length between the Parkway East and 2nd Ave. Ignore the traffic noise and appreciate the great views up the Monongahela River and back toward downtown. With a cliff on one side, a river on the other, and no cross traffic, this is a superb in-town trail. You can look up at Duquesne University on the bluff overlooking the jail, across 2nd Av at industrial yards and the campus of the Pittsburgh High-Technology Center, and across the Monongahela River to the homes on the slopes on the South Side.

Eliza Furnace Trail	
Location	Pittsburgh, Allegheny County
Trailheads	Downtown, Hazelwood
Length, Surface	2.4 miles developed, 6 planned; paved and packed crushed stone
Character	Busy, urban, sunny, flat
Usage restrictions	No motorized vehicles; no horses
Amenities	Rest rooms, food, fishing
Driving time from Pittsburgh	In Pittsburgh

Development plans

A steep, switchbacked trail from the end of Boundary St up to Locust Trail (the running trail below Overlook Drive) in Schenley Park has been graded and surfaced; it should open early in 1999. The connecting trail from the end of Boundary St to Neville St in Oakland will be developed in spring 1999 as part of the Junction Hollow soccer field development. A ramp to the Pittsburgh High Technology Center is under consideration; for now use the Bates St exit, turn right toward the river, and ride carefully on Bates St across 2nd Av.

The City of Pittsburgh is considering an extension to the north end of the Glenwood Bridge and a connection across that bridge to the Three Rivers Heritage Trail.

There is also discussion of connecting the north end of the Glenwood Bridge to the Nine Mile Run area and thence to the lower end of Frick Park .

Access points

Vicinity: Directions begin on 2nd Av, on the north side of the Allegheny River just east of downtown Pittsburgh.

Downtown Pittsburgh trailhead: Go west on 2nd Av (toward downtown). While you're under the Blvd of the Allies, turn left on Ross St, go two blocks, and park in the 1st Av parking lot. Go toward the river to the edge of the parking lot, then go left to the jail. The trail starts between the jail and the Parkway.

Swinburne (Hazelwood) trailhead: Go east on 2nd Av (away from downtown). This will become PA885. Just before PA885 jogs left under the railroad tracks at the edge of Hazelwood, turn left at an inconspicuous opening in the retaining wall on an orphaned block of Swinburne St. A small trail sign on the retaining wall marks the intersection. Go up a short hill and take the first right into the trail parking lot.

Amenities

Rest rooms, water: Rest room at 1s Av lot; chemical toilet at Swinburne St trailhead.

Bike shop, rentals: None

Restaurant, groceries: Downtown restaurants within a few blocks of the trailhead. Big Jim's is along road connection to Schenley Park.

Camping, simple lodging: No camping. Hotels in town.

Swimming, fishing: Swimming pool in Schenley Park. Fishing in Panther Hollow Lake

Winter sports: Cross-country skiing

Wheelchair access: Gates at both ends completely block paved portion of trail; adequate clearance on packed crushed stone portion. Bates St accessible via crushed stone ramp.

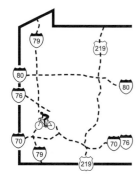

Steel Valley Trail

Along Monongahela River in Allegheny County

The Steel Valley Trail will provide the critical link that allows smooth transition among the major Pittsburgh-area trails. It will connect with the Youghiogheny River Trail at McKeesport, with the Montour Trail at Clairton, with the Three Rivers Heritage Trail at Sandcastle, and with the Eliza Furnace Trail at the Glenwood and Hot Metal bridges.

The trail will run through the industrial heartland of Allegheny County, passing through 4 former and current steel operations: the former Homestead, USS Duquesne, and National Tube Works, and the still-active Clairton Coke Works. It will stay close as possible to the riverfront, but the final route of the Mon-Fayette expressway will affect the ultimate trail alignment.

The first section should open by June 1999 to fill the 4-mile gap between McKeesport and Clairton. Although we don't usually include descriptions of trails we haven't actually ridden, this link is so important (and so imminent) that we make an exception.

The trail will begin at McKee Point Park in McKeesport. The initial leg will run south-westward, crossing the Youghiogheny River on the 5th Av bridge and then running parallel to 5th Av, which becomes Monongahela Av, to Glassport. It will cross the Monongahela River on the Glassport-Clairton Bridge and work through back streets and alleys of Clairton to connect with the Montour Trail near the mouth of Peters Ck.

Steel Valley Trail	
Location	Allegheny County
Trailheads	McKeesport, Clairton, Sandcastle
Length, Surface	4 miles to open 1999, 12.5 miles planned; some segments along roads
Character	Busy, urban, sunny, flat; some automobile traffic
Usage restrictions	No motorized vehicles on off-road portions
Amenities	Rest rooms, water, bike rental, food, lodging, fishing
Driving time from Pittsburgh	In and adjacent to Pittsburgh

Development plans

Sections will be opening through 1999 and 2000; the trail council hopes to complete the leg from McKeesport to Pittsburgh on the south side of the Monongahela River by the end of 2000. Later development will provide trail on both sides of the Monongahela and more river crossings.

The Steel Valley Trail is one of seven trails in the Allegheny Trail Alliance. The Alliance is coordinating the effort to establish a trail system connecting Pittsburgh with Washington DC via rail-trails and the C&O Canal Towpath.

Access points

Vicinity: Directions begin on PA837, the Green Belt, on the south side of the Monongahela River passing Kennywood Park southeast of downtown Pittsburgh.

McKee Point trailhead: Go southeast on PA837. In Duquesne, turn left to cross the McKeesport-Duquesne Bridge. Turn right on PA148 (Lysle Blvd) and continue to McKee Point Park.

Clairton trailhead: Go southeast on PA837 and continue to follow it as it bends south-westward and goes through Dravosburg and Coal Valley and into Clairton. The trailhead is about a mile past the Glassport-Clairton Bridge.

Amenities

Rest rooms, water: McKee Point Park

Bike shop, rentals: McKee Point Park

Restaurant, groceries: Downtown restaurants within a few blocks of the trailheads.

Camping, simple lodging: No camping. Hotels in town.

Swimming, fishing: For now, the available water is the Monongahela River and the mouth of the Youghiogheny River. People fish in these waters, but we wouldn't want to swim there. When the trail is extended to Pittsburgh, it will pass Sandcastle Waterpark.

Winter sports: None

Wheelchair access: Parts of the trail will share roads with automobiles.

Trail organization

> Steel Valley Trail Council
> Steel Industry Heritage Corporation
> 338 E 9th Av, 1st Floor
> Homestead PA 15120
> (412) 464-4418
> web: trfn.clpgh.org/sihc/

Maps, guides, other references

USGS Topographic Maps: McKeesport, Glassport.

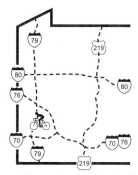

Montour Trail

Coraopolis to Clairton in Allegheny and Washington Counties

The abandoned rights-of-way of the Montour RR and the Peters Creek Branch of the Pennsylvania RR make a sweeping crescent around the western and southern suburbs of Pittsburgh, dipping back and forth between Allegheny and Washington Counties. The Montour Trail system follows this route and will offer 54.5 miles of trail, including 46.5 miles of main line and 8 miles of spurs. The planned route runs from Coraopolis on the Ohio River to Clairton on the Monongahela River. From Coraopolis along Montour Run to Imperial the trail is primarily rural except for the area near the Parkway. From Imperial south and west, under US22 into Washington County south to McDonald then east to Cecil, it's extremely rural and agricultural, with some restored strip mines and small mining towns. As it enters Peters Township and approaches US19 it becomes suburban residential until it reenters Allegheny County near South Park. From South Park to Clairton it's again more rural.

Six sections are now open in Moon-Robinson-Findlay-North Fayette, Quicksilver-McDonald, Cecil, Arrowhead (Peters Township), the Bethel Park Spur, and South Park. Together they cover 25.9 miles. Most of the trail will be packed crushed limestone, some parts with a parallel dirt treadway for horses. Peters Township is developing the Arrowhead Trail in asphalt. The trail segments and their status are:

Coraopolis to Groveton	1.0 miles	under consideration
Robinson-Moon-Findlay-N Fayette	11.4 miles	finished (packed crushed stone)
US22 Champion area	3.0 miles	2.2 miles being mined early 1999
Quicksilver-McDonald	3.0 miles	finished (packed crushed stone)
Mt Pleasant	5.2 miles	original ballast
Westland Mine Spur	3.9 miles	original ballast
Cecil	5.9 miles	finished (packed crushed stone)
Muse Spur	1.3 miles	original ballast
Cecil/Arrowhead Gap	2.5 miles	original ballast
Arrowhead to Brush Run Rd	3.2 miles	finished (paved)
Peters-Bethel Park Spur	2.6 miles	0.9 miles finished (crushed stone)
Peters/Bethel Gap	1.5 miles	original ballast
South Park-Jefferson-Clairton	10.0 miles	1.5 miles finished (crushed stone)

The Montour Trail Council has a cue sheet for routes that connect the completed sections of the trail. Unfortunately, there are often no good low-traffic alternatives, so you may encounter moderate traffic. They are available from the trail council (you are a member, aren't you?) or on their web site at http://trfn.clpgh.org/mtc/roads.htm

In a public/private partnership, Montour Trail Council and Allegheny County will have easements or ownership of the 28 miles of trail within the county (including 10 miles yet to be acquired). The Montour Trail Council owns 21 miles within Washington County. Peters Township owns a 7.5-mile segment.

Development plans

The Montour Trail Council holds regular volunteer trail development activities for improving the established segments and for preparing new segments for development. The trail council now has funding to support project planning and engineering for the remaining portions of the trail.

Plans to extend and improve the currently trail segments are described with those segments. Mining in the US22 area should be completed in late spring 1999 and trail construction to close the gap between the BFI trailhead and Quicksilver should follow soon thereafter. The trail council is working with PennDOT and DCNR to plan for bridges to cross over several roads, especially over PA980 at Quicksilver and over Morganza Rd in Hendersonville.

The trail council holds title to the two miles of railroad right-of-way between PA51 and PA837 in Clairton; these two miles are unimproved but open for mountain biking. Final routing of the trail near PA51 depends on completion of plans for the interchange of PA51 with the impending Mon-Fayette Expressway and on possible future availability of the parallel Wheeling and Lake Erie Railway. In cooperation with Jefferson Borough and the city of Clairton, the trail council hopes to start construction in 1999.

The Montour Trail is one of seven trails in the Allegheny Trail Alliance. The Alliance is coordinating the effort to establish a trail system connecting Pittsburgh with Washington DC via rail-trails and the C&O Canal Towpath.

Trail organization

> Montour Trail Council
> PO Box 11866
> Pittsburgh PA 15228-0866
> (412) 257-2328 for voicemail system
> (412) 831-2030 for information
> web: trfn.clpgh.org/orgs/mtc/
> Membership: $25/year individual, $35/year family

Maps, guides, other references

Trail Users' Guide to Montour Trail.

USGS Topographic Maps: Ambridge, Oakdale, Clinton, Midway, Canonsburg, Bridgeville, Glassport.

Robinson-Moon-Findlay-North Fayette Section

Along Montour Run from near Coraopolis on the Ohio River to west of Imperial in Allegheny County

The longest completed segment of the Montour Trail is the westernmost, running from mile 0 near Coraopolis to mile 11.4 at Boggs, west of Imperial. This segment follows Montour Run from near its mouth on the Ohio River, passing under the Parkway West to Imperial, then continuing west along South Fork Montour Run to a point near the intersection of US22 and PA980 at the Allegheny County line. It's finished in crushed limestone, 10 feet wide.

The trail begins in Moon Township near Coraopolis, at Groveton alongside Montour Run under the PA51 bridge. From here to Beaver Grade Rd (mile 3.2), the trail runs largely through woods alongside Montour Run, punctuated occasionally with single houses. You'll also see a few industrial sites: a superfund site (mile 0.3), Snyder's scrap metal (mile 0.6), and Moon Township Water Pollution Control Plant (mile 1.3), which smells like most sewer plants.

At mile 1.7 the trail passes through the Forest Grove Sportsman's Association. Shooting ranges occupy both sides of the trail, so exercise caution here by staying on the trail. From Beaver Grade Rd (mile 3.2) to Cliff Mine (mile 5.9), the trail is within sight (and sound) of Montour Run Rd and Cliff Mine Rd on one side, but the other is all woods. In this section the trail crosses Montour Run three times. It also crosses the roads to Robinson Town Centre and two other commercial areas.

Montour Trail, Moon-Robinson-Findlay-North Fayette Section	
Location	Along Montour Run in Robinson, Moon, Findlay and North Fayette Townships, Allegheny County
Trailheads	Groveton, Montour Run Exit of Parkway, Enlow, Boggs Rd near BFI landfill
Length, Surface	11.4 miles, packed crushed stone
Character	Uncrowded, rural to wooded, mixed shade and sun, flat
Usage restrictions	Horses ok on grass—stay off improved surface; no motorized vehicles; no snowmobiles
Amenities	Rest rooms, water, bike rental, food, lodging, fishing
Driving time from Pittsburgh	30 minutes west

At Cliff Mine (crossing Steubenville Pike-Enlow Rd), the trail passes behind a salvage yard and some houses then crosses Cliff Mine Rd (mile 6.2). Here the trail works away from roads into the woods, crossing Montour Run four times before entering the 558-

foot Enlow Tunnel (mile 7.2-7.3). Just west of the tunnel, cattails grow in a small wetland (mile 7.5). The trail emerges at the old Enlow ballfield just before the Five Points intersection (mile 8). Go early on a summer morning to watch the rabbits. The Findlay Water Authority will install a water fountain at the Enlow ballfield in early 1999.

After Five Points, the trail runs in a short cut full of wildflowers, then enters the out-skirts of Imperial with houses on the east and a construction yard on the west. Soon it parallels the streets of Imperial. From the embankment you can look down onto the shopping district and future community center along Main St or up on the other side to the houses along Station St. After crossing the trestle over US30 (mile 8.9) the trail en-ters a residential area, then reclaimed strip mines. A farm with a fine barn provides visual relief (mile 11.1). The finished trail currently ends at mile 11.5, near the BFI Imperial landfill on Boggs Rd.

Enlow Tunnel, mile 7.2

Local history, attractions

The Montour RR was started in 1877 to haul coal from Santiago, near Imperial, to the Ohio River. It also hauled general goods. In 1913 it was extended beyond Santiago to West Mifflin. Some bridges on this section are dated 1924, when realignment shortened the line by about a mile. This section of the Montour RR was abandoned between 1962 and 1984.

The BFI Imperial Sanitary Landfill near mile 11.5 offers tours. Call (724) 695-0900.

Development plans

The Montour Trail Council holds titles or easements to the 3 miles of right-of-way between the Boggs/BFI trailhead and the segment that begins at Quicksilver. Strip mining for the coal under 2 miles of the trail started in Nov 1998 and should be completed in spring 1999. The trail, including both the mined area and the last mile from Beagle Club Rd to Quicksilver will be installed as a side effect of the mining operation. This link should open sometime in 1999.

At the other end of the trail, the Montour Trail Council is investigating the possibility of extending the trail from Groveton (mile 0) back to Coraopolis. This would provide access to the amenities in Coraopolis.

The Hollow Oak Land Trust is developing an extensive greenway along Montour Run. The Montour Valley Alliance is working to preserve the valley's environment. The trail will follow the spine of the greenway, which will also include some tributaries.

Access points

Vicinity: Directions begin at the interchange of I279/US22/US30 (Parkway West) with I79. To reach this point from Pittsburgh, go west on I279/US22/US30 (Parkway West).

Groveton trailhead (northeast): At the intersection of I279/US22/US30 with I79, go north on I79 to Exit 17, PA51. Exit northbound on PA51. After less than half a mile, PA51 crosses Montour Run on a high bridge. Immediately after crossing the bridge, make an extremely sharp right onto Montour Rd. The intersection is marked with a large sign for H. Snyder Scrap and a small sign for Montour Trail. Go 0.1 mile on Montour Rd to trailhead parking under the PA51 bridge. Park well clear of the narrow road.

Montour and Cliff Mine trailheads (Parkway west): At the intersection of US22/30 with I79, continue west on the Parkway for 5.8 miles (it will change number to PA60). Exit onto Montour Run Rd at Exit 2. *For Montour trailhead:* At Exit 2, follow signs for Montour Run Rd. Just after you get clear of the intersection, there is plenty of parking on the wide shoulder of Montour Run Rd within sight of the trail. You will be on the north side of the Parkway near the entrance to Wickes Furniture. *For Cliff Mine trailhead:* Follow the signs from Exit 2 to Cliff Mine Rd and follow Cliff Mine Rd about a mile to parking at the intersection with Steubenville Pike-Enlow Rd.

Enlow trailhead: At the intersection of US22/30 with I79, continue west on the Parkway for 7.9 miles (it will change number to PA60). After passing the Montour Exit, follow PA60, the Airport Expressway, rather than Business 60. Exit onto McClaren Rd at Exit 4, following signs for Imperial. Go 1.5 miles to parking at Enlow ballfield, just before Five Points (the first major intersection).

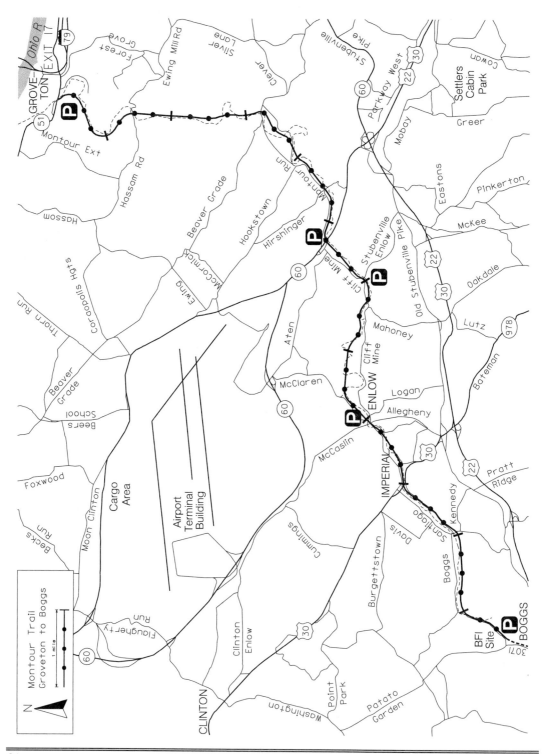

N
Montour Trail
Groveton to Boggs
1 mile

Free-Wheeling Easy in Western Pennsylvania

Boggs Rd (BFI) trailhead: At the intersection of US22/30 with I79, continue west on the Parkway for about 3.8 miles. At the interchange with PA60, exit westbound on US22/30. Continue westbound on US22 for about 6.8 miles, staying on US22 where US30 splits off. Take the PA980 exit and go north on SR3071 for about half a mile. Turn right across a bridge on SR3070 (Boggs Rd) toward the BFI landfill. Shortly after the turn, go straight into trailhead parking (Bugay Dr) instead of following the road slightly left up the hill.

Amenities

Rest rooms, water: Seasonal chemical toilets at most trailheads. The Sportsman's Club at mile 1.7 offers the courtesy of their rest rooms. Seasonal water fountain below Robinson Town Centre, at the trail crossing near the intersection of Park Manor Blvd and Montour Run Rd. Another water fountain will be installed near Enlow ballfield in spring 1999.

Bike shop, rentals: Trail Blazers near the trail on Old Beaver Grade Rd at mile 3.1. Imperial Bike Rental, beside the trail near mile 8.5. Coraopolis Bike and Hobby Shop in (where else?) Coraopolis. Another shop planning to open beside the trail near mile 5.3.

Restaurant, groceries: In Coraopolis, but it's a mile or so on a busy road with poor shoulders. In Robinson Town Centre on top of the hill near the Parkway, accessible from mile 4.2 on a narrow, busy road. Schmidt's Restaurant near mile 5.8. Two bars (both closed on Sunday) and a pizza carryout at mile 8.9 near the trestle in Imperial; a pedestrian tunnel under the trail at mile 8.6 (there's a sign for this side trail) may help you get there. Snacks at bike shops.

Camping, simple lodging: Motels near Montour Run exit to Parkway West.

Swimming, fishing: Swimming depends on whether you're willing to swim in Montour Run. A few spots might be deep enough, but the water quality may discourage you. Lower Montour Run is stocked with trout by the Sportsman's Club.

Winter sports: Cross-country skiing is encouraged. Snowmobiles prohibited

Wheelchair access: OK along whole section

Maps, guides, other references

Trail Users' Guide. Trail map/brochure available at trailheads and local bike shops.

USGS Topographic Maps: Ambridge, Oakdale, Clinton.

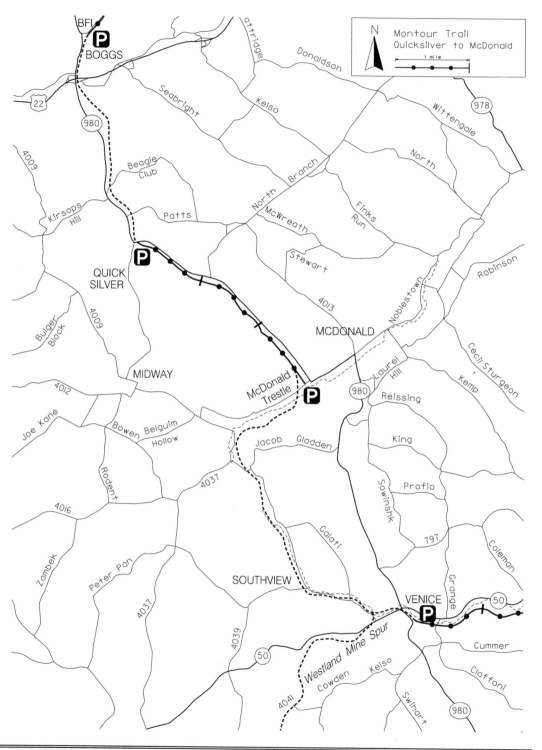

N
Montour Trail
Quicksilver to McDonald
1 mile

BFI
P
BOGGS

22

980

4009

Seabright

Kelso

Donaldson

Attridge

978

Wittengale

Beagle
Club

Kirsops
Hill

Patts

North Branch

North

McWreath

Finks
Run

North

Robinson

P
QUICK
SILVER

Bulger
Block

4009

4009

MIDWAY

4012

Joe Kane

Bowen

Belguim
Hollow

Stewart

4013

MCDONALD

Noblestown

Laurel
Hill

980

Reissing

Cecil Sturgeon

Kemp

McDonald
Trestle

P

Jacob

Gladden

King

Rodent

4037

4016

4037

Zambek

Peter Pan

Southview

Galati

Profio

Sowinshk

797

Coleman

VENICE
P

Grange

50

4039

50

Westland Mine Spur

Cowden

Kelso

Cummer

Claffoni

4041

Swihart

980

Free-Wheeling Easy in Western Pennsylvania

Quicksilver-McDonald Section

Quicksilver to McDonald Trestle

One of the more remote stretches of the Montour Trail, this section parallels PA980 through an area of former strip mines. The road is never far away, but it is never intrusive. A creek and often some buildings separate the trail from the road, so you can concentrate on the surrounding scenery and nature's success in restoring the land.

This section actually begins just north of Beagle Club Rd on the east side of PA980 at a point with no road access. The trail is largely on a raised embankment and the trail surface has not yet been laid, so it's pretty rough. After 0.8 mile it reaches PA980 just south of the entrance to Quicksilver Golf Course. There's no bridge here, just a steep hill to the busy road with poor sight lines for traffic. This is, for now, a dead-end stretch. The trail council is working toward laying trail surface and installing a bridge here in 1999.

Things change on the other side of PA980. A dirt driveway climbs a short hill to a small parking area on the west side of PA980 (mile 15). This is just south of the turn to Quicksilver, and it's the start of three miles of smooth trail with no road crossings. Heading south from this parking area, you pass behind a few houses, through a cut, and behind some more houses. The trail then swings away from the road. A creek and swampy area separate the trail from the road. The houses give way to light industry, chiefly storage areas for construction equipment and chemicals used in the tinplate industry. After a few of these, nothing obstructs the views across the valley.

As you approach the McDonald trestle (which is unfinished and closed) the trail bends left and descends to Noblestown Rd (mile 18). At Noblestown Rd the trail emerges near the base of the high trestle that will eventually carry the trail across this valley.

Extensions of the ride

PA980 is too busy for our taste, but if you want to ride in traffic you can follow PA980 (named SR3071 after crossing US22) north from the Quicksilver crossing about 3 miles to the BFI end of the northern section of the trail. Half a mile after US22, turn right on SR3070 toward the BFI landfill. Shortly after the turn, go straight into trailhead parking.

Development plans

The Montour Trail Council holds or is acquiring titles or easements to the 3 miles of right-of-way between the Boggs/BFI trailhead and the segment that begins at Quicksilver. Coal under 2 miles of the trail is scheduled to be strip-mined in early 1999. The trail will be installed as a side effect of the mining operation, and the last mile from Beagle Club Rd to Quicksilver will also be finished. A bridge for the Quicksilver crossing is being designed; construction should start in 1999.

Montour Trail, Quicksilver-McDonald Section

Location	Robinson Township, Washington County
Trailheads	Near Quicksilver, under McDonald trestle
Length, Surface	3.0 miles, packed crushed stone
Character	Little-used, rural, sunny, flat
Usage restrictions	No motorized vehicles; no snowmobiles
Amenities	Rest rooms
Driving time from Pittsburgh	40 minutes south-southwest

Access points

Vicinity: Directions begin headed west on Noblestown Rd from the Carnegie Exit (Exit 13) of I79. To reach this point from Pittsburgh, go west on I279 and turn south on I79.

McDonald Trestle trailhead (south): From I79 Exit 13, go west on Noblestown Rd for 10.6 miles. Be careful not to lose track of Noblestown Rd in Oakdale; it's a little tricky. Continue through McDonald to the point where PA980 turns right (but don't turn). Trailhead parking is just ahead on the left (before the trestle). The trail starts on the right, directly across from the parking lot.

Quicksilver trailhead (north): From I79 Exit 13 go west on Noblestown Rd for 10.6 miles as for the South trailhead. Turn right on PA980 and go north for 3.0 miles. Just before the sign marking the Quicksilver entrance, a small sign indicates trailhead parking.

Amenities

Rest rooms, water: Chemical toilet at McDonald trailhead.

Bike shop, rentals: None on this section. Closest is in Imperial, along the Montour Trail.

Restaurant, groceries: A dairy stand and a restaurant on PA980 about halfway between the trailheads. Unfortunately, they aren't easily accessible from the trail.

Camping, simple lodging: None

Swimming, fishing: None

Winter sports: Cross-country skiing is encouraged. Snowmobiles are prohibited.

Wheelchair access: OK at north end, but long steep ramp from McDonald parking to trail.

Maps, guides, other references

Trail Users' Guide to the Montour Trail. Available at trailheads and local bike shops.

USGS Topographic Maps: Clinton, Midway, Canonsburg.

Cecil Township Section

Cecil Township Park to Hendersonville in Washington County

After a 5-mile gap from McDonald, the Montour Trail resumes behind Cecil Township Park. To reach the trail there, start from Cecil Park on the south side of PA50, in the village of Venice. From here it runs 4.4 miles to Hendersonville and an additional 1.5 miles to Chartiers Ck. The trail itself is packed crushed limestone 10 feet wide, except in the tunnel. It is complemented by extensive signage and landscaping.

Behind the tennis courts in Cecil Park a footbridge crosses the creek into a small glade. At the opposite end of this glade a path rises from left to right to meet the rail-trail at grade level at mile 24.7. From here the trail passes eastward through the former mine towns of Cowden (mile 25.4) and Bishop (mile 26.1). Swinging away from residential development, you enter the cut that leads to the curved National Tunnel (mile 27 to 27.1). This major feature of the trail is 633 feet long, at an elevation of 1138'. The tunnel is sometimes called "National Cave" in the winter because of the ice formations that develop there. The trail in the tunnel is loose ballast to improve drainage, so cyclists should be prepared to dismount and walk. Past the tunnel the cut opens up and the trail runs through open farms and woods. Four and a half miles east of Cecil Park, the trail is interrupted at Hendersonville (mile 29.1), where the bridge over SR1009 (Washington Pike on maps, Morganza Rd on the ground) was removed. To continue, descend to road level and cross carefully. You get ice cream and snacks at The Hendersonville Shops, also called "the company store", just across the intersection.

Montour Trail, Cecil Township Section	
Location	Cecil Township, Washington County
Trailheads	Cecil Township Park, Dacor Dr, McConnell Rd, Hendersonville
Length, Surface	5.9 miles, packed crushed stone
Character	Busy, suburban to wooded, sunny, flat
Usage restrictions	Horses ok on grass—stay off improved surface; no motorized vehicles; no snowmobiles
Amenities	Rest rooms, water, food
Driving time from Pittsburgh	35 minutes south-southwest

Picking up again behind The Hendersonville Shops (use the driveway on the far side of the building), the trail continues east for another 1.5 miles to the trestle over Chartiers Ck. The trestle is undecked, fenced off, and closed. Eventually the trail will continue from here to Arrowhead Trail in Peters Township.

Extensions of the ride

From the eastern end of the trail 1.4 miles past Hendersonville, the trail will eventually continue 2 miles to the western end of the Arrowhead trail. However, another tunnel, two closed and fenced high trestles, two more missing bridges, and a poor crossing for US19 (all in the space of 2 miles) currently prevent a direct trail link. Instead, you can connect from Hendersonville to Arrowhead Trail on roads, but you'll have to deal with hills and traffic. Here's how: From Hendersonville, follow the road parallel to the trail (it's Hahn on maps, Georgetown on the signs) for 0.3 miles east; turn left to pass under the trail, go 0.8 miles, then turn right at the T intersection (Baker Rd). Follow this road for about 3 miles past the Greenmoor Riding School, down the hill through Lawrence (also called Hill Station), under US19, to Pelipetz Rd. The road becomes Valley Brook Rd as you cross Chartiers Ck between Lawrence and US19. At Pelipetz Rd, 0.5 mile after you cross under US19, turn right to the Arrowhead trailhead. Be careful in traffic on Valley Brook Rd, especially near US19.

National Tunnel, mile 27

Development plans

In 1999 the trail council expects to resurface the trail between Hendersonville and National Tunnel in fine crushed limestone.

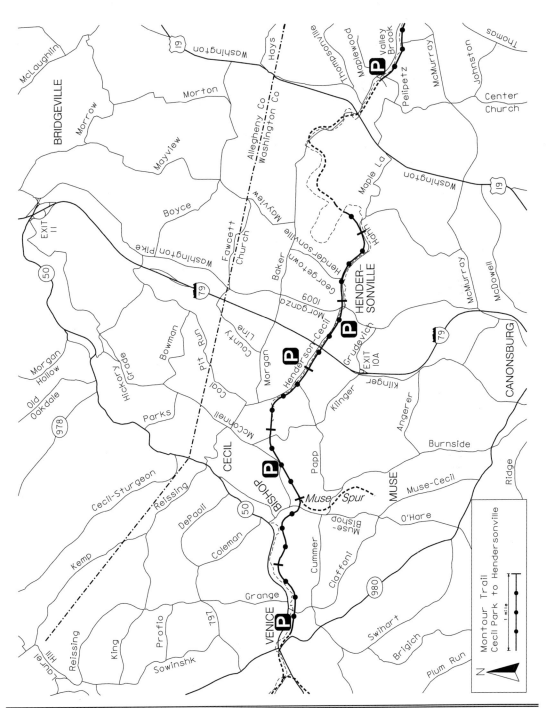

Montour Trail: Cecil Township Section   41

The missing bridge at Hendersonville will be replaced soon, but PennDOT wants the remaining abutment to be removed. The Montour Trail Council plans to complete the connection between this section and the Arrowhead trail eventually.

At the other end of the trail, westbound from Cecil Park, two bridges need extensive work before the trail can be extended the half-mile to the intersection of PA980 with PA50 in Venice. This won't be done until PennDOT realigns PA980.

Access points

Vicinity: Directions begin headed south from I279/US22/US30 (Parkway West) on I79 toward the Bridgeville Exit (Exit 11, PA50). To reach this point from Pittsburgh, go west on I279 and turn south on I79.

Cecil Park trailhead (west): From I79, take the Bridgeville Exit (Exit 11, PA50) and go west on PA50 6.7 miles to the Cecil Township park. The park is actually in Venice, 2.7 miles west of Cecil, on the south side of the road. On weekends, please park in the township building parking lot at the west end of the park, leaving park parking for park users.

Dacor Dr trailhead: From I79, take the Bridgeville Exit (Exit 11, PA50) and go west on PA50 5.5 miles, past Bishop. Turn south on Dacor Dr and go 0.25 mile to parking area.

McConnell Rd trailhead: From I79, take the Bridgeville Exit (Exit 11, PA50) and go west on PA50 4.9 miles to Bishop. Turn south on Muse-Bishop Rd, then left (east) on McConnell Rd. The parking area is just over half a mile east of this intersection.

Kurnick and Hendersonville trailheads (east): From I79, take the Southpointe-Hendersonville exit (Exit 10A). At the bottom of the ramp, turn left (east) and follow signs to Hendersonville. The signs will lead you east for 0.5 mile to SR1009 (Morganza Rd), then left (north) on Morganza Rd for 0.5 mile to Hendersonville. For the Hendersonville trailhead, turn left at the Hendersonville Shops, just *before* the road goes through the cut where a bridge once carried the railroad and a new bridge will eventually carry the trail. For additional parking at the Kurnick lot, turn left on SR1010 (Hendersonville-Cecil Rd) just *after* the road goes through this cut. Follow Hendersonville-Cecil Rd 0.8 mile to the Kurnick parking area on the left.

Amenities

Rest rooms, water: Rest rooms and water at Cecil Park in season. Chemical toilets all year at Cecil Park and seasonally at the Kurnick parking lot and the ball field near Hendersonville.

Bike shop, rentals: None

Restaurant, groceries: Convenience stores along PA50 in Cecil (traffic, alas). Snacks and sandwiches at the Hendersonville Shops. Restaurant at intersection of PA980 and PA50.

Camping, simple lodging: None

Swimming, fishing: None

Winter sports: Cross-country skiing is encouraged. Snowmobiles are prohibited.

Wheelchair access: At Dacor Dr, McConnell Rd, and Kurnick Rd. Steep ramp from Cecil Park to trail. Loose ballast in National Tunnel is not wheelchair-friendly. Morganza Rd crossing is busy and uncontrolled.

Maps, guides, other references

Trail Users' Guide to the Montour Trail. Trail map/brochure available at trailheads and local bike shops.

USGS Topographic Maps: Canonsburg.

Get out and ride!

Arrowhead Trail

Town of McMurray in Washington County

This popular trail runs through residential areas of Peters Township. Frequent informal side routes provide local access. Expect lots of company on the trail, including pedestrians, dog-walkers, and rollerbladers. It's well laid out, with a good asphalt surface and extensive landscaping. The northern part is 11' wide; the southern end 8'. There is so much traffic that a striped center line has been added to remind people to stay right. Although nearly flat, the trail has enough curves and alternations between residential and wooded areas to remain interesting. Trees keep it reasonably well shaded. Considering the amount of development nearby, the trail feels very rural.

The only section of the Montour trail under separate management and the first to open, the Arrowhead Trail is being developed and managed by Peters Township. It currently includes approximately miles 33 to 36. The Montour Trail Council plans to extend the trail west toward Hendersonville, north to the Bethel Park Spur, and east to Library.

From the western trailhead at Pelipetz Rd, an access ramp goes under the trail and curls up to meet the trail at the end of the pavement. You begin in woods, separated from Valley Brook Rd by Brush Run, and climb gradually to McMurray, picking up residential development along the way. By the time you reach McMurray you're clearly in the suburbs. Just after crossing over McMurray Rd you pass the trailside Hike n' Bike shop. You remain in the suburbs until Bebout Rd, where Peterswood Park occupies the right side of the trail. A spur trail climbs to the developed parts of the park, including playing fields, restrooms, telephones, and other community park amenities.

After crossing Sugar Camp Rd, you reach Library Jct, where the trail forks. The left branch is asphalt; it climbs briskly to the parking lot on Brush Run Rd. Across the road from the parking lot, the trail continues unimproved for 0.8 mile to connect with the Bethel Park Spur. The right fork at Library Jct is coarse gravel. This is the main line of the Montour Trail, and it leads to Library.

Local history, attractions

The Montour Railroad was organized in 1877 to haul coal from Santiago, near Imperial, to the Ohio River. It also hauled general goods on the route. The Library branch was built in 1919. It was transferred to the P&LE in 1975, abandoned in 1984, and acquired by Peters Township in 1985 for development as a multi-use recreational trail

Extensions of the ride

Half a mile east of Bebout Rd, a paved spur trail starts just across the trail from the handicapped parking lot. It takes you up the hill into Peterswood Park. In the park it makes 1.2-mile loop past the soccer fields, playground, and softball field. The trail is near Pittsburgh, so all the nearby roads are likely to carry traffic. However, if you follow the spur into Peterswood Park, you can find good low-traffic riding south and west of the park.

The future continuation of the Montour Trail will leave the paved trail at Library Jct on the route now marked as "Walking Trail". It currently extends 1.7 miles before ending at the fenced-off trestle over Library Rd, which now has neither deck nor railing.

Arrowhead Trail	
Location	Peters Township, Washington County
Trailheads	Pelipetz Rd, Brush Run Rd
Length, Surface	3.2 miles paved, 7 miles planned
Character	Busy, urban, shady, flat
Usage restrictions	No motorized vehicles; no snowmobiles; no horses; 20 mph limit for bicycles
Amenities	Rest rooms, water, bike rental, food
Driving time from Pittsburgh	45 minutes south-southwest

Development plans

Westward: In 1999 the trail will continue west from Pelipetz Rd, crossing under US19 to reach the Peters Township Sanitary Facility. Extension past US19 to connect with the Cecil section at Hendersonville will require extensive, expensive construction: two bridges over Brush Run, two high trestles (now fenced off), and a tunnel. This segment is unsafe and closed to the public

Eastward: From Library Jct the trail will extend east to meet the rest of the Montour Trail as it reenters Allegheny County west of South Park. The Montour Trail Council and Peters Township are cooperating in preliminary planning and fund-raising.

Northward: The Bethel Park Spur connects with the Arrowhead Trail at the township line, 0.8 mile north of the Brush Run Rd parking lot.

Access points

Vicinity: Directions begin headed east on Valley Brook Rd (SR1010) from its intersection with US19. To reach this point from Pittsburgh, go south on US19. About 1.8 miles past Boyce Rd, or 1 mile past the Allegheny/Washington County line, or the third traffic light past the county line turn left on the ramp, then left at stop sign on Valley Brook Rd (SR1010) toward McMurray.

Pelipetz trailhead (west): After turning from US19 on Valley Brook Rd (SR1010), continue 0.5 mile and turn right on Pelipetz at the intersection of Valley Brook Rd with Pelipetz Rd and Maplewood Dr. The parking area appears almost immediately on the left.

Brush Run Rd trailhead (east): After turning from US19 on Valley Brook Rd (SR1010), continue about 1.5 miles to SR1002 (McMurray Rd) and turn left. Go about 1.4 miles and turn right on SR1004 (Brookwood Rd). Go about 0.9 miles and turn left on Brush Run Rd (T757). The trailhead parking lot is on the right, just past Scott Rd.

Other access: Along Valley Brook Rd (SR1010), there is pedestrian access at McMurray Rd (SR1002) and Bebout Rd. Other access via the spur trail in Peterswood Park.

Amenities

Rest rooms, water: Rest rooms at the playground in Peterswood Park.

Bike shop, rentals: Scones and Cones, along trail just east of E McMurray Rd.

Restaurant, groceries: Scones and Cones just east of E McMurray Rd. Deli/grocery a block from the trail at McMurray Rd near the intersection with Valley Brook Rd. This busy intersection now has a traffic light.

Camping, simple lodging: Motels along US19 or at exits of nearby I79.

Swimming, fishing: None

Winter sports: No snowmobiles. Cross-country skiing only when snowfall is 4" or more.

Wheelchair access: Handicapped access at special trailhead on Bebout Rd; look for the trailhead sign, "Handicapped access only". Moderately steep grades near Pelipetz and Brush Run parking areas.

Trail organization

Peters Township owns and independently operates this part of the Montour Trail.

Joanne F. Nelson, Director
Peters Township Department of Parks and Recreation
610 East McMurray Rd
McMurray PA 15317-3420
(724) 942-5000

Maps, guides, other references

Arrowhead Trail. Trail map/brochure from Peters Township

Trail Users' Guide to the Montour Trail. Trail map/brochure available at local bike shops.

USGS Topographic Maps: Bridgeville. Glassport for undeveloped section to Clairton.

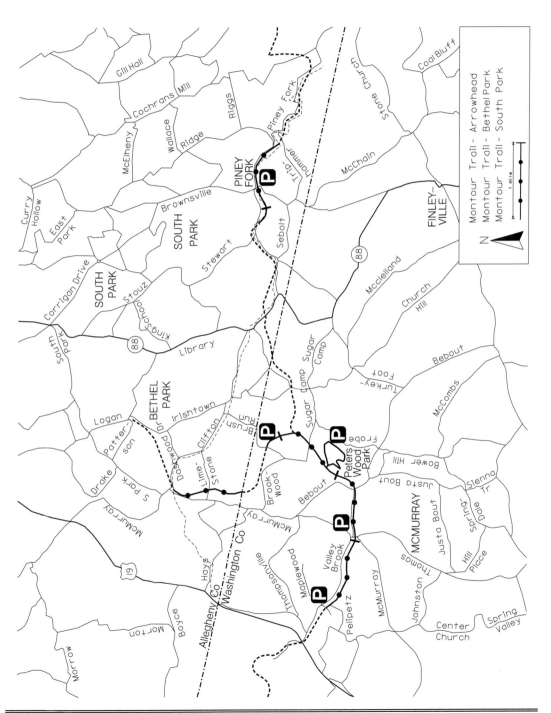

Montour Trail: Bethel Park Section

Bethel Park Spur

Southern part of Bethel Park Township in Allegheny County

The Arrowhead Trail splits at Library Junction, with the northern branch connecting with the Brush Run trailhead and the eastern branch connecting (eventually) with the main leg of the Montour Trail. Across Brush Run Rd from the parking lot, the trail goes down a short steep hill, then is mostly level as it heads west, then north, then northeast to the intersection of Logan and Patterson Rds. The first 0.8 mile is in Peters Township, hence part of the Arrowhead Trail. At the county line, the trail becomes the Bethel Park Spur, and it follows the railroad grade for 2.1 miles until the railroad grade disappears in an industrial park.

The Brush Run Rd trailhead is located where a cut has been filled in to eliminate a road trestle. Arrowhead Trail climbs steeply to the parking lot, and the continuation to Bethel Park descends quickly to original grade level. Allegheny Power (formerly West Penn Power) owns the railroad grade in Bethel Park, and the Montour Trail Council has arranged a recreational easement along the railroad grade, sharing space with the power line.

Currently, the mile between the county line and Clifton Rd is finished in packed crushed stone. At Clifton Rd a ramp descends to the road. Eventually a ramp will go up the other side to resume the route to Logan Rd. There's a walk cycle on the traffic light here.

Montour Trail, Bethel Park Spur	
Location	Bethel Park Township, Allegheny County
Trailheads	Brush Run Rd
Length, Surface	1 mile packed crushed stone; 2.1 miles under design
Character	Little-used, suburban, shady, flat
Usage restrictions	No motorized vehicles; no snowmobiles
Amenities	Food
Driving time from Pittsburgh	45 minutes south

Access points

Vicinity: Directions begin headed southeast on McMurray Rd (the Orange Belt) from its intersection with US19. To reach this point from Pittsburgh, go south on US19. About a mile past South Hills Village shopping center, take the Orange Belt/McMurray Rd exit and go southeast.

Clifton Rd Trailhead: After turning from US19 on McMurray Rd (the Orange Belt), continue about 1.8 miles to the intersection with Clifton Rd, where the Orange Belt goes straight and McMurray Rd turns right. The trail comes down a ramp to this intersection. Look for someplace inoffensive to park.

Brush Run Rd Trailhead: After turning from US19 on McMurray Rd (the Orange Belt), continue about 1.8 miles to the intersection with Clifton Rd, where the Orange Belt goes straight and McMurray Rd turns right. Turn right to remain on McMurray Rd. Go just over a mile and turn left on SR1004 (Brookwood Rd). Go about 0.9 miles and turn left on Brush Run Rd (T757). The trailhead parking lot is on the right, just past Scott Rd.

Amenities

Rest rooms, water: None

Bike shop, rentals: None

Restaurant, groceries: Restaurants and convenience store at the crossing of Clifton Rd

Camping, simple lodging: None

Swimming, fishing: None

Winter sports: No snowmobiles.

Wheelchair access: Steep ramp at Clifton Rd, short steep hill at Brush Run Rd

Maps, guides, other references

Trail Users' Guide to the Montour Trail. Trail map/brochure available at local bike shops.

USGS Topographic Maps: Bridgeville.

South Park Section

Along Piney Fork in South Park Township in Allegheny County

The seed of the South Park section of the Montour Trail has been sown with a mile and a half of trail. It runs beside Piney Fork Ck, parallel to Brownsville-Library Rd and Piney Fork Rd. There are currently two access points, one near the Bethel Park and South Park sewer plant on Piney Fork Rd, and the other at Triphammer Rd. Access at the west endpoint won't be available until a bridge is rebuilt.

For now, the west end of this trail segment is on the south side of a bridge over Brownsville Rd near Stewart Ed. This bridge is closed pending replacement, and there's no trail access here. The surfaced trail starts at the south end of the bridge. Here the trail is next to a golf driving range here; beware of flying golf balls. Trail fencing is being installed to protect you, so stay on the trail. Aside from the golf area, the trail runs alongside Piney Fork creek for a secluded half-mile to Brownsville Rd Extension, where it crosses at grade. The bridge over Catfish Run here was the first bridge from which rust and paint were removed using the new ElectroStrip method.

Another 0.3 mile brings you to the entrance road for the sewer plant. The 10-car parking lot here is for trail use. After this lot, the road climbs away from the creek and you're left again in relative solitude with the woods and the creek. Too soon (in half a mile) the trail crosses a newly decked and painted bridge and arrives in the Triphammer Rd. parking area. Eventually the trail will be extended at both ends.

Montour Trail, South Park Section	
Location	South Park Township, Allegheny County
Trailheads	Stewart Rd, Piney Fork Rd, Triphammer Rd
Length, Surface	1.5 miles developed; packed crushed stone
Character	Little-used, suburban, shady, flat
Usage restrictions	No motorized vehicles; no snowmobiles
Amenities	Rest rooms, water, food
Driving time from Pittsburgh	45 minutes south

Access points

Vicinity: Directions begin headed south on Clairton Rd (PA51) from its intersection with Library Rd (Blue Belt). To reach this point from Pittsburgh, go south through the Liberty Tubes and turn left on PA51.

Piney Fork trailhead: Follow PA51 to the Yellow Belt and turn right on Curry Hollow Rd (toward South Park). Turn left on Brownsville Rd just after crossing a creek. Follow Brownsville Rd through South Park. Where Brownsville Rd makes a sharp right at Piney Fork Rd (at the CoGo store), turn left on Piney Fork Rd. In 0.5 mile, turn right into trail parking at the entrance to the Bethel Park/South Park wastewater treatment plant.

Triphammer Rd trailhead: Follow PA51 to the Yellow Belt and turn right on Curry Hollow Rd (toward South Park). Turn left on Brownsville Rd just after crossing a creek. Follow Brownsville Rd through South Park. Where Brownsville Rd makes a sharp right at Piney Fork Rd (at the CoGo store), turn left on Piney Fork Rd. In 0.8 mile, turn right on Triphammer Rd. Trail parking is on the right side in 0.1 mile.

Amenities

Rest rooms, water: CoGo at the crossing of Brownsville Rd Extension

Bike shop, rentals: West of the trail, on Library Rd.

Restaurant, groceries: CoGo at the crossing of Brownsville Rd Extension

Camping, simple lodging: None

Swimming, fishing: None

Winter sports: No snowmobiles.

Wheelchair access: Good at both trailheads

Maps, guides, other references

Trail Users' Guide to the Montour Trail. Trail map/brochure available at local bike shops.

USGS Topographic Maps: Bridgeville, Glassport.

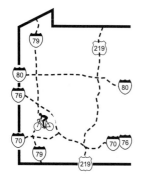

Shorter Trails and Bike Lanes

In addition to the trails that get you away from roads, several areas of Pittsburgh offer bike lanes that provide some separation from traffic. Bike lanes are established along Beechwood Blvd in Point Breeze and Squirrel Hill, and also in Riverview, North, and South Parks. A short trail in Schenley Park has been developed on the former bridle trails; this one is separated from motor vehicle traffic.

Most of these trails are in parks run by Allegheny County and the City of Pittsburgh.

Schenley Park Trails

Park Loop on Former Bridle Trails, Schenley Park

Nearly two miles of the Schenley park trail system have been finished in packed crushed limestone. This makes a good surface for most bicycles. The trail forms a loop that begins and ends near the only traffic light in Schenley Park. Begin just south of the intersection where Overlook Dr ends on Greenfield Rd. Drop gently down the hill and bear right into the woods. You'll be on a gentle downhill that has great views to the south, overlooking the Parkway. After 0.6 mile you pass a sharp left side trail that drops steeply into a series of switchbacks; this is the link to the Eliza Furnace Trail. Staying on the main trail, you emerge at a 3-point trail junction near the swimming pool (fee); this is the midpoint of the trail. Right takes you to the pool; left takes you down a short slope to pass under the Blvd of the Allies Bridge. Go left here. After going under the Blvd of the Allies you'll swing right, get a look down at Panther Hollow Lake, pass the entrance to a small parklet, and cross under Panther Hollow Bridge (the one with the panther statues). After 1.9 miles you'll reach another 3-point trail junction. The right branch takes you into the picnic area next to the traffic light where you started.

In summer, 1999, the trail will connect with the Eliza Furnace Trail. The side trail to the Eliza Furnace Trail will drop steeply through several switchbacks (be careful!) and emerge on Boundary St. To go to Oakland, you will turn right and follow the trail; it will come out near the south end of Neville St. To go to the Eliza Furnace Trail, you will turn left on Boundary St, go two blocks, turn right on Saline St, and follow Saline St to the stop light at Second Av. Cross carefully under the railroad, turn right for 50 yards, then turn right again at the first opening in the retaining wall. This road leads to trailhead parking.

Other, rougher, trails are also available. For example, at the 3-point trail junction near the stoplight in the park, you can continue another mile in the park to Panther Hollow

Lake instead of returning to the traffic light. This trail, however, is dirt and sometimes rutted.

Rest rooms and drinking water are available at many picnic groves near the trail. Swim in season at the park pool. Other amenities are available not far outside the park.

Access points

Anderson Playground: There is only one traffic light in Schenley Park. It's at the intersection of Greenfield Rd, Hobart St, Bartlett St, and Panther Hollow Rd (which you probably think is the extension of Boulevard of the Allies into the park). It's actually a simple intersection, but everything changes names here. This is the best access point for the trail, as there is no other road crossing. Overlook Drive runs into Greenfield Rd just south of this intersection. You can park on Overlook Drive or Bartlett St.

There is also some parking and trail access at the Anderson Playground at the midpoint of the trail. This is near the intersection of Panther Hollow Rd and Blvd of the Allies.

Beechwood Blvd Bike Lanes

Along Beechwood Blvd from Fifth Av to Browns Hill Rd

Signs and white lines along Beechwood Blvd set off both sides of the road as bicycle lanes. Beechwood Blvd takes you through several traditional Pittsburgh neighborhoods, including some quite fine homes. For the most part it is wide enough for cars and bikes to co-exist. It runs almost entirely in residential areas.

The bike lanes start at 5th Av at the tennis-court entrance to Mellon Park. They wind along Beechwood Blvd for 4.0 miles up and down hill across Forbes, along the edge of Frick Park, over Squirrel Hill, and down to the intersection with Browns Hill Rd. Unfortunately, the bike lanes also serve for parking. Unless you're collecting driver-side car doors, this is not an advantage.

Extensions

Along Beechwood Blvd you'll pass Frick Park Parklet, with playground. You can ride into the playground along the fitness course. At the bottom of the sled-riding bowl, you can enter a network of mountain biking trails. Alternatively, you can follow the paved trail in the playground to the end of the pavement and continue on a gravel trail into the "roller coaster", the most difficult single-track mountain biking trail in the park.

Access points

Beechwood Blvd: Anywhere along Beechwood Blvd in Point Breeze or Squirrel Hill.

Lawrenceville Trail

From 43rd to 36th Sts in Lawrenceville, City of Pittsburgh

Tucked away behind Lawrenceville industrial plants near the Washington Crossing Bridge, this pleasant trail offers a short walk beside the Allegheny River. Half the trail runs behind the Carnegie Mellon Robotics Consortium; the other half is behind a warehouse. The trail is well above the river, but close to it. Between the trees you'll get a good view of whatever is happening on the river.

Although this trail is currently only 7 blocks long, the Lawrenceville Development Corporation hopes to extend it to 31st St, where it will connect via the 31st St Bridge with the Washington Landing end of the Three Rivers Heritage Trail.

Access point

40th St: From downtown Pittsburgh, go east on Penn Av to 40th St. Turn left on 40th St. Keep right to avoid crossing the Allegheny River on Washington Crossing Bridge. There is parking for a few cars near the entrance to Carnegie Mellon Robotics Consortium at 40th St

Riverview Park Bike Lane

Along Riverview Drive, Riverview Park

Riverview Park is perched on the side of one of the North Hills, overlooking the Ohio River. Riverview Dr is a paved 2.1-mile loop road that includes a bicycle lane. Picnic groves are perched not far from the road wherever they can find a toehold. The bike lane is popular with pedestrians and joggers. However, the loop road is wide and one-way. Since this isn't a through route, traffic is slow and there's plenty of room to pass.

The trail is on the hillside, so it's far from flat. From the entrance near Allegheny Observatory, it runs downhill for a mile to the intersection of Riverview Drive and Woods Run Rd, then back uphill for 1.1 miles to the start. It loses 140 feet of elevation on the way down and regains it coming up.

Rest rooms and drinking water at many picnic groves near the trail. There's a swimming pool at the top of the hill. Other amenities available not far outside the park.

Access points

Vicinity: Directions begin headed northbound from Pittsburgh on US19, at the corner where US19 turns left from Marshall Av to Perrysville Av about 3 miles north of the West End Bridge.

Riverview Av: About a mile north of where US19 turns onto Perrysville Av, turn left on Riverview Av just before the Byzantine Seminary. In a tenth of a mile, turn right on Riverview Dr. Park along Riverview Dr.

North Park Lake Bike Lane

Around North Park Lake, North Park

Bicyclists, joggers, walkers, skaters, baby buggies, dogs, kidcycles, and anything else that moves can be found on this very popular 5-mile loop alongside the road around North Park Lake. The lake forms an irregular "Y", and the trail follows the lake shore. Sometimes it is alongside the lake, sometimes picnic groves lie between the trail and the lake. Aside from the traffic, it's pleasant and scenic. Since this is a loop trail, it has no official ends. People start at any parking area and go either direction.

This is really a bike lane rather than a bike path, as it isn't very well separated from the automobile traffic. For the most part, the paved trail is directly adjacent to the road, separated only by white lines. It's narrow, too—as much as 7' wide, but don't count on more than 6'. Think of this as a 5-mile sidewalk with cross traffic minimized. The adjacent road is fairly busy, too.

Rest rooms and drinking water are available at many picnic groves near the trail. Swim in season at the park wave pool. Other amenities are available not far outside the park.

The Western Pennsylvania Conservancy offers a detailed 2-page description of the trail.

Access points

Vicinity: Directions begin from the intersection of US19 with the Yellow Belt (Ingomar Rd). To reach this point from Pittsburgh, go north on US19 for approximately 10 miles.

North Park Lake: From the intersection of US19 and the Yellow Belt (Ingomar Rd), go east on the Yellow Belt for 1.6 miles following signs for North Park. At this point the lake and trail will be on your left. Park at any convenient place around the lake.

Alternate route: You can also reach the trail from PA8. From the intersection of PA8 and the Yellow Belt (here called Wildwood Rd), go west on the Yellow Belt for 2.8 miles to North Park.

South Park Bike Path

Along Corrigan Drive, South Park

A paved path runs 2.2 miles through the park on the east side of Corrigan Drive. Like North Park, this path is popular with walkers, joggers, dog walkers, and everything else. Even on a December weekday it will be busy. In addition to the path, at the north edge of the fairgrounds, a 0.75-mile paved path goes over the hill to the "heart course", a 0.75-mile exercise trail. On the other side of the heart course, a 0.25-mile path returns to Corrigan Drive at McConkey. You can use these to stretch the trip out to a bit over 3 miles.

Rest rooms and drinking water are available at many picnic groves near the trail. Swim in season at the park wave pool. Other amenities are available not far outside the park.

An undeveloped leg of the Montour Trail is only a mile to the south. Unfortunately, there is no good way of getting there.

Access points

Vicinity: Directions begin headed southbound from Pittsburgh on PA88 (Library Rd) about a mile south of the Yellow Belt.

Corrigan Dr: At well-signed Corrigan Dr, turn into South Park. Corrigan Dr runs through the park. Use any handy parking lot.

Downtown from North Shore

Trails South & East: Laurel Highlands

Fifty miles east of Pittsburgh, rolling hills rise into the folds of the Appalachian mountains. Although the terrain is rugged, the region is laced with rail-trails. Like the railroads that preceded them, these trails follow rivers on gentle grades. The major trail system in this region combines the Youghiogheny River and Allegheny Highlands Trails. The route runs upstream along the Youghiogheny River, going southeast from McKeesport to Confluence, then along the Casselman River northeast to Rockwood and southeast to Meyersdale. These trails should be complete from McKeesport to Meyersdale in 1999. Eventually the system will continue southeast to meet the C&O Canal at Cumberland MD and south from Connellsville to Pt Marion, where it will connect with an extensive system that's growing in West Virginia.

Additional trails in the area follow US119 near Greensburg, Indian Creek near PA381, and Linn Run and Summit Rds east of Ligonier.

The Pittsburgh to Washington DC Connection

McKeesport PA to Cumberland MD and thence to Washington DC in Allegheny, Westmoreland, Fayette, Somerset Counties PA; Allegany, Washington, Frederick, and Montgomery County MD; and Washington DC

Soon after the turn of the century, it should be possible to ride for over 300 traffic-free miles from Pittsburgh PA to Washington DC. From Pittsburgh the trail will climb gently along the Youghiogheny River, Casselman River, and Flaugherty Run to the spine of Big Savage Mountain. Here it will cross through the mountain into Maryland north of Frostburg, then descend to Washington via Jennings Run, Wills Ck and the C&O Canal Towpath along the Potomac River. In Pennsylvania, one continuous stretch of 71 miles and another of 21 miles are now open, and construction is progressing steadily.

Development of the corridor between Pittsburgh and Cumberland is being coordinated by the Allegheny Trail Alliance. This organization is a coalition of the seven trail organizations that are directly responsible for segments of the trail.

This route between Pittsburgh and Washington DC will involve several distinct trails:
- Allegheny County trails connecting to McKeesport, including Montour, Three Rivers Heritage, and Steel Heritage Trails along the Monongahela River. Distances depend on where you start. Trail organizers are now identifying routes to connect existing segments of the Montour and Three Rivers trails.
- Northern, or flatwater, section of the Youghiogheny River Trail, 43 miles from McKeesport to Connellsville. It's open from Boston to Connellsville now. By late 1999, the connection from McKeesport to Boston should be complete.

- Southern, or whitewater, section of the Youghiogheny River Trail, 28 miles from Connellsville to Confluence. This is complete except for short road links in Confluence and Ohiopyle.
- Casselman River section of the Allegheny Highlands Trail, 32 miles from Confluence to Meyersdale. In early 1999, 21.3 miles from Meyersdale around the Pinkerton Horn were complete; the whole section should be finished in 2000.
- Flaugherty Run section of the Allegheny Highlands Trail, 11 miles from Meyersdale to the state line. Construction from Meyersdale toward Deal should begin in late 1999 or 2000.
- Maryland section of the Allegheny Highlands Trail, 21 miles across Big Savage Mountain from the state line to Cumberland. The 5 miles from Frostburg to the state line are scheduled for 1999 development, and development of a bike trail along the scenic railroad line awaits funding.
- C&O Canal Towpath from Cumberland to Washington. This 185-mile trail has been open for many years. For variety, the paved 10-mile Western Maryland Rail Trail parallels the towpath for 10 miles south from Hancock

These trails all follow rivers except for the section that crosses through Big Savage Mountain. The trail leaves Flaugherty Run near Deal, follows an old railroad grade (with tunnels) along the eastern flank of Big Savage Mountain, and emerges near Frostburg to parallel Jennings Run.

In this guide, we describe each trail in the direction suggested by its mileposts. Unfortunately, this is not consistent: the northern section of the Youghiogheny River trail counts from west to east; the others count from east to west.

By summer of 2000, the trail system should be complete except for a gap between Meyersdale and Frostburg, where the Savage Mountain Tunnel will be the major remaining obstacle. Until then, you can connect the trails on roads: From Meyersdale follow SR2006 for 8.5 miles to Flaugherty Run Rd, then Flaugherty Run Rd for 3.3 miles to the state line and Mason-Dixon Campground; there's little traffic on these roads. Turn left on MD946 and follow it through Finzel for 3.5 rolling miles to AltUS40; you'll see somewhat more traffic. Take the ramp to go east on Alt US40 and be prepared to endure real traffic for 3.5 miles into Frostburg; fortunately it's mostly downhill and there's a smooth shoulder. From Frostburg to Cumberland you can ride in traffic on MD36 or AltUS40—or you can buy a one-way ticket on the Western Maryland Scenic RR. We recommend the train; they'll take your bike, it's a nice trip, and you can preview the route of the future trail. We wish someone would offer a shuttle service between Frostburg and either the state line or Meyersdale.

Even with the Frostburg gap, the trail offers an excellent opportunity for either a camping or a motel/B&B trip, provided you're willing to ride a few miles in traffic near

Frostburg (or you can find someone to shuttle you). You already can ride this trip if you're also willing to use PA281 between Confluence and Ft Hill or Markleton.

Here's a sample itinerary for an 8-day camping trip at a leisurely 40 miles a day:

Day 1	McKeesport to Adelaide	40 miles
Day 2	Adelaide to Confluence	29 miles
Day 3	Confluence to Finzel	41 miles
	(using low-traffic roads from Meyersdale to the state line)	
Day 4	Finzel to Potomac Forks Hiker-Biker Camp	40-45 miles
	(hills and traffic to Frostburg, then take the scenic RR)	
Day 5	Potomac Forks to Little Pool Hiker-Biker Camp	45 miles
Day 6	Little Pool to Horseshoe Bend Hiker-Biker Camp	41 miles
Day 7	Horseshoe Bend to Marble Quarry Hiker-Biker Camp	42 miles
Day 8	Marble Quarry to Washington DC	38 miles

If you prefer longer days and more luxurious nights, you can stay in B&Bs and motels. They're not as well spaced as the campsites, though. Here's a 5-and-a-half-day itinerary at about 60 miles a day:

evening	McKeesport to Smithton	24 miles
Day 1	Smithton to Rockwood	57 miles
Day 2	Rockwood to Paw Paw	64 miles
Day 3	Paw Paw to Williamsport	56 miles
Day 4	Williamsport to Whites Ferry (stay in Leesburg, VA)	64 miles
Day 5	Whites Ferry to Washington DC	36 miles

Trail organization

Allegheny Trail Alliance
419 College Ave
Greensburg PA 15601
(724) 853-BIKE (853-2453)
(888) ATA-BIKE (282-2453)
e-mail: ATAmail@westol.com
web: www.ATAtrail.org

C&O Canal National Historical Park
Box 4
Sharpsburg MD 21782
(301) 739-4200

web: www.nps.gov/choh

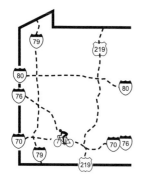

Youghiogheny River Trail

Once trains wound their way up both sides of the Youghiogheny River Gorge en route to the Potomac basin. Now only the CSX (formerly B&O) line on the north side of the river operates. On the south side, a rail-trail connects McKeesport with Confluence on the routes of the former Pittsburgh and Lake Erie (P&LE) and Western Maryland lines. By late 1999 the trail will be open all the way from McKeesport to Confluence. The Youghiogheny River Trails North and South are two of seven trails in the Allegheny Trail Alliance. The Alliance is coordinating the effort to establish a trail system connecting Pittsburgh with Washington DC via rail-trails and the C&O Canal Towpath. The northern section of the Youghiogheny River Trail is owned and operated by the non-profit Regional Trails Corporation with help from the Southwestern PA Heritage Preservation Commission. The southern part is developed and managed by Ohiopyle State Park. Several volunteer organizations support the trail.

Allegheny County

Mon/Yough Trail Council
PO Box 14
McKeesport PA 15135-0014
(724) 872-5586
Membership:
    $10/year individual; $15/year family

Fayette County

Yough River Trail Council
PO Box 988
Connellsville PA 15425-0988
(724) 626-5994

Membership:
    $15/year individual; $25/year family

Ohiopyle State Park

Ohiopyle State Park
PO Box 105
Ohiopyle PA 15470-0105
(724) 329-8591
web: www.dcnr.state.pa.us/stateparks/parks/ohio.htm
e-mail: ohiopyle.sp@a1.dcnr.state.pa.us

Westmoreland County

Westmoreland Yough Trail Chapter
PO Box 95, 101 North Water St
West Newton PA 15089-0095
(724) 872-5586
Membership:
    $15/year individual; $25/year family

Operations, Boston to Bruner Run

Regional Trails Corporation
PO Box 95, 101 North Water St
West Newton PA 15089-0095
(724) 872-5586
e-mail: youghrtl@westol.com
web: www.youghrivertrail.com/
Membership:
    $25/year individual

Hotline for trail problems

(724) 872-5586
In the evenings, this number also takes voicemail for each of the councils

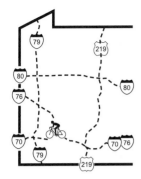

Youghiogheny River Trail, Northern Section

McKeesport to Connellsville, in Allegheny, Westmoreland, and Fayette Counties

By late 1999, the trail will be completed all the way from McKeesport to Connellsville. The final gap, just south of McKeesport, should be closed in early fall of 1999. The trail begins in McKeesport's McKee Point Park on the east side of the Youghiogheny River just south of its confluence with the Monongahela River. This is Pittsburgh and Lake Erie (P&LE) milepost 15; if milepost 0 existed, it would be under the Smithfield St Bridge in Pittsburgh. The trail runs through McKeesport and crosses to the west side of the Yough at the 15th St bridge. From there it remains on the south side of the Youghiogheny all the way to Connellsville. Volunteer trail monitors ride the trail carrying first-aid kits, basic tools, and cellular telephones. Flag one down if you need assistance or have questions.

McKee Point Park in McKeesport (mile 15) is the official northern terminus of the trail. From the park, the trail runs south past the marina on Water St to 9th St, Here it stays off the streets on packed crushed limestone between Kane Hospital and the river's edge for a quarter-mile. It turns away from the river to join Saunders St for two blocks. At Market St the trail leaves the street, returning to packed crushed limestone. It crosses 11th St and parallels 11th St to Walnut St (PA148) for two blocks. Just before Walnut St, the trail turns to run alongside Walnut St to 13th St, where it jogs toward the river to pass behind a building, soon returning alongside Walnut St to the 15th St Bridge. The large round building just below the trail is the old water softening plant. The trail crosses the 15th St bridge; you have a choice between walking on a narrow sidewalk and riding on a wide shoulder. At the end of the bridge the trail turns left on River Rd, which has been widened a bit and posted as a bike route. If in doubt about the route, follow signs for Durabond Coatings. The trail follows River Rd for just over a mile to the Durabond plant gate. By late 1999 the trail will turn right at the Durabond gate, go uphill for about 200', and turn left, clinging to the hillside to skirt the back side of the Durabond plant for half a mile to Deadman's Hollow. This section will climb about 75 feet on a 5% grade. At present, however, it is mostly graded but unsafe, with shale and mud on the surface and steep unprotected dropoffs to the side.

The trail resumes at Deadman's Hollow (mile 18), which is currently accessible only from Boston. A network of hiking nature trails (no bikes) runs up Deadman's Hollow. Our trail remains level and goes through woods for a mile to the trailhead at the Boston Riverfront Park (mile 19.1). Until the Durabond connection is finished, most people will prefer to use the Boston trailhead. From here the trail runs along the edge of Boston, with light industry on the river side and residential back yards on the land side. The warehouse at mile 20.8 has doors to match boxcars on some long-gone adjacent siding.

The scrap yard at mile 21.2 has three large bells hiding in the shrubbery. Wildflowers proliferate along the shoulders. After fifteen road crossings, including four in the residential area of Greenock (mile 21.3-21.6), the trail leaves civilization and runs along the river in splendid isolation for 5 miles to Buena Vista. In early May trillium carpet the slopes of the 300-foot hillside near miles 22-23.

The trail emerges on the flats in a curve of the river and passes the site of the Dravo Methodist Church (mile 24.9). This church was founded in 1801 and once drew a congregation from both sides of the river. It was the oldest in the area until fire destroyed it in 1920; the cemetery remains. The trail's first campground, Dravo Landing, is between the cemetery and the river, accessible by the wide trail to the right of the cemetery. It has two fire rings and shares the chemical toilet with trail users at the cemetery. The trail council hopes to have a well soon. This campground is for trail users and canoeists; share the space. For a group of 20 or more, contact the Regional Trail Council first.

Youghiogheny River Trail, Northern Section	
Location	South Versailles and Elizabeth Townships, Allegheny County; Rostraver Township, Westmoreland County; Perry, Franklin, and Dunbar Townships, Fayette County
Trailheads	McKeesport, Boston, West Newton, Cedar Creek Park, Smithton, Dawson, Connellsville
Length, Surface	43 miles planned; 2 miles complete McKeesport-Durabond, 40 miles complete Deadman's Hollow-Connellsville; packed crushed stone
Character	Busy to crowded, wooded, shady, flat
Usage restrictions	Horses ok beside trail—stay off improved surface; no motorized vehicles; no snowmobiles
Amenities	Rest rooms, water, bike rental, food, camping, lodging, swimming, fishing
Driving time from Pittsburgh	45 minutes to 1 hour 30 minutes

Half a mile past Dravo Cemetery is the ghost town of Stringtown, marked only by a few inconspicuous foundations. This village once strung out for half a mile along the railroad. Also near here was Indian Queen Alliquippa's summer village.

The trail enters Buena Vista at the Dapul Company (mile 26.4). A picnic pavilion (mile 26.6) greets you in Buena Vista, not far from the swimming pool. For the next 4.8 miles, the trail passes frequently through small towns, alternating between woods and residential communities. In Industry (mile 27.5), note the stained glass windows in the Merritt Primitive Methodist Church. As you pass through Industry, Blythedale (mile 29), and later Smithdale (mile 30), notice the uniform basic shape of the houses—a sign of company towns—and the way subsequent owners have individualized them. The trail emerges on SR2017 at mile 29.5, next to the bridge to Sutersville.

From Sutersville, the trail runs half a mile between the cliff and the river to Smithdale (mile 30). Smithdale is one of several company towns along the trail and a particularly good example of how a production-line town can evolve into a community of homes with quite distinct personalities. After leaving Smithdale, the trail returns to the bench along the cliff to pass into Westmoreland County at mile 31.4. It emerges in a residential area of Collinsburg (mile 32.3), which blends into West Newton (mile 33.2).

Dravo Cemetery, mile 24.9

In West Newton, the trail council's combine car—a rail car that's part passenger, part baggage—sits beside the trail near PA136; this car is being restored, largely by volunteers, to become an environment learning center. You'll see some fine old homes in West Newton just before reaching a major trailhead at PA136. There are stores across the Youghiogheny River, across the PA136 bridge. Be careful at the PA136 intersection; there's a lot of traffic but no signal. At West Newton, the trail leaves civilization for most of a mile, until Buddtown (mile 34), where Joseph and Joshua Budd once operated a ferry across the river (mile 34.1). Just after leaving Buddtown you pass the remnants of the Banning #4 coal mine and coal cleaning plant (mile 34.5, private property). The mine is closed, but the water treatment plant still runs. Note the cattails across from the water treatment plant.

Then the cliff approaches the river and the trail runs on a wide flat bench between the cliff and the river. A wooden bridge marks the entry to the Manderino Riverfront section of Cedar Creek Park (mile 36.5), where you'll find heat in the restrooms and snacks in restored Cedar Creek Station. The Cedar Creek gorge has superb wildflower displays through the year. The trail continues through the waterfront section of the park to the access road (mile 37.1), then re-enters the woods between the cliff and the river for another mile to Smithton (mile 39.3). Group camping is available by prior arrangement and fee; contact Westmoreland Co. Parks at (724) 830-3959 for information and permit. Across the river at Smithton you can see the Jones Brewing Company, built in 1907 as the home of Stoney's beer.

Past Smithton, the trail continues along the Youghiogheny River through old company towns and their mines, beginning with Van Meter (mile 40.1 to 41.2) and Whitsett (mile 42.7 to 44.5). Van Meter (mile 40.5) served the Darr Mine, whose coal cleaning plant you'll see at mile 41.4. Van Meter became a virtual ghost town almost overnight in December 1907, when disasters in both the Naomi and Darr Mines claimed first 34, then 239 lives. The large building on the west side of the trail near the road intersection is the former Company Store; you can still buy soft drinks at the vending machine nearby. The residence across the street that looks like a train station once was the train station. A suspension footbridge once crossed the Youghiogheny River from Van Meter to Jacob's Creek. At 432 feet in length, it was believed to be the longest such bridge in the world when it opened in 1926.

After Van Meter, you pass under the Norfolk and Western High Bridge (mile 41.5), The Banning #2 mine (office at Whitsett Rd, mile 42.7) was served by Whitsett (mile 43), another coal patch town. Ralph Whitsett Sr., the town founder, built the large red house on the road near the river (mile 43) in 1873. An exhibit at the Pittsburgh Regional History Center features Whitsett.

The most remote section of the trail runs from Layton (mile 45.7) to Dawson/Dickerson Run (mile 52.8). There is no road access in this 7-mile stretch, just the woods and the river. Be prepared to do your own repairs here; it's a long walk to the nearest road. The trail council hopes to develop a campground at Round Bottom (mile 47.5) some day. Just past Layton you'll pass the remains of a brick factory and its associated kilns (mile 46.2) and cross several small streams.

Dickerson Run (mile 52.8), across the river from Dawson, was once a major switching yard. The P&LE operated the 2500-car yard under a joint switching agreement with the Western Maryland RR from 1912 to 1970. It has a large parking lot and trailhead. For 2.5 miles south from here, to Adelaide (mile 55.2), the trail again runs close to the river.

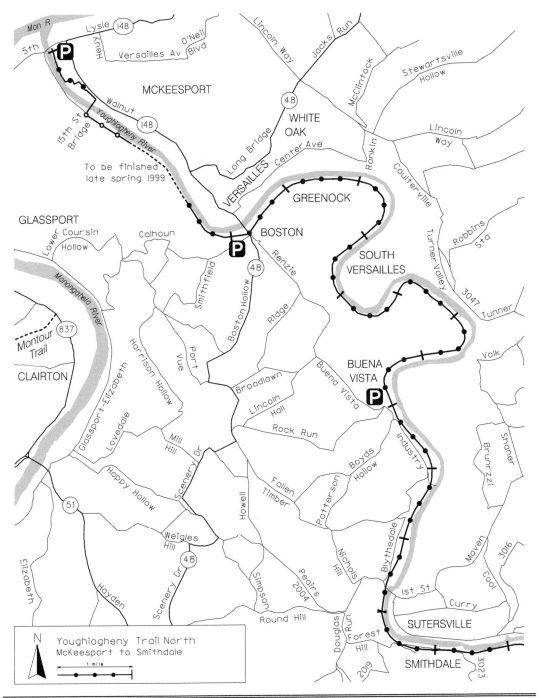

Youghiogheny Trail North
McKeesport to Smithdale

1 mile

This area was once known as the coke capital of the world. Hundreds of coke ovens in one or two rows dot the hillsides just above the trail. An interpretive sign at mile 54 describes their history.

At Adelaide (mile 55.2) the trail emerges from the woods at River's Edge Campground, passes through a small town for about a mile, and re-enters the woods. At mile 57.2 a side trail leads to a (closed) railroad bridge across the Youghiogheny. The trail emerges into a large cindered parking lot at mile 58. At the edge of the lot a former railroad yard office is being refurbished as a trail information center; eventually there will be rest rooms here.

From the left edge of the cinder lot a ramp winds down the hill to Yough River Park near the William Crawford cabin. Here it connects with the bike trail along 3rd St through Connellsville to the southern section of the trail. At Connellsville the river leaves the farm and mining lands in the valley and enters the water gap through Chestnut Ridge. As you cross to the southern section, the character of the trail changes from flatwater to whitewater, and the setting changes from rural mining towns to near-wilderness gorge.

Local history, attractions

The railroad that once ran here opened for business as the Pittsburgh, McKeesport, & Youghiogheny Railroad—PMc&Y, also known as the "P-Mickey"—in October 12, 1883. Almost immediately, on January 1, 1884, it became part of the Pittsburgh and Lake Erie Railroad (P&LERR). In 1887 it became a New York Central (NYC) line, which merged with the Pennsy in the 1960s to become the Penn Central. The collapse of the Penn Central made the P&LE independent again in 1978. P&LE filed to abandon the line in 1990, after the decline of the coal industry reduced traffic too much. Most of the P&LE's business was related to steel-making: coal, ore, coke, and limestone. P&LE boxcars bore the slogan "Serves the Steel Centers."

Industrial activity in the valley revolved around the steel industry, and the trail shows conspicuous remnants of both steel and mining activity. In some areas piles of mine tailings (also called gob, or red-dog) dominate the landscape. Several ruins of coal-processing plants remain. Less obvious, but still visible, are a number of areas of mine drainage. Spot these by the bright orange soil under the waterfall or creek. Remains of coke ovens lie near the trail at several locations. Several of the towns along the trail are former company towns.

A short-lived canal served the Youghiogheny River between West Newton and McKeesport. The Youghiogheny Slackwater Navigation Company built two dams of logs and stone. Locks allowed steamboats to overcome a 27-foot change in elevation and created a slackwater navigation system. The canal began operations around 1850 but was destroyed by a flood in January 1865.

Dawson was the center of Philip Cochran's coke empire. Remains of coke ovens fill the hillside by the trail for miles nearby; there were over 34,000 of them in the area. The Cochran's Queen Anne Victorian home, Cochran House, still stands in Dawson.

Two miles uphill from Dawson via River Rd and Stone Bridge Trail, Linden Hall sits atop the hill. The great Tudor mansion at Linden Hall was built for Sarah Cochran, the widow of the coke and coal pioneer. The Tudor mansion's 35,000 square feet contains beautiful period pieces, Tiffany windows, and an Aeolian pipe organ—one of three in the world. Linden Hall is the centerpiece of a resort/conference center and is open for tours (fee).

Connellsville was close to the head of navigation on the Youghiogheny, so it was a good place for businesses such as flat boat building and associated raw materials such as lumber and ironwork. Such businesses flourished in the late 18th and early 19th centuries.

Coke oven, near mile 54

Extensions of the ride

Linden Hall Resort has developed a trail to provide bicycle access from Dawson. Using the Stone Bridge Trail, you can climb 500' from river level to the Cochran mansion atop the hill. Leave the Youghiogheny River Trail at Dickerson Run, mile 52.8. Climb the road ramp to PA819, then turn left on PA819 and carefully cross the bridge to Dawson. At the Dawson end of the bridge, turn left on River Rd. Ride carefully in traffic for a level half-mile and cross the railroad tracks. Just after you cross the tracks, turn left to stay on River Rd; it's marked "No Outlet" and there's less traffic on this section.

Follow River Rd, which now is slightly hilly, 1.2 miles to the mouth of Laurel Run. Here the road turns away from the river and starts climbing; the surface deteriorates seriously. This was originally the main road to Linden Hall. The road does a switchback across the trail's namesake stone bridge and ends at a fork after 0.1 mile and 80 feet of climb. The right fork is private; the left fork, now traffic-free, climbs another mile to Linden Hall. The first half-mile climbs 180 feet, including two steep sections of about a tenth of a mile. A large overlook with rustic railing marks the end of the steep climbs. Another half-mile (and only 100 feet of climb) brings you onto the southwest corner of the Linden Hall grounds, near the maintenance shed. Now you can ride on the resort's hilly roads to the mansion, swimming pool, restaurant, or whatever. We enjoyed both soup and sandwich at the restaurant.

Development plans

The trail organizations hold regular volunteer trail development activities on most Saturdays with decent weather. Several Boy Scouts have improved the trail through their Eagle Scout projects. These projects include restoration of mileposts, interpretive displays, and environmental work.

In addition to completing the trail, plans call for development of river access areas for camping, fishing, and boating. Historic sites will be preserved and developed. Overnight facilities for through travelers will include B&Bs, hostels, and primitive campsites at several locations along the trail.

Access points

Vicinity: Directions begin headed southeast on PA51. Except for the McKeesport trailhead, the directions start at Elizabeth, where PA51 crosses the Monongahela River. To reach this point from Pittsburgh, pick up PA51 anywhere in the South Hills and turn south or southeast.

McKee Point (northern) trailhead: Go southeast on PA51 from Pittsburgh. Turn east on the Yellow Belt (Lebanon Church Rd) toward Allegheny County Airport just north of Century III Mall. Follow the Yellow Belt for about 5 miles to cross the Monongahela River on Mansfield Bridge and then another mile to cross the Youghiogheny River. Turn right after crossing the Youghiogheny to McKee Point Park.

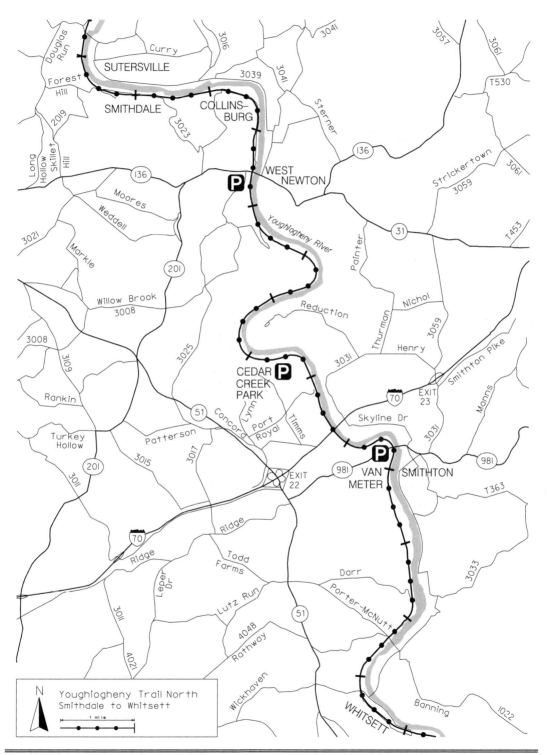

Youghiogheny Trail North
Smithdale to Whitsett

N

1 mile

Boston trailhead: Go southeast on PA51 from the Monongahela River for about 4 miles to PA48 near Round Hill Regional Park. Turn north on PA48, and follow its twists and turns for 6-8 miles to a 5-way intersection in Boston, just before you cross the Youghiogheny River. At this point (the south end of Boston Bridge), turn west (left), then immediately back north (right, toward the river). In less than a block, the road crosses the trail, and there is plenty of parking at this point. If you go a bit farther, you'll come to a PA Fish Commission boat ramp. *Alternate route:* If you're coming from the east side of Pittsburgh, it's quicker to reach Boston via PA48 south from the Parkway and US30.

West Newton trailhead: Go southeast on PA51 from the Monongahela River for about 6 miles to PA136. Turn east (left) on PA136 and continue about 5 miles into the outskirts of West Newton. Just before crossing the Youghiogheny River, turn south (right) into the parking area at the west end of the PA136 bridge. There's additional parking on the north side of PA136, along Collinsburg Rd.

Cedar Ck trailhead: Go southeast on PA51 from the Monongahela River for about 10 miles and follow signs to the Park. In quick succession you'll turn left on Concord Lane, left on Lynn Rd, and right on Port Royal Rd. Just after passing Timms Lane, turn left at the main entrance to Cedar Creek Park. Follow this road downhill until it reaches the flood plain. There's one parking lot just before you cross the trail and several more a little farther along the road.

Smithton trailhead: Go southeast on PA51 from the Monongahela River for 11 miles. Just after passing I70, turn east (left) on PA981 toward Smithton. Follow PA981 for 1.5 miles, to a point just before crossing the Youghiogheny River (the west end of the PA981 bridge). Immediately before the bridge's guard rail starts, turn down a short road that leads sharply down to the parking area near the river.

Whitsett trailhead: Go southeast on PA51 from the Monongahela River for 13-14 miles. Half a mile after passing Wickhaven, turn east (left) on T495 toward Whitsett. When you reach river level in about a mile, look for a right turn to trail parking and the pavilion at the trail, a block away from the river.

Dawson/Dickerson Run trailhead: Go southeast on PA51 from the Monongahela River for 18 miles to the PA201 interchange for Connellsville. (Note: this will be the second intersection of PA51 and PA201; watch your mileage and don't be fooled.) Take PA201 south toward Vanderbilt and Connellsville for 7 miles. In Vanderbilt, turn north (left) on PA819 and follow it 0.7 mile downhill almost to the Dawson-Liberty Bridge across the Youghiogheny River. Just before crossing this bridge, turn left (northwest). Almost immediately turn left down a ramp, making a 270-degree descending left turn. This ramp leads back under the road and into trailhead parking. The trail is at the far side of the parking lot.

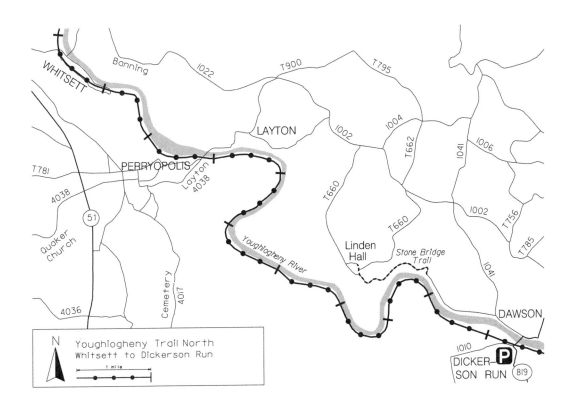

N
Youghiogheny Trail North
Whitsett to Dickerson Run
1 mile

Connellsville trailhead: Go southeast on PA51 from the Monongahela River for 18 miles to the PA201 interchange for Connellsville. (Note: this will be the second intersection of PA51 and PA201; watch your mileage and don't be fooled.) Take PA201 south for 10.7 miles toward Vanderbilt, then Connellsville. Just before the intersection with the southbound lanes of US119, turn north (left) into the vast cindered area between US119 and the termination of PA201. Go back beyond the produce stand and the caboose to where the cable closes off the area. This is trailhead parking. The northern section of the trail takes off on the other side of the gate, past the restored yard office. The connection to Yough River Park and the southern trail drops off the plateau toward US119 and crosses under the highway. To reach the parking near Yough River Park, continue on PA201 to the intersection with US119. Turn left on PA711 (Crawford Av) and continue several blocks to the traffic light at 3rd St. Turn left on 3rd St and follow signs to trailhead parking in the gravel lot just before Connellsville Bottling Co.

Other trailheads: There are additional trailheads at Buena Vista, Sutersville, Layton, and Adelaide (fee parking at campground). These are reached by various back roads. Take a good map with you.

Amenities

Rest rooms, water: Seasonal chemical toilets at Boston, West Newton, Smithton, and Dawson/Dickerson Run trailheads and at ballfields in Greenock, Industry, and Blythedale. Rest rooms at Cedar Creek Park all year, at Linden Hall, at Yough River Park (may be closed in winter), and eventually at the restored yard office near mile 58. Drinking water at playground in Industry, in Cedar Creek Park, and at River's Edge Campground in Adelaide.

Bike shop, rental: Bike shops with rentals at several shops in Boston, Greenock, West Newton, and Connellsville. Rentals at the restored train station in Cedar Creek Park (mile 36.7) and Adelaide Campground (mile 55.1). More shops are opening all the time.

Restaurant, groceries: Boston has a Foodland grocery store near Boston Bridge and Boston Diner, three blocks toward Greenock. There are several other restaurants along the trail near Boston, along Smithfield St parallel to the trail in Boston, and just across Boston Bridge; the church near the trail sometimes serves dinner, too. A trailside shop just before Greenock offers snacks. Three blocks from the pavilion at Buena Vista, the Volunteer Fire Department operates a seasonal snack bar next to the swimming pool. Just south of Buena Vista, near mile 27.0, Ped-L-ers Market (the former Valle[y] Dairy) has groceries and a deli counter. Sutersville, across the Yough at mile 29.5, has restaurants. A dairy stand half a block from the Sutersville trailhead offers ice cream and sandwiches. Half a block from the West Newton trailhead are a deli store, an ice cream store, and a Rite-Aid offering snacks and light groceries. West Newton, across the river at mile 33.2, has a Giant Eagle 0.7 miles north of the bridge plus several restaurants, including a Dairy-Land on N Water St near the Giant Eagle, the Second St Cafe on 2nd St just south of PA136, and several pizza shops. The rental shop at Cedar Creek Park (mile 36.7) has snacks (seasonal). At Layton (mile 45.3), snacks are seasonally available at Hazelbaker Canoe livery, across the river and a quarter mile up the road. Dawson (across the river, at mile 52.8) has groceries, snacks, and restaurants. There's a restaurant at Linden Hall, at top of the Stone Bridge Trail spur. The campground at Adelaide (mile 55.1) has a small store with groceries, and a restaurant (The Coke Oven). In Connellsville, a Sheetz market and a Wendy's are just across the PA711/US119 intersection from the trailhead; there are many others in town. Soft drink or juice vending machines have been installed at Dapul Company (mile 26.4), Ped-L-ers Market (mile 27.0), and near the old company store in Van Meter (mile 40.8).

Camping, simple lodging: Primitive camping at Dravo Landing (mile 24.9). Primitive group camping at Cedar Creek Park (mile 36.7) by prior arrangement with Westmoreland County Parks at (724) 830-3950. River's Edge Campground lies along the trail near Adelaide (mile 55.1). *Trail Book '96* contains ads for Bed-and-Breakfasts close to the trail at Buena Vista (1 mile up the hill) and Dawson. Linden Hall, at the top of the Stone Bridge Trail spur, has motel rooms. Several motels uphill from Smithton near PA51.

The trail council hopes to develop another primitive campsite at Round Bottom (mile 47.5).

Swimming, fishing: Pools at Buena Vista, Linden Hall, and River's Edge Campground (all fee). The Youghiogheny may look enticing for unsupervised swimming, but it carries a considerable amount of raw sewage. Exercise caution, especially if the water is high. Swimming is prohibited at the Fish Commission access at Boston and at Cedar Creek Park. Signs at Connellsville Riverfront Park remind you that the park was not created to entice swimming and you do so at your own risk. Fishing is good to excellent all along the trail. Common catches are trout and small-mouth bass plus other varieties including catfish. The Yough is stocked with trout at West Newton. Record-size bass have been caught near Smithton. We see fisherfolk all along the river; one day we met a fisherman with a 35" muskie.

Winter sports: Cross-country skiing. No snowmobiles

Wheelchair access: OK at most trailheads, though many parking lots are gravel. Ramp down to Yough River Park is steeper than most of the trail; avoid this by parking in the upper lot. Wide gates; the ones we measured were all 44" or wider.

Maps, guides, other references

Trail Book '96: A Users Guide to the Youghiogheny River Trail and the Allegheny Highlands Trail. Available from the trail councils and many local businesses.

Tim Palmer. *Youghiogheny, Appalachian River.* University of Pittsburgh Press, 1984.

USGS Topographic Maps: McKeesport, Donora, Smithton, Fayette City, Dawson, Connellsville.

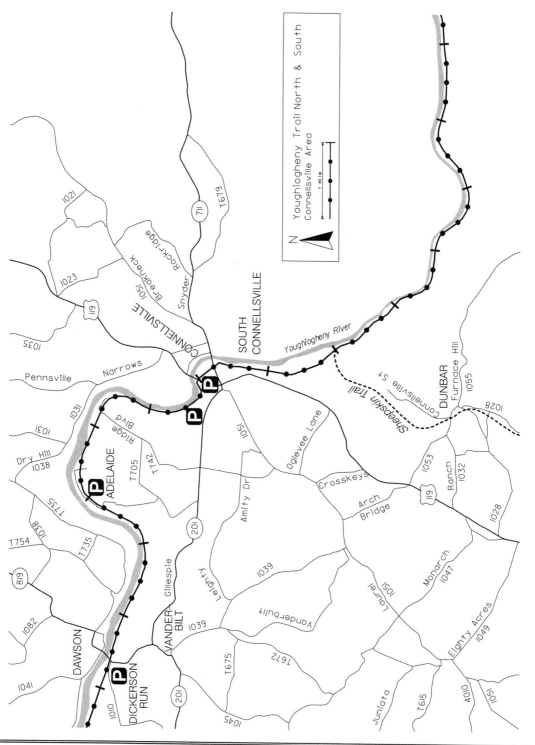

Free-Wheeling Easy in Western Pennsylvania

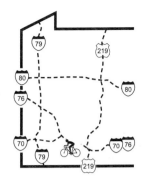

Youghiogheny River Trail, Southern Section

Confluence to Connellsville, in Fayette County

George Washington followed the Youghiogheny to Ohiopyle in 1754 in his search for a water route to Fort Duquesne (now Pittsburgh), but he gave up when he encountered the falls at Ohiopyle and the rapids below. Modern visitors cycle this route through the Appalachians on the former route of the Western Maryland Railroad.

This trail has been named as one of the best walking trails in the world. Writing in the October 1994 issue of *Travel and Leisure Magazine*, Rita Ariyoshi named the Youghiogheny River Trail among 19 paths from France to New Zealand as "The World's Best Walks". It's a popular trail, and hence can be a busy one. In 12 years from 1986 to 1998 the number of user-days grew from 45,000 to 300,000.

The zero milepost of the trail is at the PA281 bridge over the Youghiogheny River in Confluence; the trail runs northwest from here toward Connellsville. For about 0.6 miles the trail goes downstream on Ramcat Hollow Rd to a right turn onto the trail, which is finished in crushed limestone. After a couple of road crossings, the trail passes through the Ramcat Hollow trailhead. From here to Ohiopyle, the trail is isolated. The river is frequently visible, and you can enjoy watching the canoeists in the easy rapids between Victoria and Ohiopyle. Along this portion of the trail you'll notice remnants of the railroad, most notably cuts through hills such as the one at mile 2.5, fills that kept the railbed nearly level over hollows such as the one at mile 2.7, and retaining walls like the one at mile 5.7. You'll also see traces of old farms, such as the fruit trees in the field at mile 6.3 and the long stacked fieldstone fence that runs from mile 6.5 to mile 6.7. Half a dozen or so benches along the trail provide chances to rest and watch the traffic go by.

At mile 9.8 the trail enters the Ohiopyle parking lot. A restored railroad station at mile 10.1 hosts the information center. Ohiopyle is a popular tourist area and has bike rental facilities. The trail is likely to be very busy with both pedestrians and bicyclists in the vicinity of Ohiopyle. From the information center the trail follows roads across the Youghiogheny River (be alert to automobile traffic) and into the parking area for the Ferncliff Natural Area, a wildflower preserve. Signs at the end of the parking area direct you back onto the trail at mile 10.4. The American Youth Hostel is to the right at the end of the parking area.

Although it's only half a mile across Ferncliff peninsula before you cross the river again, the river takes 2 miles to go around the peninsula, dropping 80 ft in the process. As the trail leaves Ohiopyle it crosses the Youghiogheny River on a converted trestle. Notice how much farther above the river you are here than in Ohiopyle. This trestle is a good place to watch raft trips negotiate (or fail to negotiate) Railroad Rapid just upstream. From Ohiopyle to Bruner Run (mile 16) the trail runs well above the river, and the woods are too thick for good views of the rafting and kayaking action. However, you'll hear, if not see, the rafting crowds. Signposts with cryptic 2-letter abbreviations mark paths down the steep hill to some of the named rapids. You can also enjoy the maturing deciduous forest, the cascading feeder streams, and the June display of laurel and rhododendron. Note especially the rock face with coal seams at mile 13.7 and the railroad ties remaining alongside the trail at mile 15. Half a dozen benches provide resting places. Several hiking trails intersect our trail: Great Gorge at mile 10.6, Beech at mile 10.7, Jonathan Run at mile 13.5, and Kentuck at miles 13.5 and 13.7. Bicycles are forbidden on most of these, though it is permitted to take bikes up the trail to the campground. The trail gradient is more noticeable between Ohiopyle and Bruner Run than elsewhere (not surprisingly, as that's also the more difficult whitewater section). Bruner Run is the termination of the very popular whitewater trip that begins at Ohiopyle.

Youghiogheny River Trail, Southern Section

Location	Confluence to Ohiopyle to Connellsville, Henry Clay, Stewart, and Dunbar Townships, Fayette Counties
Trailheads	Confluence, Ohiopyle, Connellsville
Length, surface	28 miles, packed crushed stone
Character	Busy to crowded, wooded, mostly shady, flat to gentle grade
Usage restrictions	No motorized vehicles; no snowmobiles; no horses
Amenities	Rest rooms, water, bike rental, food, lodging, fishing
Driving time from Pittsburgh	1 hour 30-45 minutes southeast to Ohiopyle; 1 hour 15 minutes southeast to Connellsville

---

From Bruner Run for about 8 miles to Wheeler Bottom (mile 24.7), the trail is isolated in the Youghiogheny gorge. A spectacular view opens at mile 16.9, where a huge cement wall holds up the hillside at a pipeline crossing. The solitude is interrupted only at mile 19.4 by Camp Carmel, a small church camp that is rarely occupied. At mile 25, just before crossing the first trestle, you pass an unfinished cinder path along Dunbar Ck that will eventually become the Sheepskin Trail. For now, stay on the finished trail and cross the first of two high trestles that take you into Connellsville. As you cross the second of these trestles, look down into the animal farm below the trestle.

In Connellsville the trail emerges behind the former Connellsville Sportswear plant on First St (mile 27). It moves over to Third St in a bike lane separated from auto traffic by landscaped planters. The trail follows Third St through mixed residential and commercial areas of Connellsville to parking near Yough Riverfront Park, about 28 miles from

---

Confluence. The crossing of busy PA711 is protected by a traffic signal. At Connellsville the river leaves the water gap through Chestnut Ridge and enters the farm and mining lands in the valley. Here you cross to the northern section of the trail, the character of the trail changes from whitewater to flatwater, and the setting changes from near-wilderness gorge to rural mining towns. The northern section of the trail starts on the far side of Riverfront Park.

River view, mile 16.9

Local history, attractions

Monongahela Indians lived in the basin between 900 and 1600 AD. After they left, Delaware, Shawnee, and Iroquois Indians used the area as a hunting ground. Old records indicate that the name Ohiopyle was derived from the Indian word "Ohiopehhle", which means "white frothy water", a reference to the large falls on the Youghiogheny River. If you find the spelling of these names daunting, take heart: The river was called Yok-yo-gane in its first appearance on a map, in 1737. Since then it has been called Yawyawganey (1751), Joxhio Geni and Yoxhio Geni (1755), Yehiogany (1784), and even Yuh-wiac-hanne (early land grant).

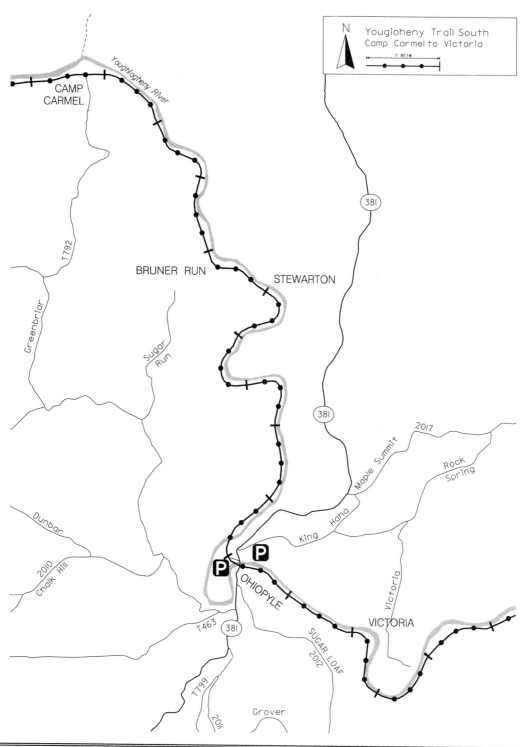

Yougioheny Trail South
Camp Carmel to Victoria

1 mile

N

CAMP CARMEL

Youghiogheny River

T792

Greenbriar

Sugar Run

BRUNER RUN

STEWARTON

381

381

2017

Maple Summit

Rock Spring

Dunbar

2010

Chalk Hill

King Haha

Victoria

VICTORIA

P

P

OHIOPYLE

T463

381

SUGAR LOAF

2012

T799

2011

Grover

In the 19th century, the falls made Ohiopyle a commercial center. Water power supported variously a sawmill, a gristmill, a planing mill, and an electric power plant. After the Western Maryland Railroad arrived in 1914, Ohiopyle became a popular resort destination. Round trip fare from Pittsburgh was $1.00.

In years past, two railroads used the Youghiogheny valley to pass through Laurel and Chestnut Ridges — the Baltimore and Ohio on the north bank, and the Western Maryland on the south bank. The B&O merged with the Chesapeake and Ohio and the Western Maryland to become part of CSX. The B&O tracks are still in use, now as part of CSX on Conrail tracks, but the Western Maryland tracks were abandoned in the 1970's.

Now Ohiopyle relies primarily on tourism. The State Park offers over 19,000 acres of natural beauty, including the Falls, Ferncliff Natural Area, whitewater rafting and kayaking, and hiking. A 10-mile mountain bike trail (Sugarloaf Snowmobile and Mountain Bike Area) has been established on the southwest side of SR2012 between Ohiopyle and Confluence. Only roads connect the mountain bike area and the river trail.

Development plans

The trail is complete from just north of Confluence to Connellsville except for a short section on roads in Ohiopyle.

A 1999 construction contract covers improvements in Ohiopyle and Confluence. Ohiopyle improvements will include a bike-pedestrian bridge, improvements in the Train Station visitor center, and parking in Ferncliff. In Confluence, the construction project will move the trail off-road from the present end to the Youghiogheny River crossing, and it will separate the bike routes for the river crossing from the automobile traffic. There will be two ways to cross the river: a bike-pedestrian bridge where the old road bridge was and a bike lane on the upstream side of the new bridge. You'll prefer the former if you're going into Confluence, the latter if you're continuing on the Allegheny Highlands Trail. Please be patient if construction causes temporary inconvenience.

In conjunction with planning for the Sheepskin Trail, a feasibility study for a 1.2-mile side spur to Dunbar is also underway. The Sheepskin Trail will eventually connect the Youghiogheny River Trail with the West Virginia rail-trail system at Pt Marion, where the Monongahela River crosses the state line.

Access points

Vicinity: Access is at Confluence (southern trailhead), Ohiopyle (central trailhead), and Connellsville (northern trailhead).

For Confluence and Ohiopyle, directions begin southbound on PA381 entering Ohiopyle. To reach this point from Pittsburgh take the PA Turnpike (I76) to Donegal. Turn east (left) on PA31. About 2 miles later turn south (right) on PA381. Follow PA381 about 18 miles to Ohiopyle.

Ramcat Hollow trailhead (southern): Follow PA381 through most of Ohiopyle and turn southeast (left) on SR2012 at the Boater's Change house. Go 8.1 miles to PA281 and turn north (left) on PA281. When PA281 turns right to cross the Youghiogheny River, you may either continue straight on River Rd to trailhead parking at Ramcat Hollow or else follow PA281 across the bridge to park in Confluence and ride back across this bridge. *Alternate route:* For a shortcut to Ramcat Hollow trailhead, turn left off SR2012 onto Ram Cat Rd 7.3 miles from Ohiopyle.

Wheeler Bottom Trestle, mile 25

Ohiopyle trailhead (central): As PA381 enters Ohiopyle, it crosses an active rail line, then the Youghiogheny River. A right turn just before the bridge takes you to the Ferncliff parking lot, access for the Ohiopyle-Bruner Run section. The first left turn after crossing the river takes you past the old train station to parking for the Ohiopyle-Confluence section.

For Connellsville, directions begin at the intersection of PA711 and US119 in Connellsville. To reach this point from Pittsburgh take the PA Turnpike (I76) to New Stanton. Follow signs to go south on US119 about 16 miles to Connellsville.

Connellsville trailhead (northern): From the traffic light at the intersection of PA711 (Crawford Av) and US119 in Connellsville, go north on PA711 for a few blocks to Third

St. You'll recognize it by the traffic light, the bike shop, and the separate bike lane. Turn left on Third St and follow the bicycle trail to trail parking.

Amenities

Rest rooms, water: Rest rooms and water at trailheads.

Bike shop, rentals: Bike shops and rentals in Confluence, Ohiopyle, and Connellsville.

Restaurant, groceries: Groceries and restaurants in Confluence, Ohiopyle, and Connellsville. In Confluence, River's Edge Cafe is popular for meals and Dannie's Place is popular for ice cream and snacks.

Camping, simple lodging: Camping at Outflow Campground, at the base of Youghiogheny Dam, near Confluence. There's also a campground at Ohiopyle State Park high on the ridge above the trail. You wouldn't want to ride up the steep, narrow, busy road, but the State Park advises us that you can take bikes up the trail marked "To Campground" at the north end of the bridge at mile 10.6. In Ohiopyle, American Youth Hostel on Ferncliff Peninsula and at a motel and Falls Market in town.

Swimming, fishing: The State Park does not allow swimming (to do so would require lifeguards). Wading is permitted, however. Be careful of the current in the Youghiogheny River. The north side of the river at Ferncliff is popular. If you enter the water near Confluence, be aware that the water is probably freshly released from the bottom of Youghiogheny Lake and hence quite cold, even in summer. Fishing is good to excellent all along the trail, in part because it's cool all summer. Common catches are trout and small-mouth bass plus other varieties including catfish.

Winter sports: Cross-country skiing. No snowmobiles.

Wheelchair access: Steeper-than-normal grade just south of Connellsville. Lips on curbs at Bruner Run Rd crossing.

Maps, guides, other references

Trail Book '96: A Users Guide to the Youghiogheny River Trail and the Allegheny Highlands Trail. Available from the trail councils and many local businesses.

Ohiopyle State Park information brochure.

Tim Palmer. *Youghiogheny, Appalachian River.* University of Pittsburgh Press, 1984.

USGS Topographic Maps: Confluence, Ohiopyle, Mill Run, South Connellsville, Connellsville.

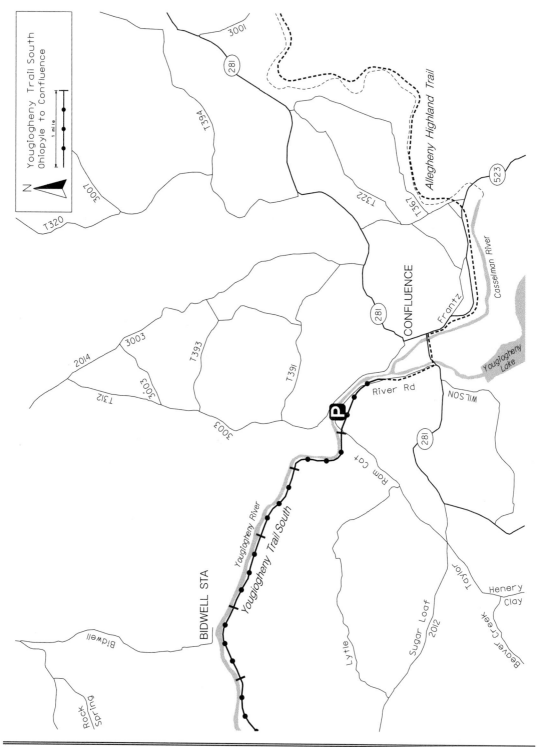

Youghiogheny Trail South
Ohiopyle to Confluence

N

1 mile

T320
3007
3001
281
T394
T312
2014
3003
3003
T393
3003
T391
3003
Bidwell
Rock Spring
BIDWELL STA
Youghiogheny River
Youghiogheny Trail South
River Rd
Ram Cat
Lytle
Sugar Loaf
2012
Taylor
Henery Clay
Beaver Creek
P
281
WILSON
Frantz
CONFLUENCE
281
T322
T361
Allegheny Highland Trail
523
Casselman River
Youghiogheny Lake

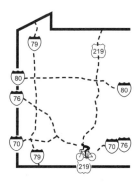

Allegheny Highlands Trail

Cumberland MD to Frostburg MD, over Big Savage Mountain into PA, then along Casselman River to Confluence in Somerset County PA

The Allegheny Highlands trail will run for 62 miles through woods and small towns, climbing from the terminus of the C&O Canal Towpath at Cumberland MD along Wills Ck and Jennings Run to Frostburg MD, then up the eastern flank of Big Savage Mountain. After crossing under the crest of the mountain in a kilometer-long tunnel, it will descend along Flaugherty Run to the Casselman River at Meyersdale PA, then follow the Casselman to Confluence. The Allegheny Highlands Trails in Maryland and Pennsylvania are two of seven trails in the Allegheny Trail Alliance. The Alliance is coordinating the effort to establish a trail system connecting Pittsburgh with Washington DC via rail-trails and the C&O Canal Towpath.

Initial development is concentrating on the Casselman River section. The continuation along Flaugherty Run will follow. The exact routing of the Maryland section is now being established. Since the sections of this trail that are not officially open are officially closed to the public, we give only short descriptions of the future routes.

Salisbury trestle soars over the Casselman valley

Allegheny Highlands Trail of Maryland

From Cumberland to Frostburg, then along Big Savage Mountain to Maryland state line in Allegany County MD

The Maryland Department of Natural Resources is planning to develop the trail from Cumberland to the Maryland/Pennsylvania state line. They expect to share the right-of-way of the active Western Maryland Scenic Railroad for 15.2 miles to Frostburg, then use the right-of-way of the former Western Maryland RR for 5 miles north to the Mason-Dixon line. Engineering design is underway.

The wildest, most remote part of the trail lies in western Maryland. Here you find rugged mountains, hardwood forest, high wooded ridges, and narrow stream valleys. The parallel ridges and valleys run from northeast to southwest, and over 55% of the land in the county is on slopes greater than 25%. Nevertheless, the grade on the right of way is less than 3%. Since the trail will traverse mountainous sideslopes, the views will be spectacular. Unsurprisingly, the trail winds 20 miles to cover the 9-mile straight-line distance from Cumberland northwest to the PA state line on Savage Mountain.

When this section of trail is completed, it will provide unique glimpses into western Maryland's prehistoric and early industrial past. In Cumberland, the trail will connect with the C&O Canal Towpath at the Western Maryland RR station, which also serves as the eastern terminus of the Western Maryland Scenic RR. From Cumberland, the trail will arch northwest, then southwest to Frostburg, sharing the railroad grade with the Scenic RR's steam train. The trailhead at Frostburg will be the Cumberland and Pennsylvania RR Depot. Built in 1891, it is also the western terminus of the Scenic RR. From Frostburg the trail will climb the flank of Big Savage Mountain to join the Pennsylvania section of the trail. You can now preview the Cumberland to Frostburg route by taking a ride on the Scenic RR.

The trail will feature two unique natural areas: the Narrows and the Bone Cave. The Cumberland Narrows is the mile-long gorge of Wills Ck, 1.5 miles northwest of Cumberland. The highway, the creek, a CSX railroad line, and the scenic railroad all squeeze through this spectacular slot between Haystack and Wills Mountains. The Cumberland Bone Cave is a limestone cave recognized as one of the most significant deposits of Pleistocene animal remains in the eastern US. About 4 miles northwest of Cumberland, it was discovered during railroad construction in 1912. Excavation yielded fossils of 46 animal species, 28 of which are extinct. The railroad grade itself is notable for its Horseshoe Curve, the second-tightest open horseshoe curve in the east (after the more famous one at Altoona PA). The trail also passes the S&S Maple Camp, one of the largest maple sugar operations in the state.

Trail organization

Trail Manager for Allegheny Highlands Trail of Maryland

Allegheny Highlands Trails of Maryland
PO Box 28
Cumberland MD 21502

Maryland Department of Nat'l Resources
Public Lands and Forestry
Greenways and Resource Planning
580 Taylor Av, D-3
Annapolis, MD 21401
(410) 974-3654

e-mail: ATAmail@westol.com
web: www.mdmountainside.com

Maps, guides, other references

Trail brochure

USGS Topographic Maps: Cumberland MD-PA, Frostburg MD-PA.

Allegheny Highlands Trail in Maryland will be alongside the scenic steam railroad

Allegheny Highlands Trail, Flaugherty Run Section

Along Flaugherty Run from Maryland state line near Deal to Meyersdale in Somerset County

From the Mason-Dixon Line (the PA/MD state line), the trail will continue for 11 miles on the Western Maryland route to Meyersdale. The major development challenge will be the kilometer-long Big Savage Tunnel, which takes the trail under the mountain and saves 250 feet of climb. This tunnel is partially collapsed and dangerous. Emerging from the woods at Deal, the trail will descend along Flaugherty Run to Meyersdale. The trail council hopes to complete the trail from the state line to Meyersdale in 2000.

Until the trail is complete, a decent alternative from Deal to Meyersdale is SR2006. There's no really good alternative from Cumberland to Deal. The direct route uses AltUS40 from Cumberland through Frostburg uphill in heavy traffic to MD546, then MD546 to the state line and Flaugherty Run Rd to Deal. Flaugherty Run Rd has almost no traffic, but AltUS40 and MD546 are too busy for our tastes.

Trail organization

Trail Manager for Allegheny Highlands Trail (Flaugherty Run Section)

Somerset County Rails to Trails Association
829 North Center Av
Somerset PA 15501-1029
(814) 445-6431
(814) 443-4313 (fax)
e-mail: somchmbr@shol.com
web: www.shol.com/smrst/somrst.htm
Membership: $20/year individual or family

Maps, guides, other references

USGS Topographic Maps: Frostburg MD, Wittenburg, Meyersdale.

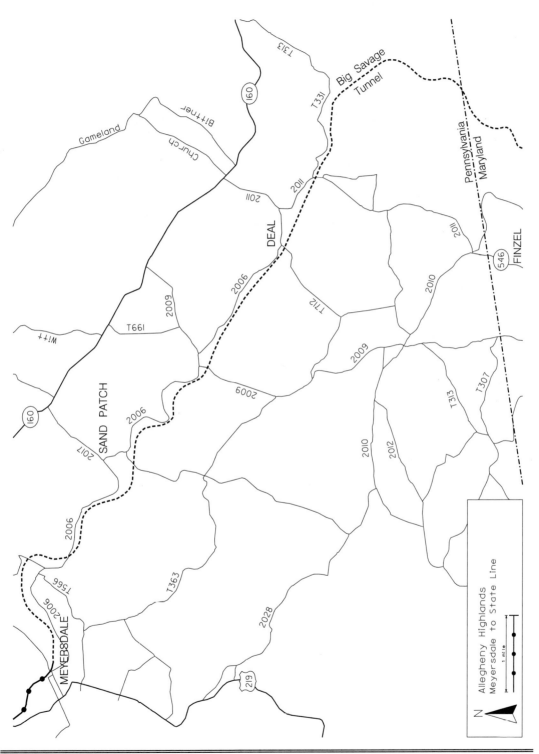

Allegheny Highlands Trail, Casselman Section

Along Casselman River from Meyersdale to Confluence in Somerset County

The completed trail will follow the Casselman River for 29 miles from Meyersdale to Confluence, where it will connect with the Youghiogheny River Trail. In early 1999, the trail was open from Meyersdale through Rockwood, Garrett, and Markleton, then around Pinkerton Horn. This provides a continuous 21.3-mile section, from mile 11.4 to mile 32.7 of the final trail. The additional 2 miles from the Pinkerton high trestle to Ft Hill are scheduled for completion by early summer 1999. From Meyersdale north for 1.6 miles to the Salisbury trestle, the trail is scraped level but otherwise unimproved. The trestle itself is concrete. Most of the rest is surfaced in packed crushed limestone, a generous 11-12 feet wide with an additional two feet of ballast on the shoulder; the Pinkerton bypass is coarser limestone without shoulders. Several benches beside the trail offer a chance to admire the scenery.

The trail currently begins at the railroad station in Meyersdale (mile 11.4). This is the restored Western Maryland station; there's another station on the active railroad a few blocks away. From this station, the trail is unimproved but rideable for 1.6 miles through a cut and along the edge of a hill. Then it emerges to cross the Casselman River valley on the Salisbury trestle. This wonderful 1900-foot structure soars as much as 100 feet above the wide valley, providing great views in both directions. At the other end of the trestle (mile 13.4), the trail is finished in packed crushed limestone. Here the trail runs through farmland for about two miles. Watch for peacocks in the farmyard near the trail. After another small cut, the trail arrives at Garrett. Here the railroad grade has been filled in to support the road, and you'll have to make a short detour to the road (SR2037). When you reach the road, turn right and immediately left (before crossing the river). Follow this dirt road to the Garrett trailhead parking.

At Garrett, the trail begins near the waterworks (mile 16.3). From here to Rockwood, little intrudes on the woods and river. The trail is generally 20-40 feet above the Casselman River, affording views of the moderate rapids and, in season, of canoeists and kayakers. During early spring snowmelt, waterfalls and creeks cascade over the adjacent cliffs and out of the hollows. At mile 18.5, a fine rock cliff forms the side of the trail. Across the river, five rectangular openings mark the location of an old mine. The gob heap that appears at mile 22.8 signals that you're approaching Rockwood.

The trail drops from the railroad grade to cross the road (Bridge St) at Rockwood (mile 23.3). A large parking lot provides the most convenient access from the PA Turnpike. Past the Rockwood parking lot, the trail passes the remnants of a mining complex and coal tipple (mile 23.7). It remains close to the river, with periodic views of the river and the canoeists. At mile 24.2 a bench provides a perch from which to watch the cascade leaping off the cliff, and at mile 24.8 another stream emerges in a wooden trough. The trail continues in woods to mile 26.5, where the town of Casselman comes into view across the river. Just north of milepost 27 (which is out of place, at mile 27.14), a waterfall gurgles gently down the cliff face.

Allegheny Highlands Trail, Casselman Section	
Location	Addison, Lower Turkeyfoot, Upper Turkeyfoot, Black, Summit Twps, Somerset County
Trailheads	Meyersdale, Garrett, Rockwood, Markleton
Length, Surface	19.7 miles developed, packed crushed stone; 1.6 miles open but rough
Character	Uncrowded, wooded, mixed sun and shade, flat
Usage restrictions	No motorized vehicles; no snowmobiles
Amenities	Rest rooms, bike rental, food, lodging
Driving time from Pittsburgh	1 hour 45 minutes southeast

At mile 29.4 the trail drops to the road crossing (SR3011) at Markleton, then climbs to the parking area. Another 1.7 miles brings you to the low trestle across the Casselman River at the Pinkerton Horn (mile 31.1). Here is the outstanding feature of this trail segment: the 850-foot Pinkerton Tunnel, dated 1911, and the trestles at the ends of the tunnel. Part of the tunnel ceiling has fallen and extensive, expensive repairs will be needed before the trail can pass through. For now, the trail crosses the low trestle, goes 1.5 miles around Pinkerton Horn on an older railroad grade, and rejoins the main route at the other end of the tunnel, just before the high trestle. The river falls about 40' as it goes around Pinkerton Horn, which accounts for both the height difference of the trestles and the river's popularity with whitewater paddlers. This railbed has been used to bypass a collapsing tunnel before: it was originally graded in 1879 to bypass a collapse of the other tunnel through this ridge—the one now used by the active B&O Railroad. The Pinkerton bypass is unlike the remainder of the trail. The railbed is on a narrow shelf, so the trail feels more intimate as it winds through the trees. Be careful on this segment: The trail is 10' wide, but the surface is rougher, there are no shoulders, and a drainage channel runs at the edge of the trail. For now, the trail stops at the far end of the high trestle (mile 32.7).

The spirit of the railroad will be with you on this trail: Full-fidelity sound is provided by the frequent trains of the active Baltimore and Ohio line just across the river.

Development plans

Plans call for extending the trail both westward and eastward. To the west, the section from the Pinkerton high trestle (the second one) to Ft Hill should be open in early summer 1999.

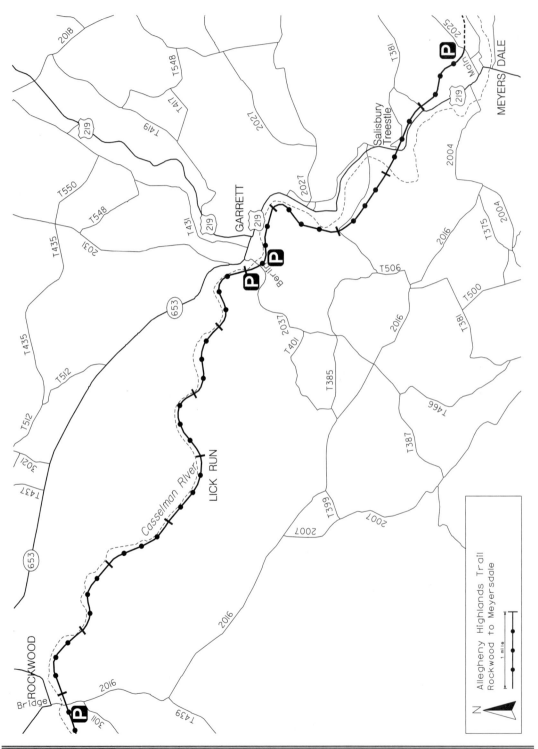

At that time, construction will start on the extension from Ft Hill through Harnedsville to Confluence, where the trail will connect with the Yough River Trail. To the east, development will start up Flaugherty Run toward Deal, probably in 1999. We hope the next edition of this guide can report an open trail all the way to Maryland.

Access points

Vicinity: Directions begin at the Somerset exit of the PA Turnpike (I76).

Meyersdale trailhead: From the Somerset Turnpike exit, go south on US219 about 20 miles to Meyersdale. Turn left on Main St and climb the hill. After 0.5 miles, just on the edge of town, the restored railroad station marks the trailhead. Park here.

Garrett trailhead: From the Somerset Turnpike exit, go south on US219 about 15 miles to Garrett. Turn right on PA653. Go 0.2 miles to Berlin St and turn left. Go 0.1 miles on Berlin St and cross the bridge. If you're riding toward Rockwood, turn right just after crossing the bridge and follow the dirt road 0.3 miles to trailhead parking. If you're riding toward Meyersdale, turn left about 100' past the bridge and go 200' to the parking area. *Alternate route:* A shortcut to Garrett uses SR2031 to avoid following US219 all the way east to the town of Berlin and back west. The intersection of SR2031 with PA653 is west of Garrett, so turn left from SR2031 onto PA653, then right on Berlin.

Rockwood trailhead: From the Somerset Turnpike exit, follow signs to go south on PA281 about 10 miles to PA653. Go east on PA653 2.7 miles to Rockwood, where it's also called Bridge St. Where PA653 turns left to avoid crossing the Casselman River, continue straight on Bridge St (SR2016) to cross the river. The entrance to the parking lot is on the right about 25 yards past the bridge. Alternate route: A shorter, but more complicated, route to Rockwood follows Coxes Ck: From the Somerset Turnpike exit follow signs to go south on PA281. At the first traffic light after joining PA281, turn left on SR3015. Follow SR3015 8.2 miles to Rockwood. At the stop sign where PA653 enters from the left, go straight on PA653. Follow this road (Main St) for 0.8 miles through Rockwood. When PA653 turns right to leave the river, turn left on Bridge St (SR2016) to cross the river and park as above. Signs in Rockwood direct you to the trail.

Markleton trailhead: From the Somerset Turnpike exit, go south on PA281 about 18 miles to SR3011. Turn left on SR3011 and follow its twists and turns to cross the Casselman River. Just after crossing the river, turn right into the parking lot. This parking area also serves whitewater boaters on the Casselman River.

Amenities

Rest rooms, water: Chemical toilets, probably seasonal, at Garrett, Rockwood, and Markleton trailheads. No water.

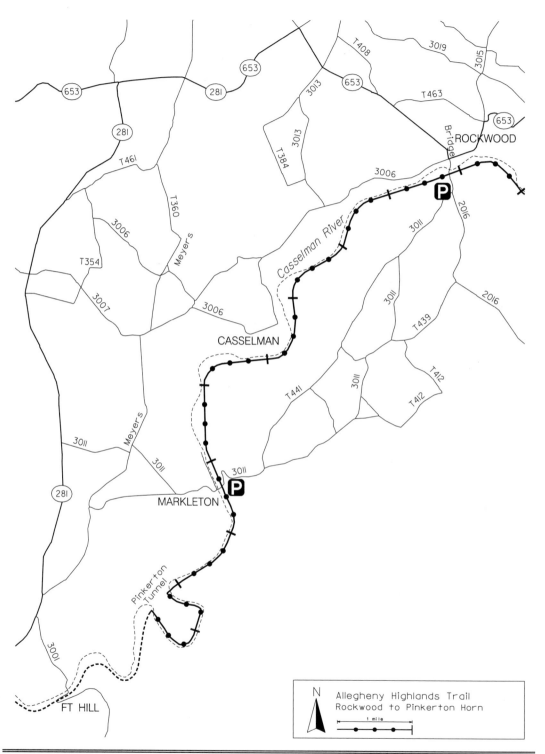

Allegheny Highlands Trail
Rockwood to Pinkerton Horn

1 mile

Free-Wheeling Easy in Western Pennsylvania

Bike shop, rentals: Rentals at The Country Trail in Rockwood just across the bridge from the trailhead.

Restaurant, groceries: The Garrett Country Store/BP gas station in Garrett (near the intersection of PA653 and US219). In Rockwood, just across the bridge from the trailhead; also restaurants in Rockwood proper.

Camping, simple lodging: B&Bs in Rockwood and Confluence. Very small motel in Meyersdale. Several bed-and-breakfast inns are being planned along the route. The Corps of Engineers operates Outflow Campground at the base of Youghiogheny Dam, about half a mile from Confluence. We also understand that private owners are considering campgrounds along the trail near Meyersdale and Rockwood.

Swimming, fishing: Unsupervised swimming in the Casselman River. Unfortunately, a mine acid accident has degraded the water quality. This problem is being actively remediated. Many sections of the river have whitewater rapids, so be careful, especially when the water is high.

Winter sports: No snowmobiles. Cross-country skiing is good, as the trail is sheltered and holds snow. The parking lot at Rockwood is plowed regularly.

Wheelchair access: Some narrow gates—as narrow as 31" at Markleton. Fairly steep ramps down to roads at Rockwood and Markleton.

Maps, guides, other references

Trail Book '96: A Users Guide to the Youghiogheny River Trail and the Allegheny Highlands Trail. Available from the trail councils and many local businesses.

USGS Topographic Maps: Meyersdale, Burdock, Rockwood, Markleton, Confluence. When the undeveloped sections are finished, you'll also need Frostburg and Wittenberg.

Trail organization

Trail Manager for Allegheny Highlands Trail (Flaugherty Run Section)

Somerset County Rails to Trails Association
829 North Center Av
Somerset PA 15501-1029
(814) 445-6431
(814) 443-4313 (fax)
e-mail: somchmbr@shol.com
web: www.shol.com/smrst/somrst.htm
Membership: $20/year individual or family

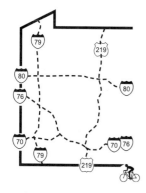

Chesapeake and Ohio Canal Towpath

Cumberland Maryland to Washington DC

The Chesapeake and Ohio Canal Towpath was built between 1828 and 1850, opening progressively from Washington toward Cumberland as sections were completed. These years were also the heyday of railroad development, and the C&O Canal competed with the B&O Railroad for both business and right of way. On the canal, 74 manually-operated lift locks raised the water level from nearly sea level in Washington to an elevation of 605 feet at Cumberland.

Floods in January and September of 1996 caused over $20 million in damage to the towpath. After Herculean effort by the Park Service and many volunteers, the entire towpath is open again, except for a detour near Dam 4 (mile 85) that remains from 1972 flooding. Much of the 184.5-mile length is now in good condition, but some sections still require a mountain bike or sturdy hybrid.

The canal was always vulnerable to flood damage. The devastation from the great flood in 1924, together with competition from railroads, spelled its doom. It is now a National Historical Park. The towpath has been restored, and in some areas the canal has been re-watered. Many traces of the canal era remain, most notably locks, lockmaster's houses, aqueducts, dams, and weirs that controlled water levels. Indeed, the particular attraction of this trail is the extensive evidence of a bygone transportation era.

From Washington DC to Great Falls the trail is packed crushed stone. North of Great Falls, trail use is lighter and investment in trail surfacing is correspondingly lower. The trail becomes double-track, much like a one-lane dirt road. It gets progressively rougher the closer you get to Cumberland. Avoid riding within two days of heavy rain. Road crossings are relatively far apart, and most of the busier roads cross over the towpath. The canal alongside has sometimes been restored to hold water, and the path is usually shaded by trees that have grown back since the Canal ceased operations. Wildflowers and birds are abundant. You're likely to see small furry rodents and turtles. Where the canal holds water, you'll also find abundant mosquitoes.

This is one of the finest bicycle camping trips in the region. Every 5-10 miles or so, a primitive campsite alongside the trail offers a water pump, picnic table, river access, and chemical toilet. On the northern end of the trail an active rail line is just across the river. The night trains add a special dimension to the camping experience. Cumberland is surprisingly convenient to Western Pennsylvania, so this is a great weekend option from Pittsburgh. Moreover, the distance from Cumberland to Hancock is about 40 miles by highway (I68) and 60 miles by towpath, so it's easy to set up a shuttle for a one-way trip.

The trail surface does not encourage speed, but the frequent remnants of the canal operation provide excuses to stop and examine the stabilized and restored ruins. Hahn's excellent guidebook is a good companion, especially for historical details.

Chesapeake and Ohio Canal Towpath	
Location	Washington DC to Cumberland MD
Trailheads	Hancock, Paw Paw, Cumberland, many other points closer to Washington
Length, Surface	184.5 miles; mostly dirt
Character	Usually uncrowded, rural, mostly shady, flat
Usage restrictions	Horses ok from Swains Lock to Cumberland, but not in campsites or campgrounds; no motorized vehicles; no snowmobiles
Amenities	Rest rooms, water, bike rental, food, camping, lodging, fishing
Driving time from Pittsburgh (to Cumberland)	2 hours 15 minutes southeast

Local history, attractions

This trail is perhaps the archetype for recreational trail conversions. It was conceived in 1954, when Supreme Court Justice William O. Douglas led 29 people on a hike from Cumberland to Washington along the route of the canal. At the time, the route was being considered for a scenic automobile parkway. Justice Douglas' hike called attention of Washington policy makers to the value of maintaining the route as a sanctuary—and to the need to halt the deterioration of the canal. It was named a National Monument in 1961 and became a National Historical Park in 1971.

The trail is as history-laden as any we've ridden. The remains of the canal have been carefully stabilized or restored. Hahn's guide, *Towpath Guide to the C&O Canal*, identifies even the most obscure of features, down to the hundredth of a mile (though his mile marks don't exactly match the Park Service mileposts).

The City of Cumberland is preserving and restoring the part of town that once served as the terminus of the canal. They plan to re-water a section of the canal and offer canal boat excursion rides.

Extensions of the ride

The Georgetown terminus connects to the Washington DC trail network and offers easy access to the Washington & Old Dominion and Mount Vernon trails. You can ride west on the Washington & Old Dominion some 30-odd miles to Leesburg and, at the expense of two miles downhill in fast traffic on busy US15, connect back to the C&O Canal at Whites Ferry. (Some of the W&OD supporters are trying to develop a bike trail along this section of US15).

By the end of the year 2000, the Allegheny Highlands trail should reach Cumberland to permit a traffic-free trip between Washington DC and Pittsburgh.

Access points

Vicinity: The C&O Canal follows the Potomac River from Washington to Cumberland. For access from interstate highways, use I270 from Washington to Frederick, I70 from Frederick to Hancock and I68 from Hancock to Cumberland. To reach I68 at Cumberland from Pittsburgh take the PA Turnpike east to Somerset, US219 south to I68, and I68 east to Cumberland. *Alternate route:* From Berlin on US219, it's slightly shorter to take PA160/MD36 directly to Cumberland. *Another alternate route:* Take I79 south to US40, US40 east to I68, and I68 east to Cumberland.

Williamsport trailhead: Leave I70 to go south on I81 near Hagerstown. Exit I81 on US11 in Williamsport. This is East Potomac St. Follow it 1.1 miles west to center of town, turn left for 1 block on West Salisbury St, turn right for 3 blocks into River Front Park.

Hancock trailhead: Take the Hancock exit from I68. Start east on E Main St. Turn right on Pennsylvania St, go two blocks to the end of the street, turn right, then left on a narrow bridge across the canal. This is Hancock City Park, and you cross the towpath on the way into the park.

Cumberland trailhead: Take the main Cumberland exit from I68 and follow signs to the Western Maryland Train Station. Park in the lot. The trail leaves from the platform one story up. If you're using the alternate route and entering Cumberland on MD36, continue straight to the train station; don't follow AltUS40 over the overpass.

Other trailheads: For access closer to Washington, consult the park brochure. For the more obscure trailheads, consult Hahn's guidebook.

Amenities

Rest rooms, water: Rest rooms and water at information centers. Water pump and chemical toilets at hiker/biker campgrounds every 5-10 miles and also at major access points. The water is drawn from wells and treated by the park service. Sometimes it tastes strongly of iodine; we've seen oatmeal, potatoes, and other starchy foods turn blue—anyone for patriotic spaghetti? The water is tested regularly; if it fails, the pump handle is removed until it's good again. Before a camping trip, check with the Park office on the status of the pumps.

Bike shop, rental: In Cumberland, Hancock, Williamsport, Shepherdstown, Sandy Hook, Leesburg, Swains Lock, Cabin John, and the Georgetown section of Washington.

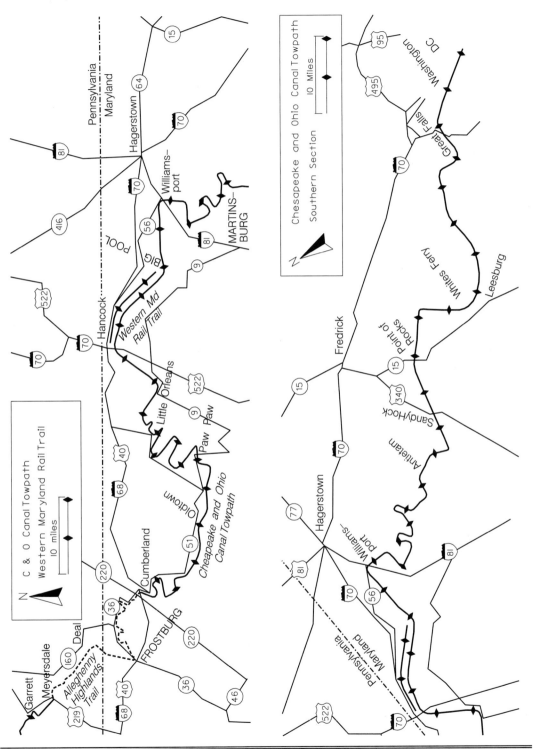

Restaurant, groceries: Within a few blocks of the trail at Cumberland, Paw Paw (WV side of river), Little Orleans, Hancock, Williamsport, Shepherdstown (WV side of river), Sandy Hook, Harpers Ferry (WV side of river), Brunswick, Point of Rocks, Whites Ferry, Seneca, and many places as you enter Washington.

Camping, simple lodging: Hiker/biker campgrounds (no road access) every 5-10 miles for tourers. Primitive automobile camping along the canal at Spring Gap, Fifteen Mile Ck (Little Orleans), McCoys Ferry, and Antietam Ck. Camping near the canal also available at Fort Frederick State Park and Brunswick. Lodging in Cumberland, Hancock, Williamsport, and Shepherdstown.

Swimming, fishing: The canal water isn't attractive, and swimming and wading are prohibited anyhow. Many swimming and fishing spots along the Potomac River, especially near campgrounds. River currents are strong, deceptive, and unpredictable, so be careful, especially if the water is high.

Winter sports: Cross-country skiing; best chance of snow is at the western end, in the mountains. No snowmobiles.

Wheelchair access: Much of the trail is moderately rough.

Trail organization

Superintendent
C&O Canal National Historical Park
Box 4
Sharpsburg MD 21782
(301) 739-4200
web: www.nps.gov/choh/

For free list of publications or to order:
Parks and History Association
PO Box 40929
Washington DC 20016
(202) 472-3083

Maps, guides, and other references

Trail brochure, *Chesapeake and Ohio Canal Official Map and Guide.* Also brochures for specific locations such as Great Falls, Four Locks, Paw Paw Tunnel.

Thomas F. Hahn. *Towpath Guide to the C&O Canal.* American Canal and Transportation Center 1991, 226 pages. (Available at Park Service information centers in Georgetown, Great Falls Tavern, Hancock, and Cumberland.)

Mike High. *The C&O Companion.* Johns Hopkins University Press, 1997.

The Railfans Guide to the Cumberland Area. Brochure with map of Cumberland showing points of interest and vantage points for WMSRR.

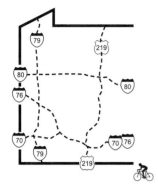

Western Maryland Rail Trail

Along C&O Canal from Big Pool to Hancock in Washington County MD

From Hancock MD to Big Pool, the only paved road is an interstate highway, and the only nearby alternative for bicyclists has long been the unpaved C&O Canal Towpath. No matter how great the charm of the Towpath (and it is indeed great), the surface isn't suitable for some road bikes. This problem has been resolved by the opening of the Western Maryland Rail Trail, a wide asphalt strip from Hancock to Big Pool.

The trail begins just west of Ft Frederick State Park, in a parking lot in Big Pool. From here it winds northwest between the canal bed and I70 for 10 miles to enter central Hancock. The highway is noticeable but not intrusive. You often get glimpses of the canal bed and towpath, including Licking Creek Aquaduct. You'll also see Little Pool, a coal tipple, and perhaps a real train between the trail and the river. Interpretive signage marks landmarks and presents railroad history.

Western Maryland Rail Trail	
Location	Hancock to Big Pool, Washington County MD
Trailheads	Hancock, Big Pool
Length, Surface	10 miles, paved
Character	Uncrowded, rural, sunny and shady, level
Usage restrictions	No motorized vehicles
Amenities	Rest rooms, water, bike rental, food, lodging
Driving time from Pittsburgh	2 hours 45 minutes southeast

Extensions of the ride

This trail connects with the C&O Canal Towpath at both ends. At the Big Pool end, go north on the trail to the intersection with Ernstville Rd. Turn left (toward the river), pass the RC cola machine and the ostrich farm, go around a left-hand bend, and look for a dirt path across the canal bed. This reaches the towpath at milepost 114.52. At the Hancock end, go to the end of the trail. Turn left on Pennsylvania St, go a block to the end of the street, turn right, then left on a narrow bridge across the canal. This is Hancock City Park, and you cross the towpath on the way into the park.

Development plans

The second phase of the project will extend the trail an additional 10.3 miles from Hancock to near Woodmont at the base of Sideling Hill.

Access points

Vicinity: Directions begin headed east on I68 between Cumberland MD and Hancock MD.

Big Pool trailhead: From I68, take I70E, then take the Big Pool exit (MD56) toward Big Pool. Follow MD56 for a few blocks, bearing left where Ernstville Rd forks right. Trailhead parking is 0.5 mile from I70.

Hancock trailhead: From I68, take the Hancock exit (MD144). Follow MD144 into town for a few blocks and turn right on Pennsylvania St. The trailhead is a block or so down, and there's parking in city lots to the south.

Amenities

Rest rooms, water: At Hancock City Park, a few blocks from the trailhead and at Big Pool trailhead

Bike shop, rentals: In Hancock

Restaurant, groceries: In Hancock

Camping, simple lodging: Car camping at Ft Frederick State Park and McCoy Ferry on C&O Canal. Camping for hikers and bikers (no cars) at hiker/biker sites along Towpath

Swimming, fishing: In nearby Potomac River

Winter sports: None

Wheelchair access: Excellent—wide gates, fresh wide asphalt.

Trail organization

Fort Frederick State Park
111000 Fort Frederick Rd
Big Pool, MD 21711
(301) 842-2155
web: www.dnr.state.md.us/publiclands/wmrt.html

Maps, guides, other references

USGS Topographic Maps: Cherry Run, Hancock.

Five Star Trail

Parallel to US119 from Greensburg to Youngwood

The Five Star Trail is named for the 5 towns that cooperated to develop it: Greensburg, South Greensburg, Southwest Greensburg, Hempfield Township, and Youngwood. It parallels US119 for 6.1 miles from Lynch Field in Greensburg to the Railroad Museum in Youngwood and then to Hollis Rd. Eventually it will continue to Westmoreland Community College and perhaps as far as Mammoth Park, running largely through the industrial areas the railroad once served. For most of its length the trail is finished in packed crushed limestone, though a mile is on a low-traffic road. Numerous trailside benches offer places to rest and enjoy the trail. Because of its urban character and location close to busy US119, this may become foremost a transportation and local recreation trail rather than a major destination.

This trail is unique in western Pennsylvania, in that it shares its corridor with an active rail line. The Southwest Pennsylvania Railroad runs 2 to 4 coal and freight trains daily. These are mostly short and slow, as trains go, but they still require caution. Please help make this combination "rail-with-trail" a success by avoiding conflict with the trains. **Stay off the tracks and out of the buffer zone between the trail and the tracks.**

The trail begins at Lynch Field in Greensburg. Bike riding in the park is restricted to the short inner oval track. The trail starts at this short oval near the rest rooms and climbs toward the swimming pool. From the pool, head toward the railroad embankment and look for the underpass that takes you beneath the active Conrail track. At the other end of the underpass, a short trail leads beside a chain link fence out to a railroad access road in an industrial yard; turn right on this access road and follow the tracks. This will take you south and across a trestle over Pittsburgh St. It's less than half a mile from the Lynch Park swimming pool to this trestle.

After the trestle the trail runs for a few blocks next to the Greensburg Shopping Center and residential back yards, then drops onto a bench. Here the hillside rises on the east, punctuated by occasional access stairs and ramps. To the west the ground drops away, providing a great view of central Greensburg. After 0.7 mile, you cross a trestle and enter the mixed residential and industrial areas of Southwest Greensburg, then pass under the Greensburg bypass and into South Greensburg, at Huff Av (PA819).

The half-mile from Huff Av to Fairview St runs close to the tracks behind industrial buildings. Be especially careful near Fairview St. Soon after Fairview St two trestles over Jack's Run have been rebuilt for the trail. The obligatory wastewater treatment plant (every trail seems to have one!) is just past the second of these trestles. Past the water plant, the trail parallels Broadway St, the residential street of Midway. A mile from Fairview St you reach the road crossing at Shady Lane in Midway.

After Midway the trail runs through woods beside Jacks Run for 0.7 miles to the entrance to the Buncher Commerce Park. You'll hear both bird song from across the creek and traffic noise from parallel US119.

The trail emerges at the entry road to the Buncher Commerce Park. The creek has been re-channeled away from the tracks, and the trail shares the low-traffic road that runs between the new creek channel and the warehouses. To continue on the trail, turn left where the trail emerges on the road, follow the road along the creek, turn right 0.9 mile later at Mt Pleasant Rd/Depot St, and almost immediately turn left onto the trail.

Where the road leaves the Commerce Park, the creek returns to its original channel and the trail leaves the road again just across the tracks from the Railroad Museum on Depot St. in Youngwood. The limestone surface resumes here, and the trail continues another half-mile along the track to Hillis Dr/Fairgrounds Rd. Eventually another branch of the trail will lead from the Depot St intersection to Westmoreland Community College and beyond.

Five Star Trail	
Location	Greensburg to Youngwood, Hempfield Township
Trailheads	Lynch Field, Highland Av near Pittsburgh St, Huff Av, Midway, Buncher Park, Youngwood
Length, Surface	5.2 miles packed crushed stone, 0.9 mile on road
Character	uncrowded, mixed residential and industrial, shady, flat
Usage restrictions	Stay off RR tracks and out of buffer zone between trail and tracks no motorized vehicles
Amenities	Rest rooms, water, bike rental, food, lodging
Driving time from Pittsburgh	50 minutes southeast

Local history, attractions

Current train traffic along the trail is operated by Southwest Pennsylvania Railroad on the former Conrail Southwest Secondary Branch, which runs from behind Greengate Mall to Connellsville. They operate 2 to 4 trains a day with 6-10 cars each; these trains shouldn't run faster than 10mph. Before Conrail took it over, the line was operated by the Pennsylvania RR.

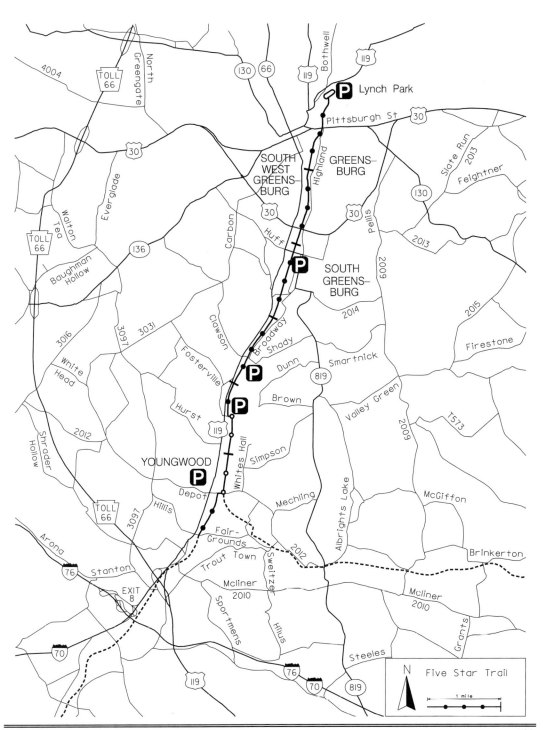

A Railroad Museum at Youngwood is open Tuesday through Saturday from 10:00 AM to 2:00 PM, possibly later on Saturday. This is the north terminus for the Laurel Highland Railroad's "Highlander", a scenic passenger train.

Development plans

Develop the trail from Depot St a mile to Westmoreland Community College, then 6 miles more to Mammoth Park.

Perhaps someday it will be possible to connect this trail to the Yough River Trail in Connellsville, 18-20 miles from Youngwood.

Access points

Vicinity: Directions begin headed east on the PA Turnpike from Exit 6 (Monroeville). To reach this point from Pittsburgh, take the Parkway East past Monroeville.

Lynch Field (north) trailhead: Get off the PA Turnpike at Exit 7 (Irwin) headed east on US30 toward Greensburg. Go east 6.4 miles on US30 and take the Pittsburgh St exit. This is the first Greensburg exit, just past Greengate Mall. Go 1.2 miles on Pittsburgh St and turn left on US119 at the county courthouse, an ornate stone building with a gold dome. Follow US119 past the Sheetz store at PA819, and look for a place to turn right into Lynch Field parking. The trail starts near the oval track and passes the swimming pool as it leaves the park.

Highland Av near Pittsburgh St trailhead: Get off the PA Turnpike at Exit 7 (Irwin) headed east on US30 toward Greensburg. Go east 6.4 miles on US30 and take the Pittsburgh St exit. This is the first Greensburg exit, just past Greengate Mall. Go 1.6 miles on Pittsburgh St, passing the county courthouse, an ornate stone building with a gold dome. A third of a mile after the courthouse, you pass under a railroad trestle. Immediately after the trestle and before the Greensburg Shopping Center, turn right on Highland St and look for inoffensive parking. The ramp up to the trail is about a block down Highland St, across from a cleaning shop.

Midway (Willow Crossing) trailhead: Get off the PA Turnpike at Exit 8 (New Stanton) following signs to go north on US119 toward Greensburg. After a mile and a quarter of highway interchanges, you'll be on US119 entering Youngwood. Follow US119 for about 1.5 miles until the northbound and southbound lanes rejoin. Continue about 1.3 mile to the second stop light (Willow Crossing Rd), turn right, and cross the creek and the trail. Parking is on the left.

Buncher Park (Trolley Line Av) trailhead: Get off the PA Turnpike at Exit 8 (New Stanton) following signs to go north on US119 toward Greensburg. After a mile and a quarter of highway interchanges, you'll be on US119 entering Youngwood. Follow US119 for 1.5 miles until the northbound and southbound lanes rejoin. Continue about 0.8 mile to the next stoplight (Trolley Line Av) and turn right into Buncher Industrial Park. The parking lot is on the left, just across the trail.

Youngwood (south) trailhead: Get off the PA Turnpike at Exit 8 (New Stanton) following signs to go north on US119 toward Greensburg. After a mile and a quarter of highway interchanges, you'll be on US119 entering Youngwood. In a few blocks US119 splits, with the northbound lanes a block away from the southbound lanes. Continue for 0.6 miles after the split to the Depot St traffic light and turn right on Depot St. This is the fourth traffic light in Youngwood; the street sign may be missing, but it's marked as the turn for the community college. Go two blocks on Depot St to the Railroad Museum; the trail and parking are just past the tracks at the museum.

Amenities

Rest rooms water: In Lynch Field

Bike shop, rental: Bike shops in Greensburg. Bike rental at Lynch Field, at the right side of the trailhead.

Restaurant, groceries: Many restaurants along US119. Lots of chain fast-food places near Huff Av. Barbecued chicken and ribs on weekend afternoons at the Railroad museum. Convenience stores within a few blocks of Lynch Field and the Railroad Museum.

Camping, simple lodging: Motels in the Greensburgs and Youngwood, including one adjacent to the trail near Huff Av

Swimming, fishing: Jacks Run is a bilious shade of grayish green, running over orange rocks. We doubt that fish live there, and we certainly aren't about to swim in it. There's a swimming pool at Lynch Field.

Wheelchair access: All trailheads accessible, but there's a steep grade from Lynch Field to the railroad underpass. There are several street crossings with moderate traffic.

Trail organization

Five Star Trail Council of the Regional Trail Corporation
RD12 Box 203
Greensburg PA 15601
(724) 872-5586
web: www.westol.com/5star/
Membership: $15/year individual, $20/year family

Maps, guides, other references

Trail brochure

USGS Topographic Maps: Greensburg, Mount Pleasant.

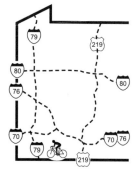

Sheepskin Rail-Trail

Connellsville to Pt Marion in Fayette County

In the 1890's, the Fairmont, Morgantown, and Pittsburgh branch of the B&O RR moved coal and coke from mines and coke ovens to the cities and steel mills where they were consumed. When the line first opened, trains startled sheep in nearby fields, and the sheep scattered in all directions. According to local legend, the unhappy shepherds responded, "Darn sheepskinners", and the nickname stuck to the rail line.

This trail will someday run on the route of the F&M&P from Connellsville to the PA state line at Point Marion. The route will be via Dunbar, Mt Braddock, Uniontown, Brownfield, Oliphant, Fairchance, Smithfield, Outcrop, Gans, Lake Lynn, and Nilan. The project is just moving from feasibility and planning into development. We include the trail here because of its role in the continuity of the trail network connecting the Youghiogheny River Trail in PA with the trails along the Monongahela in WV. From Bowest Jct to the Fairchance Industrial Park the trail may become rail-with-trail and share the right of way with a short line serving the industrial park. The Sheepskin Trail will also connect with the proposed Brown Run trail, which will run from Smithfield for about 10 miles via Shoaf to Ronco on the Monongahela River.

Construction of the first section, from the Yough River Trail North along the Dunbar spur to Pechin, should start in 1999. You'll be able to ride up with your trailer and load up with groceries at Pechin's.

Sheepskin Rail-Trail	
Location	Southward from Connellsville to Pt Marion on PA/WV state line
Length, Surface	0 miles developed, 33 miles planned
Driving time from Pittsburgh	1 hour 15 minutes southeast

Trail organization

Sheepskin Trail Chapter of the Regional Trail Corporation
108 Boulevard
Pt Marion PA 15474
(724) 725-5184
Membership: $10/year individual, $20/year family

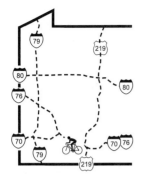

Indian Creek Valley Hiking and Biking Trail

Along Indian Creek in Fayette County

The Indian Creek Valley trail runs for 6 miles from Champion through Indian Head to the Saltlick Township line along the east bank of Indian Creek, nestled in the valley between Chestnut Ridge and Laurel Ridge. The trail has a variety of surfaces, from crushed limestone to cinders. It has more grades and curves than you'd expect from a rail-trail.

The route was developed between 1906 and 1910 as the Indian Creek Valley Railroad, which carried passengers and freight down Indian Creek to meet the B&O Railroad on the north side of the Youghiogheny River. Above Melcroft, the primary freight came from the logging industry; below Melcroft it came from the mining industry. Since the freight was mostly headed downhill, this railroad could tolerate relatively steeper grades than most.

From Champion the trail runs south for about a mile through woods, then comes into sight of Mountain Pines Resort, an immense campground. Adjacent to the swimming pool at the back of the campground, a footbridge connects the campground and the trail. The trail then passes some homes and camps near Nebo, where it's called C-H Blvd.

Half a mile later, the trail passes a lake, then crosses Fowl Hill Rd (which leads to Melcroft) and enters the woods. Just after Fowl Hill Rd, a spur trail leads right, crossing Indian Creek on a refinished trestle, to the Melcroft trailhead and the nearby G&D store on PA381/711 for amenities.

Indian Creek Valley Hiking and Biking Trail	
Location	Champion to Indian Head, Saltlick Township, Fayette County
Trailheads	Champion, Melcroft, Indian Head
Length, Surface	6 miles, packed crushed stone
Character	Little-used, wooded, shady, flat to rolling
Usage restrictions	No motorized vehicles; no horses
Amenities	Rest rooms, bike shop, food, camping, fishing
Driving time from Pittsburgh	1 hour 15 minutes south-east

Another pastoral mile and a half brings you to some picnic tables overlooking the creek. Shortly thereafter, the trail emerges from the woods at the auto junkyard just north of Sagamore. The next mile, to the Indian Head trailhead on Hull St, is more developed.

To continue on the trail, follow Hull St 300 ft to SR3089. Turn right on SR3089, go one block, and turn left on a dirt road between Resh's store and Indian Ck. This road swings left, climbs slightly, and crosses the railroad bed. Turn right here, at the sign for ICV Trail. The trail continues for about a mile to the Salt Lick Township line. Springfield Township does not currently plan to develop the portion of trail that runs from the township line to the Youghiogheny River. Even if they did, the projections about connecting this trail to the Youghiogheny River Trail are glossing over the task of crossing the Yough, unless Camp Carmel opens a ferry service.

Access points

Vicinity: Directions begin headed south on PA711/PA381 from the point where they come together near Jones Mills. To reach this point from Pittsburgh, take the PA Turnpike to Donegal and go east on PA711, then turn south on PA711/PA381.

Champion trailhead: From the junction of PA711 with PA381, follow PA711/PA381 south for about 1.3 miles to Champion. Turn left (east) on SR1058. The trailhead is across from the bagel shop about a quarter mile down SR1058. To park, continue a bit east on SR1058, cross the bridge, and park in the field on the right. The field may be unmarked.

Melcroft trailhead: From the junction of PA711 with PA381, follow PA711/PA381 south for about 3.6 miles to Melcroft. Just after passing Kessler Rd and crossing Champion Ck, turn right into trailhead parking. A spur trail runs from this parking lot, crosses Indian Ck on a trestle, and joins the main trail.

Indian Head trailhead: From the junction of PA711 with PA381, follow PA711/PA381 south for about 6 miles to Indian Head. Turn left (east) on SR1054. Just past Resh's store, turn left on Hull St, and follow this road past the trailhead to parking near the ballfield. The trailhead is on the opposite side of the ballfield from the river, along Hull St.

Amenities

Rest rooms, water: Rest rooms at C-W Park, the Indian Head access area.

Bike shop, rentals: Millers, along PA711/381 less than half a mile north of Melcroft

Restaurant, groceries: Bagel shop at Champion trailhead. Chain convenience store with restaurant is about a quarter-mile west of the Champion trailhead, at the intersection of SR1058 with PA711/PA381. If you take the spur trail to Melcroft, you can turn right on PA711/PA381 to the G&D market and a gas station just across Champion Ck, then a bit farther to the Valley Inn restaurant (only 1/8 mile on the highway). Groceries and deli sandwiches at Resh's store across from the park in Indian Head.

Swimming, fishing: Swim at Mountain Pines Resort pool (fee), just across the trail bridge. There's unlikely to be enough water to swim in the creek at any time you'd be there. Good fishing in creek.

Winter sports: Cross-country skiing.

Wheelchair access: The trail surface is a little rougher than most in this area.

Trail organization

Salt Lick Township
PO Box 403
Melcroft PA 15462-0403
(724) 455-2866

Maps, guides, other references

USGS Topographic Maps: Seven Springs, Donegal.

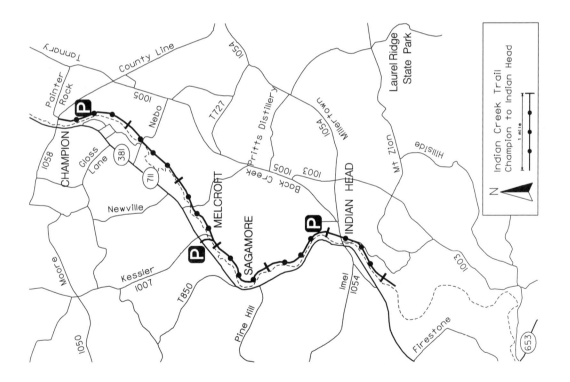

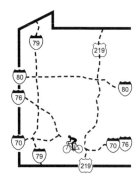

Forbes State Forest, Mountain Streams II Trail System

On west slope of Laurel Ridge between Jones Mill and Kregar in Westmoreland County

Within 3 miles of the Donegal Turnpike exit, Forbes State Forest has opened a new system of trails for mountain biking, hiking, horseback riding, cross-country skiing, and snowmobiling. This was a 1997 project of the Youth Conservation Corps. The trails lie on the western slope of Laurel Ridge, bounded on the north by the PA Turnpike and on the south by PA31. This is a State Forest, so wear blaze orange and exercise caution during small game season, and go elsewhere in deer season.

Unlike many trails in this guide, the trails in this area were developed as multi-use forest trails that provide a primitive forest experience. The lowest (western) trail follows a railroad grade along Indian Creek; the upper (eastern) end connects with the North Woods trail system on the crest of Laurel Ridge. The trails along the base of the ridge are not technically demanding, though they are rougher and significantly hillier than most rail-trails. The trails themselves are generally 6-12' wide. They don't have shoulders, and the woods come right to the edge of the trail. On a straight stretch with sun dappling through the leaves overhead, it feels like a Gothic cathedral. The effect is much more intimate than you'll find on a rail-trail, and we rather like it.

As you go farther north and east, the trail gets much rougher and steeper. This is a great place to get acquainted with mountain biking, without committing a day to something you may not enjoy—just start near PA31, work north and east until you've had enough, and return the way you came or by road on PA381.

The system includes three trails, plus a couple of connectors.

Blair Brothers Railroad Grade follows the west side of Indian Creek. It connects with Mountain Streams Trail in two places, near Camp Run and at Hunter Land.

Mountain Streams Trail starts at Camp Run Rd and parallels Indian Creek up the ridge, eventually connecting with Tunnel Rd and the North Woods trail system.

Pike Run Trail connects the south end of Mountain Streams Trail with PA31 above the Pike Run Country Club

The *Blair Brothers Railroad Grade* begins at PA381 just north of PA31. It is nearly level, often double-track, and the trail surface is good enough to ride on a hybrid bike, though not nearly as smooth as most rail-trails. It will remind you of a 1-lane country driveway, with grass growing between the wheel tracks. This trail is on the same railroad grade as the Indian Creek Valley Trail a few miles to the south. The ride through the bottomland near Indian Creek is lovely, but short enough to leave you wanting more. A right-hand turn 0.6 miles from the parking lot leads to a connector trail that crosses Indian Creek and PA381, then leads to Pike Run Trail. From this ntersection the railroad grade continues another 0.6 miles, where it crosses a tributary of Indian Creek, then another 0.2 miles to its end at Hunter La. Turn right on Hunter La, cross Indian Ck and PA381, and go up a short connector to meet Mountain Streams Trail.

Mountain Streams Trail begins at Camp Run Rd just east of PA381. The first 4 miles have some serious, but not brutal, climbs and descents. After 5 miles the surface gets very rough, and the last 3 miles of the trail climb a thousand feet to the crest of Laurel Ridge. Starting at Camp Run, the first mile has recently been scraped and graded to a width of about 12'. It climbs steadily past its intersection with Pike Run Trail to a corner, then descends quickly to Camp Run, where a splendid new bridge provides passage. You pay immediately, though, with a brisk climb that brings you back within sight (or at least sound) of PA381. The new construction ends, leaving the trail still wide but more mature. At several points gaps in the trees provide great views north and west up the valley. Soon you descend to a trailhead at Aukerman Rd, 2.3 miles from Camp Run Rd.

Forbes State Forest, Mountain Streams II Trail System	
Location	West slope of Laurel Ridge near Kregar, Fayette County
Trailheads	Various sites along PA381 between Jones Mills and Kregar
Length, Surface	10-11 miles, usually 6-12' wide, dirt to gravel
Character	Little-used, wooded, shady, some real hills
Usage restrictions	Horses and snowmobiles ok
Amenities	Fishing
Driving time from Pittsburgh	1 hour south-east

To continue from here, go right on Aukerman Rd (note: not the road marked "no outlet") for 0.15 miles and turn left at the trail signs. The trail narrows to only about 6', and it gradually becomes more technical. Folks with hybrid bikes may want to turn back here. After a delightful rolling 0.8 mile, the trail emerges at the upper Sky View Rd parking area. Turn left, go a tenth of a mile down the hill, and turn right. You're now on the railroad grade again. In another tenth of a mile, pass through a small parking area, duck under a gate, and follow the trail along the railroad grade. The trail continues fairly level for another mile or so, then starts a 3-mile climb to the ridge. Toward the end of this mile the surface gets very rough. At the somewhat precarious crossing of Little Run, we decided the surface was rougher than our taste, and we turned back.

We haven't had a chance to ride *Pike Run Trail* yet. It starts at Mountain Streams Trail 0.4 mile above the Camp Run parking area. It runs southeast, then south for about 2 miles, emerging on PA31 above Pike Run Country Club. The map suggests that most of the 300' climb is in the first mile.

Local history, attractions

The trails in this area are built on grades that once served the Blair Brothers sawmill in Kregar. The railroad along Indian Creek was used only to haul lumber from the saw-mill to market. The grades east of PA381 were narrow gauge lines for shay locomotives to haul logs to the sawmill.

Extensions of the ride

All of the trail is in Forbes State Forest. State Forest rules for bicycles allow bikes on all roads and trails (but only on roads and trails) unless they're specifically posted as closed. This is a different policy from State Game Lands, which permit bikes off-road.

Camp Run Rd, Aukerman Rd, and Sky View Rd are narrow dirt township roads. They have very little motor vehicle traffic, and they're too rough and steep for the cars to be going very fast. You may enjoy extending your ride with these roads.

Access points

Vicinity: Directions begin headed north on PA381 from its intersection with PA31 east of Jones Mills. To reach this point from Pittsburgh, take the PA Turnpike to Donegal and go east on PA31 for 2.8 miles, then turn north on PA381. Note that this is 0.6 miles east of the intersection where PA381 goes south from PA31.

Blair Brothers trailhead: From the junction of 381 and PA31, follow PA381 north for less than a tenth of a mile. Parking is on the left side of the road just before the bridge across Indian Creek or on the right just after you cross the bridge.

Camp Run trailhead: From the junction of 381 and PA31, follow PA381 north for 0.6 mile. Turn right on Camp Run Rd. Parking is about a tenth of a mile up this road on the left.

Kregar trailhead: From the junction of 381 and PA31, follow PA381 north for 2.8 miles. Turn right on Sky View Rd. Follow Sky View Rd down to the creek and start up the hill. There are two parking areas. For the first, go 0.5 miles from PA381, turn left on the marked side road, go 0.1 mile on the side road. For the second, go 0.6 miles from PA381 to parking on the right.

Amenities

Rest rooms, water: None

Bike shop, rentals: None

Restaurant, groceries: Restaurants and groceries along PA31 between Jones Mills and Donegal.

Swimming, fishing: Cold water fishing in Indian Creek

Winter sports: Cross-country skiing, snowmobiling

Wheelchair access: Trails are probably too rough for most wheelchairs

Trail organization

Forbes State Forest, District 4
PO Box 519
Laughlintown PA 15655-0519
(724) 238-9533

Maps, guides, other references

USGS Topographic Maps: Seven Springs.

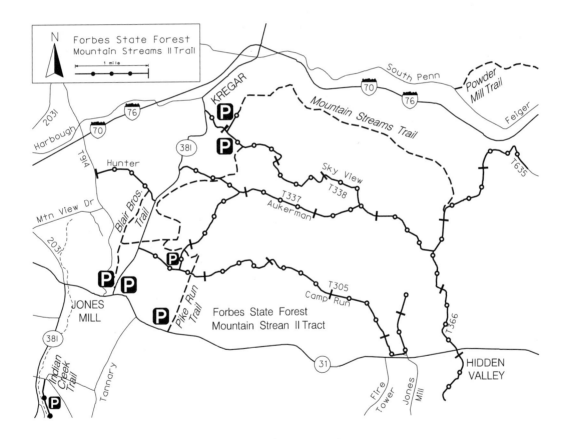

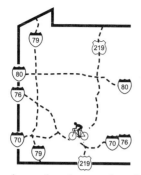

PW&S Railroad Bike Trail

Forbes State Forest and adjacent state parks in Westmoreland and Somerset Counties

Forbes State Forest and the adjacent State Parks (Linn Run, Laurel Mountain, and Laurel Ridge) maintain a network of snowmobile trails and forest service roads though the second-growth forest along Laurel Hill. Much of this network serves as a mountain biking system the rest of the year. Bicycling is allowed *only* on the designated trails (plus, of course, on roads open to automobiles). Bikes are specifically prohibited on the yellow-blazed Laurel Highlands Hiking Trail, which intersects the PW&S system at several places. Currently, the official mountain biking map shows about 15.4 miles of road (mostly dirt) and 19 miles of motor-free trail open north of the PA Turnpike (I76) and south of US30. These trails are marked to indicate their difficulty as "novice" (green ●), "advanced" (blue ■), or "expert" (black ▲). Most of the motor-free trails are rough, rocky, and steep—true mountain biking trails. Most of the wide easy trails are on lightly-traveled roads. This trail system, then, is unlike most of the other trails in this guide.

Within the PW&S network, 6.5 miles follow the route of the former Pittsburgh, Westmoreland, and Somerset Railroad. This includes 3.9 miles along Linn Run Rd, 1.8 miles along Laurel Summit Rd, and 0.8 mile closed to motor vehicles (the "Old PW&S Grade"). Linn Run Rd follows the PW&S grade for most of the way from Linn Run State Park to the top of the hill. One place where the road deviates from the railroad is near the ranger's residence; two others are at the safety switches on the steep part of the hill. The PW&S grade along Linn Run Rd is quite steep by railway standards—up to 12%. The low point on the trail system is at the eastern edge of Linn Run State Park on Linn Run Rd. Here a quarry supplied "bluestone" to make the cobblestones that paved many Pittsburgh streets. Quarry Trail emerges here after its final steep descent.

Traces of two original safety switches from the PW&S can be found about a mile southeast (uphill) from the park boundary, where Linn Run Rd crosses Linn Run (from south to north if you're going uphill). At a parking lot here, Fish Run Trail (no bikes) runs well above the road, emerging half a mile later at the lower of the two safety switches. Here Fish Run Trail crosses over to the south side of the road for half a mile and becomes a bike trail. This is the Fish Run-Water Station area; it is on the steepest part of the hill and is one of the finest segments of the original grade. The railroad grade crosses the creek four times in this half-mile, twice on original stone culverts and twice on timber replicas of railroad bridges. The remains of another safety switch and associated features can be seen on the upper end of this half-mile segment. The switches were kept in the safety position and changed manually to let trains pass. Since the train had to stop at each safety switch, these were natural places for water stops as well.

Traces of the railroad pond are about 100 yards upgrade from the upper timber bridge. An interpretive area will be developed here. Bikes are permitted on Fish Run Trail only on the half-mile section on the south side of the road. When Fish Run Trail returns to Linn Run Rd, it crosses and becomes hikers-only again; bikes must remain on the road.

At Laurel Summit, the PW&S forks. The left branch goes north on Laurel Summit Rd. The right branch is gated to exclude motor vehicles; it starts gently downhill on a wide flat trail. Regrettably, there's only 0.8 miles of it. The portions of the railroad grade on roads are surfaced in dirt and gravel; automobile traffic is light and reasonably slow. The on-road portions are not terribly interesting, but the short segments on Fish Run Rd and on the old railroad grade in the woods are quite pleasant.

PW&S Railroad Hiking-Biking Trail	
Location	Forbes State Forest and adjacent state parks, Cook and Ligonier Townships, Westmoreland County; Jenner and Lincoln Township, Somerset County
Trailheads	Linn Run Rd, Laurel Summit Rd
Length, Surface	6.5 miles of 34.3-mile network on abandoned rail line; dirt, gravel, and single-track
Character	Uncrowded, wooded, sunny, hilly, very rugged
Usage restrictions	Snowmobiles permitted
Amenities	Rest rooms, water, bike rental, camping
Driving time from Pittsburgh	1 hour 30 minutes

Of the 26.5 miles of the trail system that are not on the railroad grade, 8.3 are on dirt and gravel roads that carry even less traffic than Linn Run Rd and Laurel Summit Rd. The surfaces tend to be rough, and there are several significant hills. The elevation change on Linn Run Rd from the low point on the west to the ridge is over 1000'; on the east side the elevation change is over 600'.

This leaves a little over 18 miles of serious mountain biking. It's one of the best mountain biking systems in the region, mostly marked and signed "advanced" (blue ■), or "expert" (black ▲). Take a mountain bike and be prepared to take care of yourself and your bike in rugged and remote terrain.

The Laurel Summit Picnic area makes a good base of operations for excursions on the interconnected loops. It is, of course, near the top of the loops.

Local history, attractions

This entire area was clear-cut in the first decade of the 20th century to supply hardwood to a sawmill in Ligonier, then largely burned over. The Pittsburgh, Westmoreland, and Somerset RR was established to haul the timber: oak, hickory,

---

cherry, and hemlock. It operated from 1899 to 1916. Passenger service was added in 1901 so people could visit the mountain. Later, the railroad carried bluestone from the quarry to Pittsburgh for paving streets. The main line of the railroad ran from Rector to Somerset. It's relatively steeper than most of the area's railroads, and two level "safety switches" were built along Linn Run to stop runaway cars. Remains of these can still be seen along Fish Run trail, parallel to Linn Run Rd; one is on each side of the road (only the part of the trail to the south of the road is open to bicycles). The state acquired 6000 acres of Byers-Allen Lumber Company land in 1912 for $2/acre, rehabilitated the forest, and stocked it with white-tailed deer. This was the first forest preserve in the Ohio River drainage of Pennsylvania.

Development plans

The 1994 master plan calls for a 46-mile network including five interconnected loops between the Laurel Mountain Ski area and the PA Turnpike. Four of these loops, totaling about 34 miles, are now available. The additional loops are slated to include one at the ski area (4 miles) and a connector to the South Penn RR in Somerset County (7 miles). Expect improvements to drainage, trail surface, and signage loops in 2000.

In the winter, the snowmobile trails north of the PA Turnpike connect with the snowmobile trails to the south using the Laurel Highlands Hiking Trail bridge over the Turnpike. The ranger at Linn Run State Park advises us that this bridge is *not* open to bicycles, so this connection is not available to cyclists.

Access points

Vicinity: Directions begin at the intersection of US30 with PA711 headed east on US30 in Ligonier. To reach this point from Pittsburgh, take the PA Turnpike and exit eastbound on US30 at Greensburg.

Linn Run trailhead: From Ligonier, continue east for 2.0 miles on US30. Turn south (right) on PA381 and go 3.0 miles to Linn Run Rd in Rector. Turn east (left) on Linn Run Rd in Rector, go 2.7 miles up Linn Run Rd to enter Linn Run State Park, and park in any lot as you go up the hill. The Quarry Trail parking lot is 4.0 miles past Rector on this road, just east of the state park boundary.

Laurel Mountain trailhead: From Ligonier, continue east for about 8 miles on US30. When US30 crests the ridge, turn south (right) on Summit Rd and go about 2 miles to the large parking area at the entrance to Laurel Mountain State Park or 0.4 miles farther to parking by the Ski Patrol warming hut.

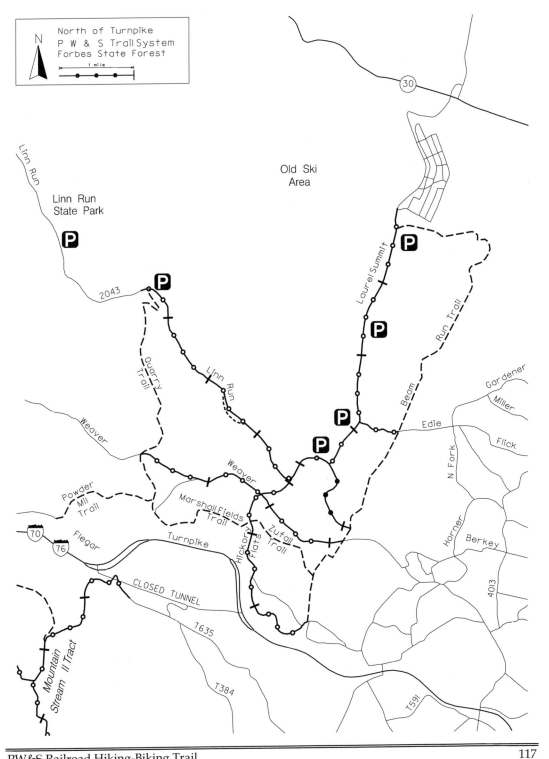

Amenities

Rest rooms, water: In Linn Run State Park and Laurel Summit picnic area.

Bike shop, rental: Rentals at large parking lot on Laurel Summit Rd near entrance to Laurel Mountain Ski Area and in Laughlintown. Bike shops on US30 near Latrobe and near Laughlintown.

Restaurant, groceries: In Ligonier, Laughlintown, and Rector.

Camping, simple lodging: Linn Run State Park has ten rustic cabins available for weekly and half-weekly rental

Swimming, fishing: No swimming. Near the lower end of Quarry Trail at Linn Run Rd, there is a set of acid rain treatment wells operated by the Loyalhanna Watershed Association and the State Park. Linn Run is stocked with trout downstream from this treatment facility

Winter sports: Most of these trails are designated snowmobile routes. A separate system of cross-country ski trails (which are not open to bicycles) weaves between the snowmobile routes in the same area.

Wheelchair access: This is principally a mountain biking area. Trails are often rough and steep; when they're not rough they're open to motor vehicle traffic.

Trail organization

Trail development

Lysle S. Sherwin, Executive Director
Loyalhanna Watershed Association
114 South Market St
PO Box 561
Ligonier, PA 15658-0561
(724) 238-7560

Operations

District Forester
Forbes State Forest
PO Box 519
Laughlintown PA 15655

(724) 238-9533

Maps, guides, other references

The PW&S Railroad Bike Trail, trail brochure, color-coded to show trail difficulty, from Loyalhanna Watershed Association ($2.00 by mail).

Trail map based on topographic map available from Linn Run State Park office and bicycle rental shops.

Forbes State Forest Public Use Map and Laurel Highlands Snowmobile Trail System Map available from Forbes State Forest.

USGS Topographic Maps: Ligonier, Bakersville.

Trails North & East: Allegheny Valley

Several networks of interconnected trails are starting to appear in the Allegheny River basin. Developers hope that some day they will grow large enough to merge.

Indiana-Cambria County System

Trail developers in Indiana and Cambria Counties are cooperating to connect the county seats of the two counties with trails in Blacklick Ck watershed. The system began with the Ghost Town Trail, which straddles the county line from Dilltown to Nanty Glo. This Y-shaped trail is planning extensions on all three ends. More recently, the Hoodlebug Trail is being developed from the town of Indiana through Homer City toward US22; its first sections should open in 1999. The final link is a possible connection from the west end of the Ghost Town to near the southern end of the Hoodlebug.

Kiskiminetas-Conemaugh Greenway

The Kiski-Conemaugh Coalition is cultivating a connection between the existing Roaring Run Trail and future trails near Conemaugh Dam to the east. They're also looking at the possibility of continuing down the Kiskiminetas River to its mouth, which is at the southern end of the Armstrong Trail. The resulting trail will be named the Main Line Trail after the nickname of the Pennsylvania Canal, whose path it follows.

Allegheny Valley Rail Trail System

Closest to Pittsburgh, the Armstrong Trail follows the Allegheny River through Armstrong County. Legal complications have slowed development, but most of the route is now open on the dirt, gravel, and original ballast. In addition, several miles near Kittanning have been surfaced, and some traffic control has been installed. The southern end of the Butler-Freeport trail reaches the Allegheny River a few miles downstream from the Armstrong Trail (and on the other side of the Allegheny).

Farther north in the Allegheny River watershed, an extensive network of rail-trails is growing in Venango and Clarion Counties under the leadership of the small but vigorous Allegheny Valley Trails Association. The main stem of this system runs along the Allegheny River as the Allegheny River Trail and the Samuel Justus Trail. The trail council would eventually like to extend the trail southward to connect with the Armstrong Trail below Kennerdell. They also hope for a northward extension along the Allegheny River through Tidioute to Warren, with various side spurs.

Long-term plans call for the spine along the Allegheny River to be supplemented with the 50-mile Clarion Secondary Trail, running from near Shippenville northwest to Sandy Lake near I79. This trail is under development from near Clarion to Pecan.

Additional plans include a connector to include the Oil Creek State Park trail, a loop connector from Franklin to Polk, and a 25-mile network in Allegheny National Forest.

The Venango County region is protected by both the National Wild and Scenic River program and the Oil Heritage Park program. The Allegheny River from Warren to Oil City and from Franklin to Emlenton is a Wild and Scenic River. The Oil Heritage Park extends along Oil Creek from Titusville to Oil City and along the Allegheny River from Oil City to Emlenton.

If it all works out, these trails will some day interconnect to provide a continuous route from near Pittsburgh to several points in the northern part of the state. Unfortunately, some parcels along the trail have passed into private ownership, and re-establishing the trail will take a lot of effort. Prospects are better for the portion of the system north of I80, not so good south of there.

In early 1999, the Oil Creek, Samuel Justus, and Allegheny River Trails are open. The Clarion Secondary Trail is under development from near Clarion to Pecan. The trails at Tidioute and Warren tantalize you with the possibility of an extension to Lake Erie.

Other trails in the Allegheny basin follow segments of Cowanshannock Ck near Rural Valley, Tionesta River along Tionesta Lake, a chain of ponds in Allegheny Forest, and the upper Clarion River and Little Toby Ck.

This part of the book includes a few other nearby trails that actually lie east of the Allegheny watershed. They are near Altoona and Clearfield.

Donkey engines lurk in the bushes

Ghost Town Trail

Along Blacklick Ck from Dilltown to Nanty Glo, with spur from Rexis to White Mill Station in Indiana and Cambria Counties

The Ghost Town Trail runs alongside Blacklick Ck and its South Branch from Dilltown to Nanty Glo, with a spur up North Branch Blacklick Ck from Rexis to White Mill Station. A 10' crushed limestone trail runs through woods, former mining towns, and the remnants of coal mines. Several benches provide resting places. The trail is named for five ghost towns, once-thriving mining towns along the railroad that were all abandoned by the 1930s. The Eliza Furnace in Vintondale still remains, as do a few original houses and foundations of mine buildings. The area shows the heritage of the Blacklick Ck valley, which includes railroads, mining, iron making, and lumbering. Much of the trail is in State Game Lands, so wildlife and wildflowers are abundant. Several original railroad mileposts remain; they're about a tenth of a mile east of the trail mileposts.

The main line of the trail follows the route of the 1903 Ebensburg and Blacklick Railroad for 12 miles from Dilltown to Nanty Glo. From Dilltown to Wheatfield the trail runs through scenic woodland, crossing Mardis Run (mile 0 from Dilltown), the new Blacklick Valley Natural Area, Clarke Run (mile 1.7), and Dobson Run (mile 2) before joining Blacklick Ck at Wheatfield (mile 2.4). A historical marker at Wheatfield describes the iron furnace that once operated near here. From Wheatfield through Wehrum to Rexis, the trail lies between a cliff and the river. The location of Wehrum (mile 3.6) can be recognized from the road crossing at SR2013, but there is scant trace of the town; the site is private and not open to the public. You can, however, see the remains of a riverside structure, the race for a coal-washing plant, a tenth of a mile to the east. Between Wehrum and Rexis two large mine gob heaps adjoin the trail (miles 4.0-4.1 and 5.0-5.6). They reflect the history of the region but detract somewhat from the scenic value of the trail. Laurel Run (mile 5) crosses just before the second gob pile. The location of the ghost town Lackawanna #3 is also in this area.

The trail forks at Rexis (mile 5.8), with the main trail going right across a bridge to the Eliza Furnace at the edge of Vintondale (mile 6.0); the left fork is the spur trail up the North Branch. On the main trail, the well-preserved Eliza Furnace (National Register Site, 1846-49) is located on the Cambria/Indiana county line. The furnace was constructed of dry fitted stone, 32 feet high, 32 feet wide, and 31 feet deep. It still boasts its original heat exchange pipes and sits in a well-tended grassy meadow ready for a picnic. A recent grant from the Southwestern Pennsylvania Heritage Preservation Commission will support preservation and historical exhibits here. An archeological site survey identified traces of some of the associated buildings; development of the

Eliza Furnace Historic Site will identify and interpret some of these. In the creek just west of the furnace, water bubbles up from the creekbed. This comes from a set of boreholes drilled to lower the water level in the mine and relieve basement flooding in some homes in Vintondale. The whitish color is an aluminum precipitate.

From Eliza Furnace, the trail follows a grassy embankment beside the road to Vintondale. Just east of the Furnace (mile 6.1) is a rest room building. Where the road crosses the bridge (mile 6.3), the trail swings left along a bench cut into the hillside for 100 ft, then enters a large flat area and passes a loading platform in front of a mine portal (mile 6.6). The trail continues across South Branch Blacklick Ck (mile 7.0) and alongside yet another gob heap (mile 7.1-7.2). The trail then passes a cattail field and cranberry bog (mile 7.3) as it enters State Game Lands #79 and enters the most scenic section. The trail begins to climb noticeably, with a gradient here of 2-3%. You pass the location of the ghost town of Bracken (mile 8.1). This area has reportedly been haunted by the "Lady in White" since she was killed by her lover in the early part of the century.

Ghost Town Trail	
Location	Along Blacklick Ck from Dilltown to Nanty Glo, Buffington Township in Indiana County, Blacklick and Jackson Townships and Vintondale and Nanty Glo Boroughs in Cambria County
Trailheads	Dilltown, Wehrum, Vintondale, Twin Rocks, Nanty Glo
Length, Surface	19.5 planned, 15.5 miles finished, packed crushed stone
Character	Uncrowded, wooded, shady, flat (2-3% grade on eastern leg)
Usage restrictions	Horses ok; no motorized vehicles; no snowmobiles
Amenities	Rest rooms, bike rental, food, camping, lodging
Driving time from Pittsburgh	1 hour 20 minutes east

After Bracken, you climb along the creek until it swings away from the trail where a railroad siding once served a strip mine (mile 9.4). Here you go through an impressive cut with a coal seam undercutting the rocks on top (mile 9.5). The trail crosses the creek again on a bridge dated 1916 (mile 9.6) before arriving at the road just south of Twin Rocks (mile 9.7). Here the trail leaves the woods and passes between homes and the river for the last two miles to Nanty Glo. The Welsh spelling is Nant-y-Glo, meaning "streams of coal". On the return trip, you can coast from the 1916 bridge (mile 9.6) almost all the way to the cattail field (mile 7.3).

Unfortunately, installation of a pipeline on the trail corridor in early 1999 disrupted the trail surface between Vintondale and Twin Rocks. The trail surface will be restored during the 1999 season, but until that's done, you may prefer to explore the Red Mill/White Mill spur to see the new bridge at Red Mill instead of going to Nanty Glo.

The spur that takes off at Rexis (mile 5.8) follows the route of the Cambria and Indiana Railroad for about 4 miles to US422 near White Mill Station. Much of the route runs through State Game Lands #79. A small pavilion with picnic table and benches overlooks the creek 1.2 miles from Rexis. A few ruins are visible along the trail. The most notable is a stone building with a railroad platform 2.3 miles from Rexis that was a stone quarry weighing station (privately owned). The bridge near Red Mill Station (2.4 miles from the fork at Rexis) was destroyed in the 1977 flood. This bridge is under construction and expected to open in April 1999. The trail has been complete for some time from this bridge for the remaining 1.6 miles to US422, where it currently ends.

Eliza Furnace greets you in winter as well as summer

Local history, attractions

The trail corridor is rich in history of the mining, iron, and lumbering industries of the valley. Five ghost towns lie along the trail:

- Armerford and Scott Glen were early mining communities west of Dilltown.
- Wehrum (Lackawanna #4) formerly provided 230 homes, a store, bank, and other services for the Lackawanna Coal and Coke Company. The town was abandoned in the 1930s, and one house remains of the 250 that once stood here. It was located where SR3013 crosses Blacklick Ck; the name still appears on some maps. It's private property now.

- Lackawanna #3 was a short-lived "coal patch" town in the area known as Edward's Flats between Wehrum and Rexis.
- Bracken was a small community between Vintondale and Twin Rocks operated by the Commercial Coal Company.

Eliza Furnace operated from 1846 to 1849. At its peak, over 90 people and 45 mules produced about 1080 tons of iron a year. Producing one ton of pig iron required about 2-3 tons of iron ore, 1-1.5 tons of charcoal, and 2.5 tons of limestone. One day's charcoal supply for the furnace required the wood from about one acre of forest. This is one of the best-preserved hot blast furnaces in the state and one of the few anywhere with its hot blast coils (the radiator-shaped metal structure on top) intact. It was never profitable. It was doomed by the poor quality of the local iron ore and the cost of transporting the iron overland to the railroad at Nineveh and Johnstown, coupled with external forces such as lowered tariffs on imported iron and discovery of the higher-quality Mesabi Range in Minnesota. An interpretive sign near the furnace provides more information. Plans call for an extensive interpretive exhibit at the furnace.

Another iron furnace was located near Wheatfield, but no traces remain. A historical marker at the Wheatfield intersection describes the furnace. A third furnace, Buena Vista Furnace, is located along the recently-abandoned railroad to the west of Dilltown. The furnaces in the valley were charcoal fired, so charcoal hearths also dotted the valley. These furnaces were built on speculation that the mainline of the Pennsylvania RR would be routed through the Blacklick Valley. When the route selected went through the Conemaugh Valley instead, this ended speculation in local iron-making.

The railroads that preceded this trail and the coal mines that they served came nearly half a century after Eliza Furnace ceased operation. Vintondale itself was established in 1894 as a coal company town.

Judy and Joseph Kovalchick have contributed land for two rail-trails in western PA, this one and the Roaring Run Trail. They own the Kovalchick Corporations and learned about the rails-to-trails movement in 1989 when Roaring Run Watershed approached them about donating a 4-mile corridor in Apollo. In 1984, they had acquired the route along Blacklick Ck for salvage. In September 1991 they deeded a 15.5-mile corridor, formerly the Ebensburg & Blacklick Railroad, along Blacklick Ck to Indiana County and the Northern Cambria Community Development Corporation (NORCAM). The trail was developed by Indiana County Parks and NORCAM with help from local citizens of the Cambria & Indiana Trail Council and grants from America's Industrial Heritage Project and ISTEA. The Cambria County portion of the trail is now managed by the Cambria County Conservation and Recreation Authority. The Cambria and Indiana Railroad donated the Rexis spur, formerly the Blacklick & Yellowcreek RR.

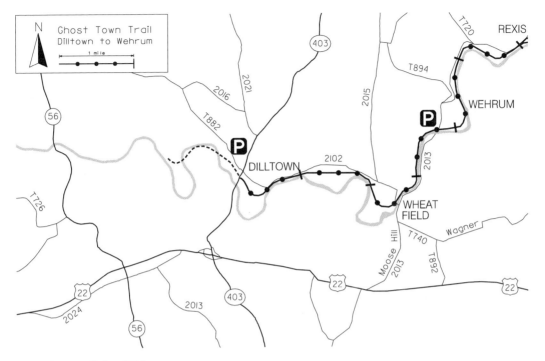

Extensions of the Ride

For variety, SR2012 and SR2013 parallel the trail from Dilltown to Rexis. Sometimes they are on the same side of Blacklick Ck as the trail, sometimes on the other. They are lightly traveled and provide a paved alternative. SR3047 parallels the trail from Vintondale to Twin Rocks. Traffic appears to be light, but it's a little heavier than on SR2012 and SR2013. The parallel road from Twin Rocks to Nanty Glo is the rather busier PA271.

Dirt roads in State Game Lands #79 may provide opportunities for extensions of the trip. Most start with brisk climbs of 300 to 600 feet, but the road that crosses the trail at Bracken provides a gentler access. If you turn at Bracken to cross the river, you can ride a 5-mile loop up, along the ridge, and back down to Eliza Furnace. This is only suitable for mountain bikers with good technical riding skills plus pathfinding and map reading ability. About half a mile after crossing the river on a forest road, take the first right. This climbs northeast for nearly 2 miles with a few steep pitches. A couple of nonobvious turns connect to the power lines on top of the hill; the route follows their cut for a little over a mile. One of the trails to the left will take you back to Bracken. Another (also not obvious) takes you about 2 miles southwest. Another obscure turn puts you on a steep, very technical half-mile hill down to Eliza furnace. If you try this, take the topo map. Coal mining in this area may close parts of this route in 1999-2000.

David and Penny Russell (co-partners in establishing the Dillweed in Dilltown) donated 675 acres to Indiana County to form the Blacklick Valley Natural Area. Hiking and equestrian trails have been developed in the area, with access across Blacklick Ck from the trail about a mile east of the PA403/US422 interchange.

Development plans

The trail is being developed by Indiana County Parks and the Cambria County Conservation and Recreation Authority with help from members of the Cambria & Indiana Trail Council and grants from Southwestern Pennsylvania Heritage Preservation Commission and ISTEA.

Plans call for access areas with parking, rest rooms, interpretive exhibits, and benches or picnic tables at Dilltown, Wehrum, Rexis/Vintondale, Twin Rocks, Nanty Glo, and White Mill Station. The missing 105-foot Red Mill Bridge that interrupts the spur trail to White Mill Station on US422 is being rebuilt and should open in April 1999. The Eliza Furnace area will be developed as an interpretive site. The trail between Vintondale and Twin Rocks will be repaired in 1999.

The master plan calls for extension of the present trail west from Dilltown, east from Nanty Glo to Ebensburg, and north from White Mill. Ultimately, this and other trails should link Ebensburg to Indiana, thereby connecting the county seats of Cambria and Indiana Counties.

The Conemaugh Valley Conservancy is working on establishing a greenway from Johnstown to Saltsburg.

Access points

Vicinity: Directions begin eastbound on US22 east of Blairsville, where US119 departs northbound. Note that US22 and US119 are the same road for over 10 miles to the west of this point.

Dilltown (west) trailhead: Go east on US22 from its intersection with US119 for 11.6 miles to PA403. Take the PA403 exit. At the end of the exit ramp turn left (north) and continue 1.4 miles to the trailhead. Parking is on the left (west) side of PA403 shortly after you cross the creek.

Wehrum trailhead: Go east on US22 from its intersection with US119 for 13.8 miles to Moose Hill Rd (SR2013). Turn north (left) on SR2013 and continue 2.6 miles to Wehrum, just after SR2013 crosses the river.

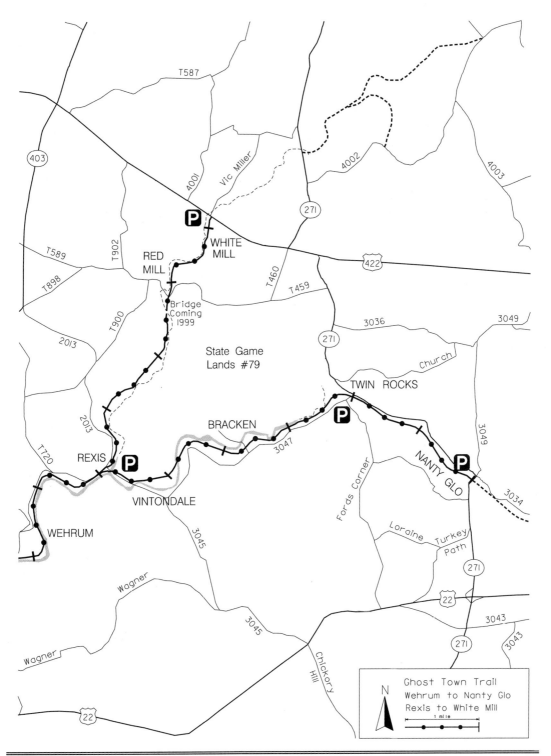

T587

403

4001

Vic Miller

4002

4003

271

P

WHITE
MILL

T589

T902

RED
MILL

422

T898

T460

T459

T900

Bridge
Coming
1999

3036

3049

2013

State Game
Lands #79

271

Church

203

TWIN ROCKS

3049

T720

203

BRACKEN

P

3047

Fords Corner

P

NANTY
GLO

P

REXIS

3034

VINTONDALE

3045

Loraine

Turkey
Path

WEHRUM

271

Wagner

22

3043

3045

271

3043

Wagner

Chickory Hill

N

Ghost Town Trail
Wehrum to Nanty Glo
Rexis to White Mill

22

1 mile

Vintondale and Rexis trailheads: Go east on US22 from its intersection with US119 for 19.0 miles to Chickory Hill Rd (SR3045). Turn north (left) on SR3045 and continue for 3.0 miles to the eastern edge of Vintondale, or 0.9 miles farther to the Rexis parking lot (100 yards west of Eliza furnace, just across the bridge).

Nanty Glo (east) and Twin Rocks trailheads: Go east on US22 from its intersection with US119 for 20 miles to PA271. Turn north (left) on PA271 and continue 1.5 miles to Nanty Glo. Just after crossing South Branch Blacklick Ck, turn left on either side of the Nanty Glo Fire Station and go about one block behind the Fire Station to the trailhead. Park behind the Municipal Building and Fire Station, at the far end of the lot. To reach Twin Rocks trailhead, follow PA271 2.1 miles through Nanty Glo to SR3047. Turn left on SR3047 to the trailhead parking lot (before crossing the creek).

White Mill (end of northeast extension) trailhead: Go east on US22 from its intersection with US119 for 11.6 miles to PA403. Exit northbound on PA403, pass through Dilltown and continue to US422. Turn right on US422 and continue to Vic Miller Rd (White Mill Station). Note that this currently provides access to about a mile and a half of trail; a missing bridge (to be completed in April 1999) separates you from the rest.

Amenities

Rest rooms, water: Rest rooms at Dilltown trailhead and 100 yards east of Eliza Furnace. Chemical toilets at Nanty Glo, and Twin Rocks. No water at trailheads.

Bike shop, rentals: Bike rental shops in Dilltown, on Main St in Vintondale, at Rexis, and in Nanty Glo. There's also a hardware store in Nanty Glo.

Restaurant, groceries: Snacks in Dilltown at the Dillweed and at bike shops in Vintondale. Convenience store on US22 just east of PA403 (1.5 miles from Dilltown). Grocery store on Main St in Vintondale. Nanty Glo is better developed, with snack shop across from the trailhead and Foodland and Subway stores half a mile or so across the river and south on PA271. The Sheetz store that used to be a block from the trailhead has moved to the intersection of PA271 and US22.

Camping, simple lodging: Dillweed Bed-and-Breakfast in Dilltown. Primitive camping at one location along Rexis spur; signs along the trail show the location. Private campground near Yellow Ck State Park (10 miles northwest).

Swimming, fishing: Blacklick Ck is the victim of long-standing acid mine pollution and is considered one of the most polluted streams in Pennsylvania. Some of the smaller creeks have clean water, but others carry the acid drainage that winds up in Blacklick Creek. Swimming is not permitted in any of the clean streams. The upper portions of several tributaries (Mardis Run, Clarke Run, and Downey Run) are stocked with trout by the East Wheatfield Cooperative Fish Nursery.

Winter sports: Cross-country skiing on trail and in State Game Lands. Snowmobiles not permitted on trail but are permitted in State Game Lands.

Wheelchair access: Good

Trail organizations

Support Group

Cambria & Indiana Trail Council
PO Box 11
Dilltown PA 15929
web: cpcug.org/user/warholic/ghost.html
Memberships: $10/year individual; $12/year family

Operations, Indiana County

Indiana County Parks
Blue Spruce Park Rd
Indiana PA 15701-9802
(724) 463-8636

Operations, Cambria County

Cambria County Conservation and
    Recreation Authority
401 Candlelight Dr, Suite 234
Ebensburg PA 15931
(814) 472-2110

Maps, guides, other references

Trail brochure

Eliza Iron Furnace interpretive brochure

Blacklick Valley Natural Area brochure

Denise Dusza Weber. *Delano's Domain: A History of Warren Delano's Mining Towns of Vintondale, Wehrum and Claghorn.* To buy reprint, write 291 Olive St, Indiana PA 15701.

Blacklick Valley Natural Area brochure

USGS Topographic Maps: New Florence, Vintondale, Nanty Glo, Strongstown.

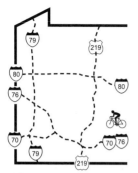

Lower Trail (Juniata River Corridor)

Along the Frankstown Branch, Juniata River from Alfarata in Huntingdon County to Williamsburg in Blair County

This valley has served as a transportation corridor since it was part of the Frankstown Path, a major Indian route connecting Harrisburg with Kittanning. In subsequent times it has supported a canal, a railroad, and a highway. The route of the former railroad and canal forms the Lower (rhymes with "flower") Trail. This trail runs alongside the Frankstown Branch of the Juniata River without road crossings for 11 miles through forest and farmland. The Juniata River here is really a creek, often running in shallow riffles near the trail.

Within sight of the Alfarata trailhead, the trail crosses under US22 and heads upstream along the Juniata to squeeze through a small gap in Tussey Mountain. The town here is said to be called Water Street because pack trains used the creek bed through the narrow steep gap. A mile later, the trail passes the foundations of structures used to bring stone down from Owens quarry, which you can see high on the hill. Another mile and a half brings you to Goodman quarry, also marked by concrete foundations. Between the two quarries, the canal channel has become the back channel of the creek, usually separated from the main channel by an island. Here, as with most of the remaining traces of the canal, a good imagination will help you visualize the former structures.

About two miles beyond Goodman quarry the trail crosses Fox Run on a handsome stone arch bridge. A view of this bridge from the creek bed is featured in many trail descriptions. Half a mile farther you make the first of two crossings of the Juniata, where the railroad took a shortcut across a peninsula. Just past the second bridge you'll reach the Mt Etna access area, including a bridge over a former mill race. The Mt Etna Iron furnace community is about half a mile from the trail here.

A mile beyond the access area the trail passes Canal Lock No 61. The walls of the lock are clearly visible. Another mile brings you to numerous foundations that mark the Juniata Limestone Company and its company town, 7 miles from Alfarata and 4 miles from Williamsburg. From here to Williamsburg the traces of the canal are more frequent, including locks and foundations of locktender's houses. Other signs of current use—farms and houses—are also more frequent.

The trail is graced by no fewer than four sets of mileage markers: three from railroads and one for the modern trail. The trail is marked from 0 to 11 in both directions in white numbers on brown posts. The railroad markers are black on white. Two such markers (with different numbering systems) are just north of the Williamsburg parking lot, and others appear along the length of the trail.

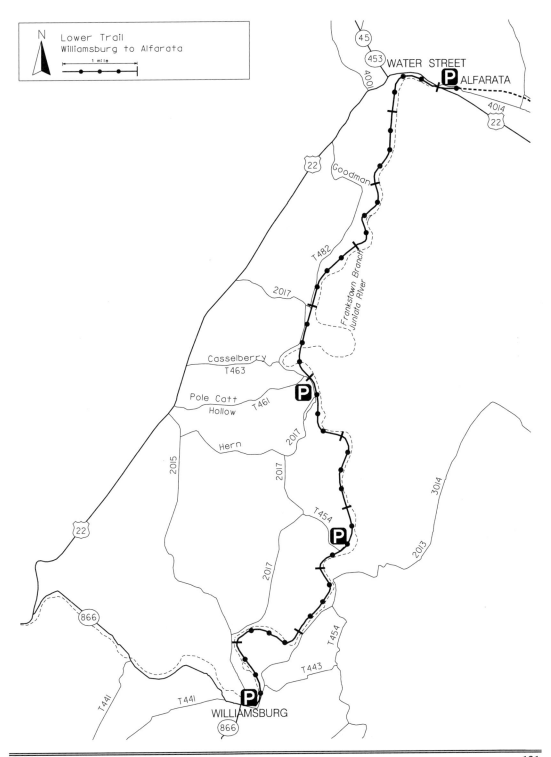

Lower Trail
Williamsburg to Alfarata

N

1 mile

Local history, attractions

The Frankstown Path, also called the Allegheny Path or Ohio Path, was the major Indian trail across this region. It connected Paxtang (now Harrisburg) with Kittanning and Forks of the Ohio (now Pittsburgh). In this area it followed approximately the same route as US22, and it's known locally as the Kittanning Path. Hunters, trappers, and pioneers later used this route to reach the frontier.

Lower Trail (Juniata River Corridor)	
Location	Alfarata to Williamsburg, Porter and Morris Townships in Huntingdon County; Catherine and Woodbury Townships in Blair County
Trailheads	Alfarata, Etna Iron Furnace, Covedale, Williamsburg
Length, Surface	11 miles, packed crushed stone with parallel mowed trail
Character	uncrowded, wooded, shady, flat
Usage restrictions	Horses ok; no motorized vehicles
Amenities	Rest rooms, food
Driving time from Pittsburgh	2 hours 20 minutes east

The canal was built in the 1830's as part of the Juniata Division of the Pennsylvania Main Line Canal, which connected Philadelphia to Pittsburgh with three canals, a railroad, and the Allegheny Portage Railway, a combination railroad and inclined plane. Traces of this part of the canal can also be seen along Roaring Run Trail. Poor management, floods, and the rise of railroads led to the demise of the canal. As technology gave railroads superiority over canals, the Pennsy RR purchased the entire Mainline Canal system in 1857. In 1879 the Petersburg Branch of the Pennsy was built on this corridor. It operated until 1979 and was abandoned in 1982. In 1990, T. Dean Lower provided funding to purchase the corridor as a rail-trail.

Access points

Vicinity: Directions begin headed east on US22 from its intersection with PA36 in Hollidaysburg. To reach this point from Pittsburgh, go east on US22 past US220, taking care to stay on US22 when it exits at the beginning of the US220 interchange.

Alfarata (north) trailhead: Follow US22 18.6 miles east from PA36. Turn left on SR4014 toward Alfarata; this turn is 0.7 miles after the intersection of US22 and PA45/453. Go 0.4 miles on SR4014 to trailhead parking.

Williamsburg (south) trailhead: Follow US22 9.1 miles east from P36. Turn right on PA866 (to Williamsburg). Follow PA866 into town, where it becomes 1st St. Remain on 1st St when PA866 turns right and go two blocks to parking at the intersection of 1st St and Liberty St. Parking is a total of 3.8 miles from US22.

Amenities

Rest rooms, water: Chemical toilets at Alfarata and Williamsburg trailheads.

Bike shop, rental: None

Restaurant, groceries: In Williamsburg, convenience store a block from trailhead

Camping, simple lodging: Family cabins at Canoe Creek State Park, just south of Williamsburg on US22.

Swimming, fishing: Swimming in Frankstown Br Juniata R. Fishing quality unknown

Winter sports: Cross-country skiing

Wheelchair access: OK

Cross-country skier emerging at Alfarata trailhead

Trail organization

Rails-to-Trails of Blair County
PO Box 592
Hollidaysburg PA 16648-0592
(814) 832-2400
Membership: $10/year individual, $12/year family

Maps, guides, other references

Trail brochure, available at trailheads

USGS Topographic Maps: Spruce Creek, Williamsburg.

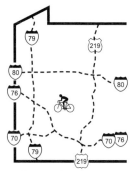

Roaring Run Trail

Southeast of Apollo in Armstrong County

Roaring Run Trail parallels the Kiskiminetas River from Cherry Lane southeast of Apollo upstream for 3.7 miles toward (but not nearly to) Edmon. The surface is finished as a 10-foot packed limestone path for 2.0 miles. After crossing Roaring Run, the trail progressively deteriorates as it approaches the Brownstown Mine (which is private property beyond the end of the trail). A side trail runs up Roaring Run for 1.4 miles to a trailhead at Brownstown Rd. At present, there is only one trailhead on the finished trail.

Most recently, this corridor served as the route of the Pennsylvania Railroad Apollo industrial extension track. The markers numbered 2 and 3 are mileage markers from the railroad. Before the railroad, though, this was the towpath for a section of the Pennsylvania Main Line Canal. Survey stones and other remains from the canal era still remain along the trail. An interpretive sign near the trailhead explains the workings of the canal. The easiest survey stones to find are near this sign.

The trail begins at a parking lot at the end of a small residential community. There's a picnic table here, and several benches dot the trail. As you head upstream, eastbound from the parking lot, you'll soon pass Milepost 1. Shortly thereafter you enter the woods, with frequent views of the Kiskiminetas River.

Roaring Run Trail	
Location	Southeast of Apollo, Kiskiminetas Township, Armstrong County
Trailheads	Apollo (no access at other end)
Length, Surface	3.7 miles along river, 2.0 finished in packed crushed stone; 1.4 miles double-track along Roaring Run; additional mountain biking
Character	Open shade along river
Usage restrictions	No motorized vehicles; no horses
Amenities	Fishing
Driving time from Pittsburgh	45 minutes north-east

Near mile 1.5 you can still see the remains of Lock 15 of the Pennsylvania Main Line Canal Its associated dam, which was originally 16 feet high, was destroyed in an 1866 flood; some remnants can be seen in the river at low water. The lock was also numbered #2 on the Kiskiminetas River. Here a "guard lock" moved barge traffic from the canal downstream to the 4-mile pool created by the dam. Upstream from the dam, the canal boats used the slackwater pool of the river instead of a separate canal prism.

Mules used the riverbank as a towpath. A lock house and inn were also located near the mouth of Roaring Run.

Long a victim of industrial pollution, especially mine runoff, the Kiskiminetas River is making a comeback. You'll find good fishing at milepost 2 and at a big hole near the mouth of Roaring Run.

The current end of the finished trail is half a mile past the bridge over Roaring Run, in the Arcadia Natural Area. The area is open for hunting, so wear blaze orange and exercise caution during hunting seasons.

Mountain bikers may ride up alongside Roaring Run on a very rough dirt road. If you start on the west side of the bridge over Roaring Run (the side closer to Apollo) you'll ford the creek once; if you start on the east side you'll ford it twice. This dirt road climbs vigorously along the creek for 1.4 miles through Roaring Run Watershed Association's parcel to a parking area on Brownstown Rd. Along the way you'll pass Rock Furnace, one of the first iron furnaces in Western Pennsylvania. It was a "tea-kettle" furnace that operated from 1825 to 1855, using charcoal, limestone, and iron ore from the adjacent hills. A model is on display at the Historical Society museum in Tarentum.

Local history, attractions

The former Pennsylvania Main Line Canal connected Philadelphia with Pittsburgh with three canals, a railroad, and the Allegheny Portage Railway, a combination railroad and inclined plane. The Western Division ran from Johnstown down the Conemaugh, Kiskiminetas, and Allegheny Rivers to Pittsburgh. Many traces of the canal can still be found along the trail. The Roaring Run Watershed Association is identifying and marking these traces and is in the process of documenting the canal remains in Armstrong County for the National Register of Historic Places. The RRWA holds numerous events along this trail; many include historical interpretation of these remains.

This is not the only trail along the former Main Line Canal: The Lower Trail, along the Frankstown Branch of the Juniata River, follows the Juniata Division of this Canal.

Extensions of the ride

The Roaring Run Watershed's property also includes mountain biking.

It's possible to add 1.3 miles to the trip by parking in Apollo and riding on Kiskiminetas Ave parallel to the river (follow the driving directions to the trailhead).

Development plans

The Roaring Run Watershed Association is working to protect the entire watershed of Roaring Run. They have extended the trail along Roaring Run to Brownstown Rd and plan (eventually) to grow upstream along the Kiskiminetas River to Edmon. They have regular volunteer activities to maintain the trail and develop amenities.

The Kovalchick family donated the initial trail segment, from the trailhead parking lot to its end 3.5 miles upstream along the Kiskiminetas River. Current activities focus on securing additional acreage in the watersheds of Rattling Run and Roaring Run and on completing half a mile of trail eastward from the Roaring Run bridge.

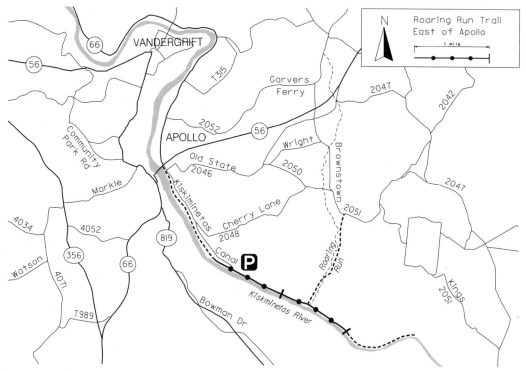

Access points

Vicinity: Directions begin on PA66 northbound across the Kiskiminetas River entering Apollo. To reach this point from Pittsburgh, take US22 east to PA286 and PA286 to PA380. Go north on PA380 to PA66. Go north on PA66 to Apollo.

Cherry Lane trailhead (the only one): After crossing the Kiskiminetas River on PA66, turn right at the first stop light onto Kiskiminetas Av. Follow this road through town to Cherry Lane. About 1 mile from the stop light take the right fork into Canal Rd instead of going up the hill. The road dead-ends in the trailhead parking lot 1.3 miles from the traffic light in Apollo.

Amenities

Rest rooms, water: None

Bike shop, rentals: None, though you can get basic hardware at the True Value Hardware or the Ben Franklin store in Apollo.

Restaurant, groceries: Within sight of the traffic light in Apollo you'll find Patrick's Pub (try the pizza and wings), a CoGo's, a Subway, and an IGA Grocery.

Camping, simple lodging: None

Swimming, fishing: The Kiskiminetas River is right next to the trail. There's good fishing at milepost 2 and the big hole at the mouth of Roaring Run (near the trail bridge). Fisherfolk report bass, catfish, drum, suckers, etc. The river often has swift currents and deep holes, and the trail managers discourage swimming.

Wheelchair access: Good for the 2 miles along the river.

Trail organization

Roaring Run Watershed Association
PO Box 40
Spring Church PA 15686
(724) 568-1483
Membership $5/year individual, $15.00/year family

Maps, guides, other references

USGS Topographic Maps: Vandergrift.

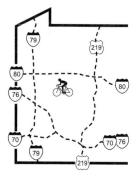

Armstrong Trail

Along Allegheny River from Schenley to Upper Hillville in Armstrong and Clarion Counties

In using this trail, you should be aware that some nearby land-owners question the trail operator's title to the trail and right to use the land. As of January 1999, this disagreement is being litigated. In addition, some sections of the trail may be obstructed or posted. We recommend against trespassing or antagonizing trail neighbors anywhere, but especially so here. Since the status of this matter changes from time to time, you may wish to check with the trail operator about the current status.

Armstrong Trail is planned to run for 52.5 miles along the east side of the Allegheny River from Schenley to Upper Hillville, primarily in Armstrong County and partly in Clarion County. Spur trails are planned westward to East Brady and eastward along Red Bank Ck. The trail was established in 1992. Two sections have been completed: 1.7 miles in Ford City and 1 mile between Manorville and Kittanning. Other areas are still primitive but passable in 1999. Modest improvements in these other areas include removing old rails and installing gates to exclude traffic. Many stretches are still rough on original ballast. Where the ballast has been removed, the trail surface is smoother.

Many original railroad mileposts remain. Mile 0 of the trail is at railroad milepost 30. Since the railroad mileposts are visible on the trail, mileages in this description refer to the railroad mileposts.

The trail begins near Schenley, at original railroad milepost 30 north of the former Schenley distillery, now the Schenley Industrial Park. At the yellow trail gate, the trail surface becomes rough gravel to Godfrey (mile 32). The Schenley distillery bottle dump is at Aladdin, between Schenley and Godfrey. Between Godfrey and Kelly you can see the remains of coke ovens on the hillside. At Godfrey the railbed is divided by a post-and-wire fence between the trail and the access road for a long series of summer cottages, camps, and trailers. These camps continue through Kelly (mile 34.8) to Lock and Dam 6 (mile 35.3; the lock is on the other side of the river) on the Allegheny River.

At Kelly the Dam Store sells ice, pop, and snacks. The road widens here to provide access to more summer camps, a handicapped-access fishing area, and the power generating plant at Dam 6. From this dam to Logansport (mile 37) and on to Crooked Ck (mile 39), the ballast has been removed from the trail, which improves the ride a little. Logansport features an industrial ruin, with the smokestack and water tower still standing. This is all that remains of the original Schenley distillery, which was active in the 1930s and was replaced by the one at Schenley.

The trail crosses Crooked Ck at mile 39 and emerges at a PA Fish Commission boat launch and parking area in Rosston, south of Ford City. The trail continues to Ford City on the railbed parallel to the road. The first completed trail section begins 1100 ft south of the mouth of Tub Mill Run, a quarter-mile south of the PA128 bridge. It's packed crushed limestone to the mouth of Tub Mill Run, then 1.4 miles of asphalt through Ford City.

The asphalt trail enters Ford City at the PA128 bridge and passes through commercial, industrial, and residential areas to 14th St. This section is very popular with many local trail users. At 14th St you may move over to parallel 3rd Av and zig and zag on local roads for 0.4 miles to Water St in Manorville. In early 1999, expect an additional 1500' of trail from 17th St to Water St.

Armstrong Trail	
Location	Along east bank of Allegheny River in Gilpin, Bethel, Manor, Rayburn, Boggs, Pine, Madison Townships in Armstrong County; Brady, Madison, Toby Townships in Clarion County
Trailheads	Schenley, Rosston, Lawsonham, East Brady
Length, Surface	52.5 miles; 1.4 mile paved, 0.3 and 1.0 miles packed crushed stone; 49.8 miles coarse gravel to original ballast
Character	Access road for river and summer homes
Usage restrictions	Horses ok while trail is still primitive; no motorized vehicles; no snowmobiles
Amenities	Food, camping
Driving time from Pittsburgh	1 hour north-north-east

At Water St the trail council recommends that you turn right on Water St, then go a quarter-mile north on Main St to old PA66, which has wide shoulders and "Share the Road" signs. Turn left (north) on old PA66 and go 0.6 mile to a large electrical substation. Turn left here (it's the end of Water St) and in about 50 feet bear right up the ramp to connect with the next finished section. Be careful of tight corners on the ramp. If you miss the ramp you'll wind up headed back into Manorville on Water St. It is also possible to ride through Manorville on Water St instead of using the recommended Main St route. Whichever route you choose, be aware that bikes on roads are regarded as vehicles under the PA Vehicle Code.

Whichever connecting road you choose, the trail resumes near the north end of Water St, now finished in packed crushed limestone. The trail is surprisingly isolated along the river for most of a mile, until it enters the Edgewood Park-and-Ride lot beside PA66. It runs beside the lot, and the finished surface ends behind King's Bowling Lanes near the end of S. Jefferson St. From here the undeveloped trail parallels Grant St through Kittanning, then moves to the riverbank along SR1033. It continues parallel to the road past Gosford (mile 47.2), where you'll see the mouth of Cowanshannock Ck, the Canfield-Holmes Preserve, and a PA Fish Commission boat ramp. The trail continues to parallel SR1033 to Mosgrove(mile 49.8), at the mouth of Pine Ck, where the main road (SR1032) swings away and the trail parallels a minor road to Lock and Dam 8 (mile 51.5).

About two miles farther along, the trail reaches the edge of the Harbison-Walker Brick Plant, which made firebrick for the steel industry but closed about 1987. The fence that encloses the brick plant blocks the trail. The route follows the road around the other side of the brick plant to the ball field and picnic shelter north of the brick plant in Templeton (mile 54). Follow Allegheny Av parallel to the river through Templeton and rejoin the trail at the PA Fish Commission boat ramp.

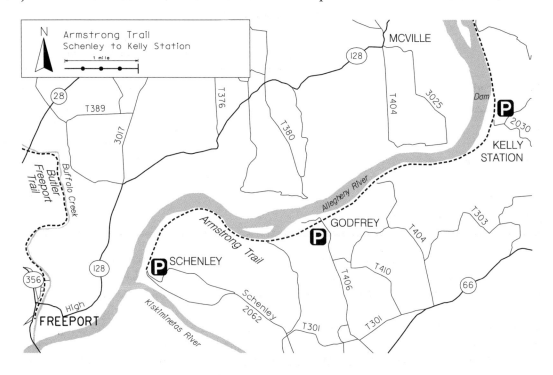

From Templeton the trail continues, still with a rough surface including loose cinders and occasional mudholes, crossing the Mahoning Ck (mile 55) and Red Bank Ck (mile 63.1). At Hooks (mile 37.2), between Mahoning and Red Bank Cks, a barrier was blocking the trail in 1999. There's no good way around, so for now plan this as an out-and-back trip; please don't antagonize nearby landowners.

On the north side of Red Bank Ck a spur goes east 4 miles to a point west of Lawson-ham. A mile past Red Bank Ck the main trail bears right to Philipston Tunnel and a spur bears left 2 miles to East Brady. The main trail will someday go through the tunnel and on to Upper Hillville. However, the tunnel is not yet suitable for use and the trail there is not completely clear. On the spur to East Brady, the trail passes under a fine relic of the days of steam, a concrete structure that was once a coaling tower for steam locomotives.

The approximate distances from the trailhead at Schenley are:

Rosston	9
Kittanning	15
Templeton	24
mouth of Red Bank Ck	33
Philipston tunnel	35
Upper Hillville	41

The additional lengths of spur trails are:

Philipston tunnel-East Brady spur	2
Red Bank Ck spur	4

Local history, attractions

The railroad was most recently part of the Consolidated Rail Corporation (Conrail) system. Prior to that the tracks belonged to the Penn Central Railroad, which had absorbed the Allegheny Valley RR in 1910. But the first attempt to develop a railroad here was the 1838 Pittsburgh, Kittanning, and Warren RR. This project failed, and so the first actual railroad was the Allegheny Valley RR, which opened the line from the Kiskiminetas River at Schenley to Crooked Ck south of Ford City in 1856. The discovery of oil in Titusville in 1863 stimulated interest in extending the route, and new construction reached East Brady in 1867 and Oil City by 1870. Part of the route beyond Hillville is now the Allegheny River Trail.

River navigation was initiated here by the construction of the Kittanning Feeder of the Pennsylvania Main Line Canal in the early 19th century. This 14-mile extension connected Kittanning with the main stem of the canal at Freeport.

Both Ford City and Kittanning have established historic sites.

Extensions of the ride

For hikers only, the Armstrong Trail connects with the Baker Trail at Schenley.

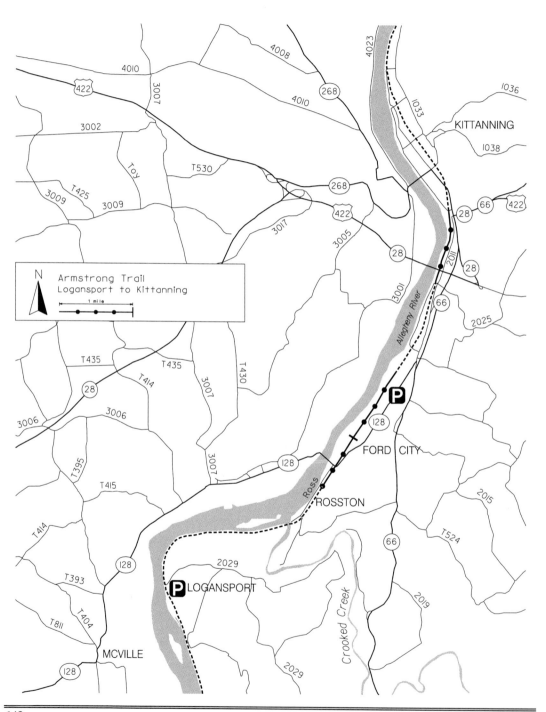

Armstrong Trail
Logansport to Kittanning

N

1 mile

Development plans

The Allegheny Valley Land Trust acquired the 52.5-mile corridor from Conrail. The trail was dedicated in June 1992. Rails and ties have been removed. Planned improvements include brush cutting, signage, trash removal, drainage repairs, barriers to motorized vehicles (though ATVs do get past), rail and tie removal, bridge and tunnel safety upgrades, and eventual installation of a packed crushed limestone surface.

The Allegheny Valley Land Trust has been selling the railbed ballast to PennDoT. In some sections (e.g., south of Rosston), the ballast has been harvested but no other development has been done. In these sections, the trail surface is noticeably improved, though still most suitable for mountain bikes.

Although much of the trail is still unfinished and often rough, a great deal of the trail is suitable for mountain bikes. Development continues steadily; 3-4 miles north from Kittanning should open in 1999 or 2000.

Access points

In the interest of good relations with trail neighbors, the trail association requests that you park only in designated parking lots. These include the Fish Commission parking lots in Rosston and Templeton, the Canfield-Holmes Sanctuary north of Kittanning, and the trail lots at East Brady and Lawsonham.

Vicinity: Directions begin at the intersection of PA66, PA28/US422, and two local streets just south of Kittanning. To reach this point from Pittsburgh, go northeast on PA28; after PA28/US422 crosses the Allegheny River, it swings north and meets PA66 at a traffic light as PA28/US422 changes from freeway to uncontrolled road.

Except for Ford City/Rosston, the Canfield-Holmes Sanctuary, and East Brady, these trailheads are fairly inaccessible. Take a good map as well as these directions.

Schenley trailhead (southern): From the PA28/US422/PA66 intersection, go south on PA66 for about 13 miles to SR2062 (Schenley Rd). Turn west (right) on SR2062 and continue about 4 miles to Schenley. Before crossing the tracks to the Post Office, turn right and continue upstream on the land side of the tracks to the aqua Eljer warehouse. Follow the road across the tracks here and continue a little farther to parking near the gate. To get to Schenley, you have to *really want* to get to Schenley.

Kelly trailhead: From the PA28/US422/PA66 intersection, go south on PA66 for about 8 miles to SR2030. Turn west (right) on SR2030 and continue about 2.5 miles to the trail, taking care to take the left toward Lock and Dam 6 at the "Y" intersection. Turn right parallel to the trail and park out of the way.

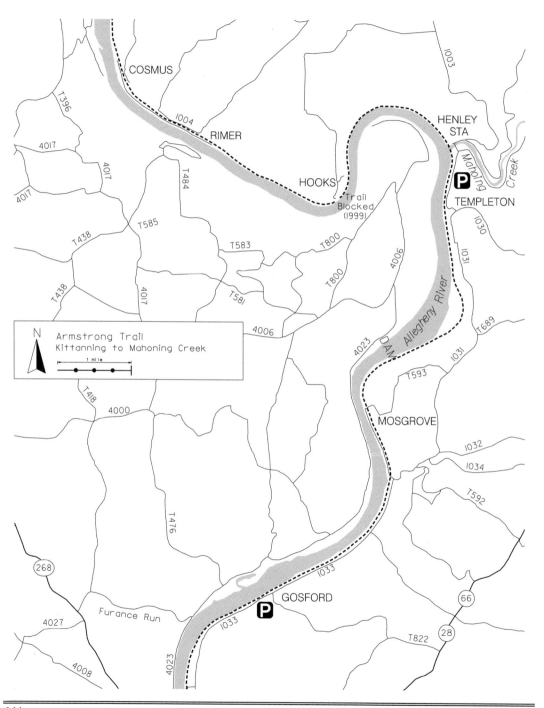

COSMUS

HENLEY STA

1003

T396

1004

RIMER

HOOKS

Mahoning Creek

4017

T484

4017

Trail Blocked (1999)

🅿
TEMPLETON

4017

T585

T583

T800

4006

1030

1031

Allegheny River

T438

T581

T800

N
Armstrong Trail
Kittanning to Mahoning Creek
1 mile

4017

4006

4023

DAM

T689

T593

1031

T418

4000

MOSGROVE

1032

1034

T592

T476

268

66

Furance Run

1033

🅿
GOSFORD

4027

1033

4023

T822

28

4008

Ford City/Rosston trailhead: From the PA28/US422/PA66 intersection, go south (left) on SR2011 (it will be called Hill St in McGrann and 4th Av in Ford City) for about 3 miles, where you will merge with PA128. Follow PA128 until it turns right to cross the Allegheny River. Instead of crossing the Allegheny, go straight on Ross Av between the tracks and the river. Continue 1 mile to the PA Fish Commission boat launching area just after Rosston and just before the trail crosses Crooked Ck.

Kittanning trailhead: From the PA28/US422/PA66 intersection, turn left into the Edgewood Park and Ride lot just the other side of old PA66.

Canfield-Holmes Sanctuary trailhead: From the PA28/US422/PA66 intersection, go north on South Water St through Kittanning (the road becomes SR1033) for about 4 miles. The sanctuary is on your right. There are good picnicking and a Fish Commission boat ramp here.

Lawsonham trailhead: From the PA28/US422/PA66 intersection, follow the instructions below to pass through East Brady on PA68. Continue east on PA68. At New Athens, turn right (south) on TR880 (Henry Rd) toward Lawsonham. Turn left on TR456 (Pinoak Rd) and follow it to the end. The parking lot is to the left at the bottom of a long hill sloping to the right. The trail goes down Redbank Ck to the west of the parking lot.

East Brady trailhead: From the PA28/US422/PA66 intersection, go north on South Water St into Kittanning. Cross the Allegheny River on the bridge at Market St. At the end of the bridge, turn left on Pine Hill Rd and follow Pine Hill Rd until it joins PA268. Follow PA268 north for about 16 miles to Kepples Corners and turn east (right) on PA68. Follow PA68 about 8 miles, back across the Allegheny River, to East Brady PA68 is called Third St in East Brady. In East Brady, turn right on Grant St, go 3 blocks, and turn left on Sixth St. Continue on Sixth St to the brown tarpaper brick covered garage. Just past this garage, turn right and follow the alley through the park, but not as far as the tennis court. The parking lot is at the bottom of the hill along the old railroad bed. To reach the trail from the parking lot, walk up the parking lot exit road, turn right on the dirt road down hill. After passing a number of campsites and going over a small bridge over a gully, this road eventually joins the old railroad bed.

Amenities

Rest rooms, water: None

Bike shop, rental: Paul's Auto Parts in Ford City

Restaurant, groceries: Restaurants in Kittanning, Ford City, and East Brady. Groceries or snacks also at Kelly, Rosston (Coleman Marina), and Widnoon General Store.

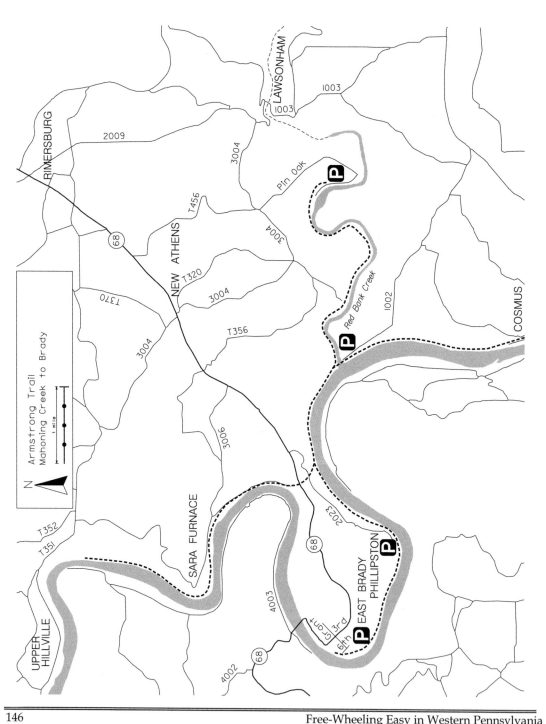

Armstrong Trail
Mahoning Creek to Brady

N

1 mile

RIMERSBURG

2009

LAWSONHAM

1003

1003

3004

Pin Oak

T456

3004

P

NEW ATHENS

T320

3004

3004

T370

Red Bank Creek

1002

T356

COSMUS

P

3004

3006

P

2023

SARA FURNACE

68

T352

T351

2023

EAST BRADY

PHILLIPSTON

P

4003

Grant

3rd

4th

UPPER HILLVILLE

4002

68

68

P

Camping, simple lodging: Campground across Allegheny River from East Brady. Primitive camping along the trail by permit only; contact the Allegheny Valley Land Trust.

Swimming, fishing: Trail runs along the Allegheny River. Swimming is unsupervised; be especially careful when the water is high. Do not trespass to get to the river.

Winter sports: Cross-country skiing. No snowmobiles.

Wheelchair access: Use finished sections only; other sections are too rough. Wheelchair-accessible fishing area at Kelly Station.

Trail organization

Allegheny Valley Land Trust
Kittanning Visitors Center
Market and Water Sts
PO Box 777
Kittanning PA 16201
(724) 543-4478
web: trfn.clpgh.org/avlt/

Membership: $10/year individual or family

Maps, guides, other references

USGS Topographic Maps: Freeport, Leechburg, Kittanning, Mosgrove, Templeton, East Brady, Rimersburg.

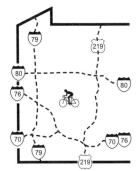

Great Shamokin Path

Along Cowanshannock Ck from Rose Valley to NuMine in Armstrong County

Both the Great Shamokin Path and PA85 run alongside Cowanshannock Ck, with the rail-trail on the south side and the road on the north. The trail connects two lakes, Devils Washbasin in the west and White Lake/Wetland to the east. The creek is well wooded, so aside from some road noise, the trail feels isolated. The surface is packed fine gravel, often double-track with grass. It is generally about 20 feet wide and well-tended, though in some places grass grows knee-high on the edges, leaving an open path wide enough for two bikes to ride abreast. The trail is properly gated and posted against motorized vehicles, with occasional signs marking it as the Great Shamokin Path.

The trail follows the route of its namesake, a traditional Indian path that connected the Susquehanna River basin with Kittanning. In this area the Great Shamokin Path followed Cowanshannock Ck. It's a pleasant, though short, ride through woods and small farms with frequent glimpses of the creek. Small wildlife is abundant: On one trip we saw chipmunks, rabbits, a groundhog, ducks, kingfishers, and a wild turkey; many other birds made a constant chirping chatter.

The west access for the trail is from a pulloff at the west end of Yatesboro, which is the east edge of Rose Valley. From the parking pulloff, go over a mound of dirt, down a formerly-paved road, across a closed bridge (the gate is too narrow for many handlebars, but you can walk your bike through), and on another 20 yards to the trail intersection. The trail actually starts about 0.3 miles west (right) of here at a missing bridge, where you can look down at Cowanshannock Ck and across at the continuation of the railbed. This is, at least for now, the end of the line.

If you don't want to visit the dead end, turn east (left) where the access path crosses the trail. From here the trail runs about two and a half miles east to NuMine. You will soon pass through the edge of a small development that appears to have been built as a company town; the originally-identical houses have acquired individual identities over the years. You soon return to the woods and see several very small ponds beside the trail. You emerge again at a cooperative fish hatchery, recognizable not only by the sign but also by the aeration cascade that prepares water for the trout. From here follow the driveway to the road intersection, where the trail resumes. The east end of the trail is at the parking lot near a ballfield, the NuMine access. From here, you can continue another 0.7 miles to White Lake.

Extensions of the ride

The ride can be extended in two ways: westward from the Yatesboro parking area and northward into the four small towns that lie just north of PA85. Both extensions are open to motor vehicles, but you shouldn't find very much traffic, and it won't be fast.

Great Shamokin Path	
Location	Near Yatesboro, Cowanshannock Township, Armstrong County
Trailheads	Yatesboro, Rural Valley, Meredith, NuMine
Length, Surface	4 miles; small gravel and dirt
Character	Little-used, rural, shady, flat
Usage restrictions	Horses ok; no motorized vehicles
Amenities	In Rural Valley
Driving time from Pittsburgh	1 hour east-northeast

Westward: When you reach the missing bridge that now terminates the trail, retrace your steps 0.3 miles to the intersection with the path to Yatesboro. Turn north on the path, crossing Cowanshannock creek and emerging on PA85. Without crossing PA85, walk west (against traffic) about 30 feet on the shoulder and turn left (south) on the abandoned railroad right-of-way. The surface is much like the rail-trail, but it now runs through open farms rather than woods. This section is open to traffic, but it appears unlikely that you will encounter any (in part because a small bridge has partly fallen in). This segment continues 1.5 miles to a large bridge with rotten ties and no deck. It's not worth going beyond this bridge; the trail deteriorates over the next quarter mile and eventually disappears into backyards and weeds.

Northward: From the Yatesboro parking area, you can follow the former railroad road-bed (the one described in the previous paragraph) north across PA85 and up the valley. After it bends to the north it gets pretty well grown up, and we quit after about 0.7 mile and came back down the paved road. You can also follow footpaths just north of PA85 into Yatesboro. This will put you on Main St. At the post office, jog over a block (you'll recognize the former railroad station) and follow the back street, which carries very little traffic, until it ends in a group of gravel driveways in Rural Valley. At that point, backtrack a couple of blocks to the main cross street (Water St), turn south, cross PA85 and Cowanshannock Ck, and return via the rail-trail.

Access points

Vicinity: Directions begin as you approach Yatesboro headed east on PA85. To reach this point from Pittsburgh, go north on PA28 through Kittanning. Follow PA28/66 north about 1.5 miles to PA85. Turn right (east) on PA85. You reach the Yatesboro trailhead in about 8.7 miles, NuMine in about 11.9.

Yatesboro trailhead (western): On PA85 the Valley Village Store marks the west edge of Yatesboro. Just east of the store, the road surface shows where the railroad was removed. Just past that point and just before the turnoff to Yatesboro, there is an unmarked parking area for about 4 cars on the right. A rideable path leads south from the parking area, across Cowanshannock Ck to the trail crossing. Beware of loose gravel as you descend from PA85 to the bridge.

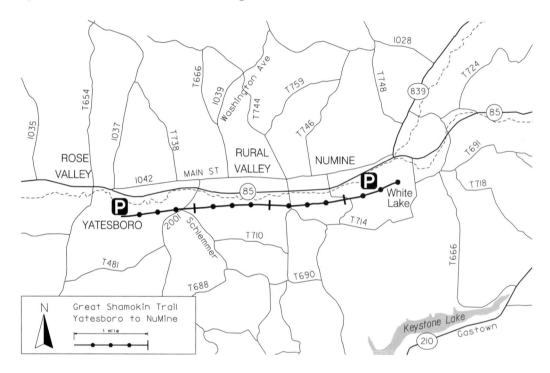

NuMine trailhead (eastern): On PA85, go about 3 miles east from Yatesboro. Turn south (right) at the intersection where you would turn north (left) to go to NuMine. Immediately cross Cowanshannock Ck, then turn right between the ballfield and the creek. You will soon see the gated trailhead. This is the easier end to identify. You can drive in a little farther to the White Lake picnic area.

Other access: Two other roads crossing PA85 are marked to turn north to Rural Valley and Meredith. If you turn south at either of these intersections you will quickly cross first Cowanshannock Ck and then the trail.

Amenities

Rest rooms, water: Rest rooms at ballfield in Rural Valley. No water, except at stores and restaurants.

Bike shop, rentals: None, but there's a hardware store in Rural Valley.

Restaurant, groceries: Rural Valley has a drug store, grocery, pizza shop, and several bars, all on Main St. We had a good dinner at Charley's Place. Valley Village Store on PA85 west of Yatesboro.

Camping, simple lodging: None

Swimming, fishing: Unsupervised swimming in the creek, if it's high enough

Winter sports: Cross-country skiing

Wheelchair access: Narrow gate at Yatesboro end; surface a little rough

Trail organization

Cowanshannock Creek Watershed Association
PO Box 307
Rural Valley PA 16249-0307
(724) 783-6692
Membership: $3.00/year individual

Maps, guides, other references

USGS Topographic Maps: Rural Valley.

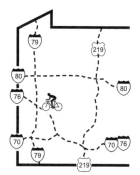

Butler-Freeport Community Trail

Along Little Buffalo Ck from Freeport in Armstrong County to Butler in Butler County

In using this trail, you should be aware that some nearby land-owners question the trail operator's title to the trail and right to use the land. As of January 1999, this disagreement is being litigated. In addition, some sections of the trail may be obstructed or posted. We recommend against trespassing or antagonizing trail neighbors anywhere, but especially so here. Since the status of this matter changes from time to time, you may wish to check with the trail operator about the current status.

The Butler-Freeport Trail is planned to follow 20 miles of the former Butler Branch Rail Line of Conrail. The planned route runs from Freeport Borough, along Buffalo and Little Buffalo Creeks to Great Belt, then down Coal Run to Butler. It passes through wooded areas, open farmland, small villages, and deep valleys. Buffalo Ck is on the registry of Scenic Waterways. It's well sheltered in a shaded valley. The trail is nearly flat, but as rail-trails go the gradient is somewhat more noticeable than usual. At present, the middle 11.5 miles plus a separate one mile have been surfaced. The 8-foot wide trail is finished in crushed limestone. Benches are liberally sprinkled along the trail, especially between Sandy Lick and Cabot. A few original railroad mileposts remain; they appear to count mileage from Laneville.

The trail begins at the new sewage treatment plant a mile south of Monroe. Indeed it was constructed as part of the sewer plant project. At this point it runs beside the main Buffalo Ck for half a mile to Winfield Jct at the mouth of Little Buffalo Ck. Halfway between the sewer plant and Winfield Jct, the undersides of overhanging rocks show fossils and drill holes left over from railroad construction. At Winfield Jct, the trail follows the left fork up the much smaller Little Buffalo Ck. After half a mile it crosses Monroe Rd, the first road access.

Just north of Monroe Rd an undecked trestle breaks the continuity of the trail; the trestle is scheduled for decking in 1999. The trail resumes on the north side of the trestle. From here to Sandy Lick (Bear Creek Rd) it runs on a narrow bench between the cliff and Little Buffalo Ck. 1.2 miles north of Sandy Lick the trail passes a lovely home set on a small lake. The creek is almost always within view or at least within hearing—the trail crosses it four times between Sarver and Cabot, and as a bonus it also crosses a small unnamed creek. 1.9 miles north of Sarver there are traces of an old industrial site on the west side of the trail. This is the first, and the most conspicuous, of several such ruins. They are part of the processing plants for the Franklin Glass and Ford Glass quarries. Foundations and walls appear on both sides of the trail for the next half-mile or so, and the remnants of two stone or concrete dams are visible in the creek on the northeast side. As the trail approaches Cabot, a series of beaver dams pool up the creek; cattails mark another wetland 0.8 mile north of Cabot.

North of Cabot there are more signs of development, with small towns, parallel roads, businesses, and farms. About two miles north of Cabot, the trail is blocked where it cuts diagonally across a field. Detour on Keasey and Jones Rds. The power substation 0.8 mile south of Great Belt was once the site of the world's then-largest oil storage facility. The railroad cut near the substation marks the end of the long climb. From here to Herman the trail traverses cuts and fills on top of the ridge. For now, the trail effectively stops at Herman, where the bridge is unfinished and blocked (scheduled for reconstruction in 1999). The intersection is dominated by St. Fidelius School, founded 1877. An additional 3/4 mile of trail extends beyond the gap, but it is not accessible from here. The other end of this segment emerges near the Summit Township municipal building, 0.25 miles west on Herman Rd, then 0.5 miles west on Bonnie Brook Rd.

Butler-Freeport Community Trail	
Location	Buffalo, Winfield, Jefferson, and Summit Townships, Butler County; South Buffalo Township, Armstrong County
Trailheads	Sarver, Cabot, Herman, eventually Laneville, Butler
Length, Surface	12.75 miles developed, 21 miles planned; 11.75 miles packed crushed stone, 1 mile tar and chips
Character	Uncrowded, wooded, shady, flat
Usage restrictions	Horses ok alongside improved trail; no motorized vehicles
Amenities	None
Driving time from Pittsburgh	45 minutes north-east

Local history, attractions

The trail follows the right-of-way of the former Butler Branch line of the Western Pennsylvania Railroad (more recently Conrail). This was the first railroad built in Butler County. It was completed in 1871 to provide freight and passenger service to Butler. The villages along the trail were built to serve the railroad, which ran as many as six passenger trains a day.

Valley Mill is just down the street from the Laneville trailhead. A similar flour mill is open to the public in McConnells Mill State Park. Cooper Cabin, a restored log cabin, is open Sundays in the summer. It is 0.3 miles west of Cabot; follow the signs. Historic Saxonburg is an old German settler village with shops, restaurants, and a museum. It is 2 miles west of Cabot.

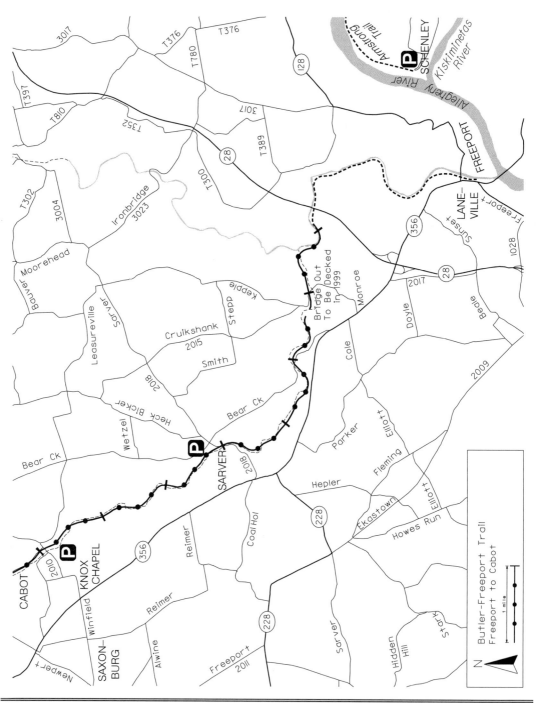

Free-Wheeling Easy in Western Pennsylvania

Development plans

Several passenger stations once adjoined the trail. The trail council hopes to rebuild the one in Cabot.

Plans for 1999 call for a wood deck and railings to be put on the trestle at Monroe and reconstruction of the bridge at Herman.

The trail will eventually begin at Laneville, the section of Freeport west of Buffalo Ck. The 3.8-mile segment from Laneville to the current start a mile south of Monroe is not officially open yet. At present its surface is raw ballast, and it includes an unfinished bridge. The area once supported numerous clay mines and the area is littered with specialty bricks. A large area of industrial ruins, which we call Kiva Town Center, is in the flats on the west side of the trail about 2 miles north of Laneville, just north of the handsome dressed-brick culvert. This is the remnant of the Harbison Brick Co brickworks; it's private property. The round kiva-like structures were kilns; five of these domed brick kilns baked bricks at a temperature of 2000°.

North of Herman, the trail is eventually planned to continue for 4 miles from the municipal building at Bonnie Brook Rd down Coal Run to near Connoquenessing Ck in Butler. This will be only about 6-8 miles from Moraine State Park. Butler County is considering a network of bike trails that may close this gap.

Access points

Vicinity: Directions begin on PA356 headed north from PA28 (except for Laneville, which begins eastbound on PA356). To reach this point from Pittsburgh, go northeast on PA28 to Exit 17 (the second Freeport exit). This is about 20 miles northeast of the Highland Park Bridge interchange on PA 28.

Monroe trailhead: Follow PA356 approximately 0.8 mile northwest from PA28. Turn right (east) on Monroe Rd and go 9.8 mile to the bottom of the hill, where it crosses Little Buffalo Ck. Just across the bridge, turn right into a small parking area. Do not block access to the service road.

Sarver trailhead: Follow PA356 3.6 miles northwest from PA28. Turn right (northeast) on Sarver Rd (SR2018). Go down the hill and along the creek for 0.8 mile. Just after crossing the creek and passing the volunteer fire department, turn left into the parking area alongside the trail.

Cabot trailhead: Follow PA356 6.5 miles northwest from PA28. Turn right (northeast) on Winfield-Cabot Rd (SR2010) at the traffic light in Knox Chapel. The trail crosses this road about half a mile later, in Cabot.

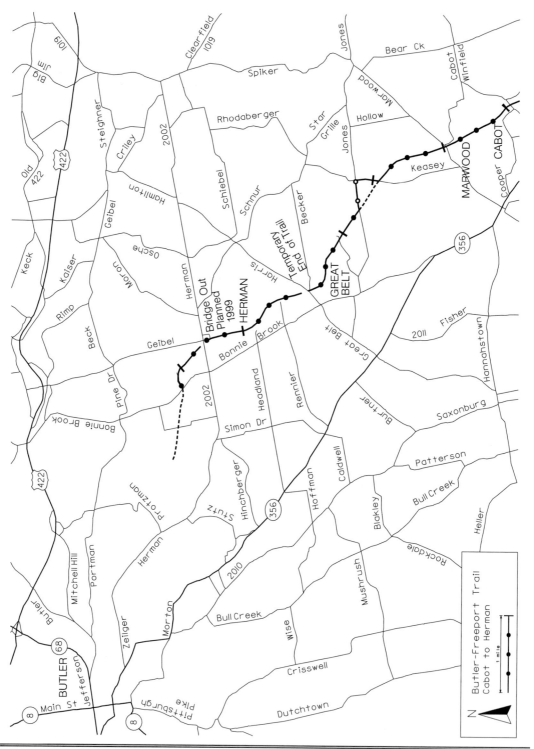

Free-Wheeling Easy in Western Pennsylvania

Amenities

Rest rooms, water: Rest rooms in restaurants for patrons.

Bike shop, rental: None at present.

Restaurant, groceries: On PA356: Risch's Market just south of Sarver Rd, Cooper Station Between Sarver Rd and Cabot, Bonello family Restaurant 0.5 mile north of PA28, and several restaurants in Knox Chapel, on PA356 0.5 mile west of Cabot. The restaurants that used to be in Cabot have closed.

Camping, simple lodging: Smith Grove Campground 1.5 miles east of trail at Herman. Hotel and Bed-and-Breakfast in Saxonburg 3 miles west of trail at Cabot.

Swimming, fishing: You might be able to swim in the creek, if it has enough water. But in the seasons when you'd want to be swimming the creek is probably almost dry. The trail council does not promote swimming. No fishing near trail.

Winter sports: The trail is protected from the sun, so XC skiing is good. No snowmobiles.

Wheelchair access: OK

Trail organizations

Butler-Freeport Comm. Trail Council
PO Box 533
Saxonburg PA 16056-0533
(724) 352-4783
web: www.nauticom.net/users/outdoor/f_trail/f_trail1.html
Membership $10/year individual, $15/year family

Buffalo Township
109 Bear Creek Rd
Sarver PA 16055
(724) 295-2648

Maps, guides, other references

USGS Topographic Maps: Freeport, Curtisville, Saxonburg.

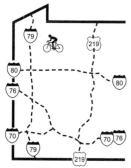

Oil Creek State Park Trail

Petroleum Center to Drake Well Museum near Titusville in Venango County

The birthplace of the oil industry supplies the setting for a ride that combines the natural beauty of Oil Creek Valley's clear trout stream and hemlock-hardwood forest with traces of the oil boom that once dominated the valley. The trail follows the path of the railroad that once carried oil from wells in this and adjacent valleys. But the intervening century has erased most evidence of the industry, and you now rely on interpretive signs along the trail and the Drake Well Museum to pick out the remaining traces.

The trail begins at Petroleum Centre near the SR1004 bridge. It shares a township road with traffic for 0.5 miles, then drops down to Oil Creek and crosses under the Oil Creek and Titusville Railroad. A mile later the trail crosses from the east side of Oil Creek to the west, remaining on the west side for the remainder of the trip. Shortly after the creek crossing, at northbound mile 1.7, is the marker for the historic site of Pioneer. There are also markers for Shaffer Farm (northbound mile 4.4), Miller Farm (northbound mile 5.2), and Boughton (northbound mile 7.5), but few visible traces remain. The most obvious is a rock foundation wall at Boughton. The trail continues northbound to mile 9.7; you can continue on the road to Drake Well Museum. It is well worth continuing, for traffic is light and the museum has a vast open-air collection of oil field equipment, which sometimes is operating.

The trail is asphalt-surfaced, 8.5 feet wide, with a few short hills. It is well populated with interpretive signs, views of Oil Creek, wildlife, picnic tables, benches, and rain shelters. It can be busy to crowded on nice summer weekends, but the seclusion of the valley and the possibility of watching herons or eagles makes it worth while.

You're likely to hear excursion trains of the Oil Creek & Titusville RR across the creek. If you want to ride one way and take the train back, your bike can join you on the train for $1 over the one-way fare (adults $6 one-way, $10 round-trip in 1999).

Development Plans

Plans for the Allegheny Valley Trail system include this trail in its Corry to Franklin leg, but it will take some creativity to get down the Oil Creek valley along PA8.

Local history, attractions

This area is the birthplace of the American oil industry. For centuries, oil occurred naturally on the surface along Oil Creek. In 1859, Colonel Edwin Drake came to the area searching for a quantity source and became the first to successfully drill for oil. On

Sunday August 28, his well just south of Titusville struck oil at a depth of 69 feet. Drake Well Memorial Park is on the site of his well.

The next dozen years saw a boom and bust in the local oil industry, with development and demise of entire towns. Petroleum Centre grew suddenly to a population of 3,000 in 1863; the town of Pithole, a few miles to the east, was built between May and September of 1865 and was already vanishing by January of 1866. Both towns are now historical sites where you can visit some of the remaining traces. There were also oil fields at Tarr Farm, Pioneer and Miller Farm, along the bike trail. The Oil Creek Railroad was created to ship oil out of the valley. Miller Farm was the terminus of railroad; the world's first successful oil pipeline connected it to Pithole, 5.5 miles to the east.

Oil Creek State Park Trail	
Location	South of Titusville, Cornplanter and Cherrytree Townships, Venango County
Trailheads	Petroleum Centre, Drake Well Museum
Length, surface	9.7 miles, paved
Character	Busy, wooded, shady, very gently rolling
Usage restrictions	No motorized vehicles, no snowmobiles, no horses
Amenities	Rest rooms, water, bike rental, food, fishing
Driving time from Pittsburgh	2 hours 30 minutes north

Oil Creek State Park provides interpretive information, including signs at many points along the trails. Additional attractions (mostly with admission fee) include the Drake Well Museum 0.4 miles from the northern end of the trail, the antique car museum 1.5 miles from the Petroleum Centre trailhead, the Pithole historical site to the east, and the Oil City & Titusville excursion train, which runs on the opposite side of Oil Creek from the trail. You may also enjoy the nitroglycerin tour at Drake Well Museum and the antique musical instrument museum in Franklin.

The valley is still an oil center: The oldest producing oil well in the country is the McClintock No. 1, located near Quaker State and owned by Drake Well Museum and located just north of Oil City. It has been producing continuously since August 1861.

Extensions of the ride

Signs at Petroleum Center indicate an antique car museum 2.5 miles east on the township road: start up the trail from Petroleum Center, and when the bike trail leaves the road, stay on the road for 1 more mile. The ghost town of Pithole (with museum) is also east of the park; the map suggests that it's accessible on back roads 2-3 miles beyond the car museum. If you find a good route, let us know.

Access points

Vicinity: Directions begin northbound on PA8 at the end of the bypass around Oil City. To reach this point from Pittsburgh, go north on I79, east on I80, and north on PA8, taking the PA8 bypass around Oil City.

Watching herons from a bench by the Oil Creek Trail

Petroleum Centre trailhead (southern): From the northern end of the PA8 bypass, continue north 3.5 miles on PA8 to the turnoff marked for Petroleum Centre at Oil Creek State Park. (The correct turnoff is just *north* of the PA8 bridge over Cherrytree Ck; do not confuse this with the turnoff for Rynd Farm and OC&T RR, which is just *south* of this short bridge.) Turn right toward Petroleum Centre on SR1007. Follow signs for 3.1 miles to a "T" where SR1007 turns left and SR1004 goes right. Turn right on SR1004 and cross Oil Creek. Trailhead parking is just ahead on the left. *Alternate route:* If you are coming southbound from Titusville on PA8, it's faster to reach Petroleum Centre by turning left at the well-marked intersection in Cherrytree, 5.4 miles after you cross Oil Creek just south of Titusville.

Drake Well Museum trailhead (northern): From the northern end of the PA8 bypass around Oil City, continue north on PA8 for 14 miles to the stop light at Bloss St, marked for Drake Well Museum. Turn right and continue for just under a mile to trailhead parking on the right (just before Jersey Bridge over Oil Creek).

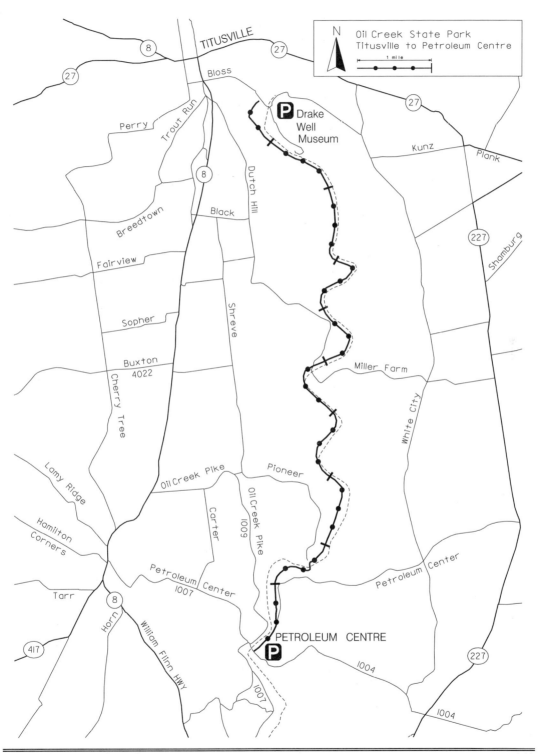

TITUSVILLE

Bloss

Drake Well Museum

Oil Creek State Park
Titusville to Petroleum Centre

1 mile

Perry

Trout Run

Kunz

Plank

Breedtown

Black

Dutch Hill

Fairview

Shamburg

Sopher

Shreve

Buxton
4022

Miller Farm

Cherry Tree

White City

Lamy Ridge

Oil Creek Pike

Pioneer

Hamilton Corners

Carter

Oil Creek Pike
1009

Tarr

Petroleum Center
1007

Petroleum Center

PETROLEUM CENTRE

Horn

William Flinn HWY

1004

1007

1004

Other access: If you're truly determined to gain intermediate access, get the park brochure and follow back roads to the Pioneer or Miller Farm historic sites.

Amenities

Rest rooms, water: Rest rooms and water at park office in Petroleum Centre. Latrine along trail just south of the intersection with Miller Farm Rd (northbound mile 4.9). Rest rooms and water at Drake Well Museum.

Bike shop, rentals: The bike shop at the Egbert Oil Office at Petroleum Center (south trailhead) is on hiatus; the park hopes to have rentals available by Memorial Day 1999. Rental season typically runs until Labor Day.

Restaurant, groceries: Light snacks and soft drinks at rental shop. Soft drink machines at Drake Well Park. Groceries in Rouseville and Titusville.

Camping, simple lodging: Oil Creek Camp Resort: from west side of Oil Creek at Petroleum Centre, up Oil Creek Pike Rd (SR1009) for just over a mile, then follow signs to jog right on Pioneer Rd for 0.1 mile then left for 0.5 miles on Shreve Rd to the campground.

Swimming, fishing: No authorized swimming area in the state park. Oil Creek is one of the largest trout streams in Pennsylvania. It offers prime trout fishing throughout the season and is stocked by the state. Deep pools alternate with productive riffles.

Winter sports: Cross-country skiing on trail and on nearby (hilly) cross-country system. No snowmobiles.

Wheelchair access: Trail surface is asphalt and gates are wide. There are a few short hills with larger-than-standard grades.

Trail organization

DCNR - Oil Creek State Park
RR 1, Box 207
Oil City PA 16301
(814) 676-5915
e-mail: oilcreek.sp@a1.dcnr.state.pa.us
web: www.dcnr.state.pa.us/stateparks/parks/o-crek.htm

Maps, guides, other references

The map in the park's information brochure shows the bike route.

Trail brochure, "Bicycle Trails of Venango County"

USGS Topographic Maps: Titusville South.

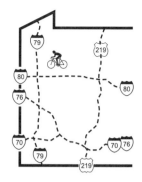

Samuel Justus Recreational Trail

Franklin to Oil City in Venango County

A 9-foot-wide strip of excellent asphalt runs along the former Allegheny Valley Railroad right-of-way, tucked between the south bank of the Allegheny River and a wooded bluff. The trail is almost completely flat and runs about 30 feet above the river, affording good views of whatever is happening on the river. Birds and wildflowers are abundant

The trail passes several oil wells, some still operating, and oil storage tanks. Two picnic areas between the trail and the river offer shade and picnic tables. They are located 0.7 mile upstream from the Franklin gate and 0.5 mile downstream from the Oil City gate.

The most prominent feature of this trail is River Ridge Farm, located two miles upstream from Franklin. This impressive mansion was built in 1913 by Joseph C. Sibley, who developed the first formula for refining crude oil and later served five terms in the US House of Representatives. The estate originally included 21 other buildings, including a stone campanile near the river. This bell tower still stands, but the eleven bells have been removed. The entrance gate, with "River Ridge Farm" carved across the top, still stands near where a railroad siding served the estate's junction. The estate is now owned by Life Ministries, Inc. If you choose to visit the grounds, please remember it is private property.

At the Oil City trailhead, the parking area adjoins the sewer plant. Be prepared to hold your nose until you're out of range.

Development plans

Oil City plans to extend the trail from its current end into Oil City. From the current end at the sewer plant, it will follow the railbed to the marina, then follow the river in a bicycle lane, cross the Allegheny River on a road bridge and Oil Creek on a former railroad trestle, and parallel Oil Creek to a park near the Holiday Inn.

Plans call for eventual extension above Oil City. The proposed route will follow the south side of the Allegheny R northeast from Silverly, cross a bridge just east of the mouth of Oil Ck, and follow the northwest side of the Allegheny R past Trunkeyville, then onward to Warren.

Plans for the Allegheny Valley Trail system also call for connecting to Oil Creek Trail as a segment of the Corry to Franklin leg, but there's no really good corridor down the Oil Creek valley along PA8.

Local history, attractions

The Allegheny Valley Railroad was established to serve the oil industry, reaching Oil City in 1868. In 1910, it was incorporated in the Pennsylvania Railroad system, and it later became part of Conrail. Service ended in 1984.

Franklin's history dates back to the early claims of French and English settlers and its strategic position at the confluence of French Ck and the Allegheny R. It's boom days, however, came in the 1860s with the discovery of oil near Titusville. The large homes, in a collection of 20 or so styles that are collectively called Victorian, that dominate the side streets date to that period. Find a copy of the walking tour guide and cruise the back streets for an interesting architectural tour.

Samuel Justus Recreational Trail	
Location	South side of Allegheny River near Franklin, Cranberry Township, Venango County
Trailheads	Franklin, Oil City
Length, surface	5.8 miles, paved with parallel gravel treadway
Character	Uncrowded, rural, mostly sunny, flat
Usage restrictions	Horses ok; no motorized vehicles
Amenities	Rest rooms, bike rental, food, fishing
Driving time from Pittsburgh	1 hour 45 minutes north

The Debence Antique Music museum has moved to Franklin, at 1261 Liberty St. It features automatic instruments such as player pianos, player organs, and music boxes.

The "salt box" house in the parking lot at the Franklin trailhead was moved there when it was rescued from a construction project at its former location on Liberty St in Franklin. This house dates to 1844 and is the only true salt box in the area. This architectural style is characteristic of certain parts of New England and is defined by the roofline, which extends farther down in back than in front. When restored, the house will serve as a visitor and information center for the trail. The Franklin trailhead also offers a "fitness cluster".

Extensions of the ride

The Samuel Justus Trail is part of the emerging Allegheny Valley Trail system. At present, you can continue south on the Allegheny River Trail 10 miles on asphalt to near Brandon (see description).

At the Oil City end, you can pick your way northward on rough fragments of the future trail and streets that parallel 1st St (which is too busy to recommend).

A loop on the south side of the river is unlikely, as the roads up from the trailheads are narrow and somewhat busy.

Access points

Vicinity: Directions begin headed north on US62/PA8 in Franklin. To reach this point from Pittsburgh, go north on I79, east on I80, and north on PA8 to Franklin.

Franklin trailhead (South): In Franklin, when US62/PA8 turns left, stay on US322. Continue 0.3 miles to the next stop light, following US322 left onto 8th St and another 0.3 miles across the Allegheny River. As you leave the bridge, trailhead parking is on your right. Access to the parking lot is a right turn about 0.1 mile past the end of the bridge; it's well marked by a sign for "Samuel Justus Recreational Trail". For bike rental, walk back under the US322 bridge. This is also the (only) trailhead for the Allegheny River Trail.

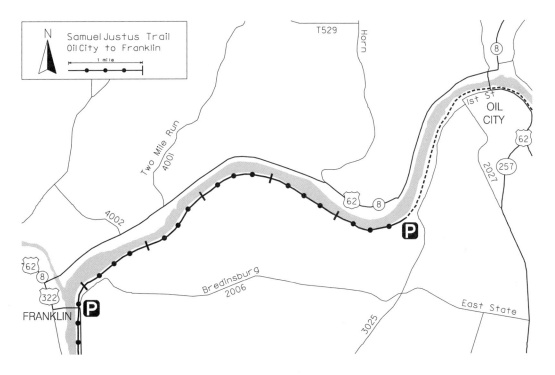

Oil City trailhead (North): In Franklin, continue on US62/PA8 about 8 miles to the outskirts of Oil City. Follow US62 North when it turns right to cross Allegheny River. After crossing the river, turn right at the second light on West 1st St (SR3025). Go 1.6 miles to the trail turnoff, which is marked "Samuel Justus Recreational Trail" and "Waste Water Treatment Plant" (this is just past the Penelec plant and across from the entrance to

Venango Campus of Clarion College). Turn right and follow the road along the sewage plant to park near the trailhead.

Amenities

Rest rooms, water: No water; chemical toilets at Franklin trailhead. Rest rooms in Oil City at the PA Fish Commission access: enter Oil City by turning left on Wyllis St, go 2 short blocks downhill to PA Fish Comm access on Front St (this is the better part of 2 miles from the trail).

Bike shop, rentals: Country Pedalers bike shop with rentals at Franklin trailhead, (814) 432-8055; Ken and Lynn Cochran are active in the Allegheny Valley Trails Association and will provide information on trails or volunteer opportunities.

Restaurant, groceries: Minimal snacks at the bike shop. Restaurants and groceries in Oil City and Franklin.

Camping, simple lodging: Motels and B&Bs in Oil City and Franklin.

Swimming, fishing: In Allegheny River. Be careful of current if it's high. Good fishing for bass and walleye.

Winter sports: Cross-country skiing.

Wheelchair access: At the Franklin trailhead, park on the north side of the US322 bridge, near the bike shop, to avoid a sharp dip under the bridge. Aside from gravel in the parking lot, there are no problems

Trail organization

> Cranberry Township
> PO Box 378
> Seneca PA 16346-0378
> (814) 676-8812

Maps, guides, other references

Trail brochure, "Bicycle Trails of Venango County"

Walking tours of Historic Franklin, America's Victorian City, Franklin Rotary Club, 1990.

USGS Topographic Maps: Franklin, Oil City.

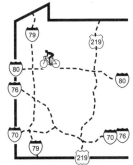

Allegheny River Trail

Franklin to Kennerdell in Venango County

The Allegheny River Trail follows the Allegheny River south from Franklin toward Belmar, Brandon, and (eventually) Kennerdell. The 10 miles from Franklin to Brandon have an 8'-wide asphalt surface and mileposts every half-mile. This trail takes you to some of the region's most outstanding rivers. The Allegheny River in this area was added to the National Wild and Scenic Rivers system in 1992. East Sandy Ck, which you cross at Belmar, is on the Pennsylvania Scenic Rivers inventory.

As you leave the parking lot at Franklin, the trail gradually bears away from US322, finally breaking away at mile 0.6 near the ruins of a former industrial plant. This building, the Whann Litha Springs building, came down in 1995. From here on you have frequent views of the river, though you share the trail with overhead power lines. The flat overgrown area at mile 1.8 is scheduled to become a campsite with Adirondack shelters, fire rings, slabs for tents, picnic tables, and canoe access. At mile 2.2 an overlook provides views up and down the Allegheny River with good birdwatching opportunities. You may see ducks, crows, or even a heron. You may also see groups of canoeists. Here and beyond you can see summer homes on the far shore of the Allegheny River. Near milepost 2.5 oil pumps and a storage tank lurk in the shrubbery beside the trail. At mile 3.8, a rest area with picnic table and fire ring lies below the trail by the river amid remnants of some sort of pipeline operation.

Allegheny River Trail

Location	Franklin to Kennerdell, Cranberry and Rockland Townships, Venango County
Trailheads	Franklin
Length, Surface	10 miles, paved
Character	Uncrowded, rural, mostly sunny, flat
Usage restrictions	Horses ok; no motorized vehicles; no snowmobiles
Amenities	Rest rooms, bike rental, food, fishing
Driving time from Pittsburgh	1 hour 45 minutes north

The finished trail surface ends at the bridge over East Sandy Ck, 5.1 miles south of Franklin. Just beyond, the trail passes under the Belmar Bridge. Built in 1907, this trestle carried the Clarion Secondary line over the Allegheny River. This line is also being developed as a rail-trail. At present, a stairway connects the Allegheny River Trail with the end of the trestle high above. There's a bench up there, but safety upgrades to the trestle itself have not been made. To reach the stairs, turn left on the rough trail just beyond the trestle and follow it up and back under the trestle. Climb up, have a snack, enjoy the view, but don't fall off.

Beyond Belmar, the trail continues toward Brandon. Views of the Allegheny River and summer homes on the far side continue. About 7.6 miles from Franklin, the power lines turn up the hill. About 8.5 miles from Franklin, you find Indian God Rock, a large rock at river's edge. It holds 50 Indian rock carvings dating to AD 1200-1750 and is listed on the National Register of Historic Places. Unfortunately, the Indian carvings are obscured by more modern "contributions". The Venango County Historical Society has constructed a viewing platform here.

Trails are friendly to many kinds of bikes

When you emerge from the trail at the Brandon gate, the roadbed continues for another mile and a half as the access road to vacation homes at Brandon. The river access here is posted.

Local history, attractions

At least half a dozen Indian paths converged at Venango (now Franklin), but none of them appears to have followed the Allegheny River. The river corridor was originally shaped by French and British fortifications. More recently it provided transportation for the oil and timber industries. The area is included in both the Wild and Scenic Rivers program and the Oil Heritage Park program.

John Wilkes Booth was part owner of an oil well near the trail a mile south of Franklin.

Kennerdell tunnel, just past the southern end of the planned trail, runs 0.75 miles through the hill, its curve assuring complete darkness.

Extensions of the ride

At Franklin, you can continue north to the edge of Oil City on the Samuel Justus Trail.

Development plans

The Belmar Bridge across the Allegheny River is scheduled for development in 1999 as the signature element of the Clarion Secondary Trail. The bridge will be repaired and re-surfaced, and a ramp will connect it with the Allegheny River Trail; for now, pedestrians can go up a stairway.

Plans for 1999 also call for building trail from the east end of the Belmar Bridge eastward toward Van.

Belmar Bridge will carry the Clarion Secondary Trail across the Allegheny River

Access points

Vicinity: Directions begin headed north on US62/PA8 in Franklin. To reach this point from Pittsburgh, go north on I79, east on I80, and north on PA8 to Franklin.

Franklin trailhead (northern): In Franklin, when US62/PA8 turns left, remain on US322. Continue 0.3 miles to the second stop light, turning left to follow US322 onto 8th St. Take US322 another 0.3 miles across the Allegheny River. As you leave the bridge, trailhead parking is on your right. Access to the parking lot is a right turn about 0.1 mile past the end of the bridge, marked by a sign for "Samuel Justus Recreational Trail". For bike rental, walk back under the US322 bridge. This also serves as a trailhead for the Samuel Justus Trail.

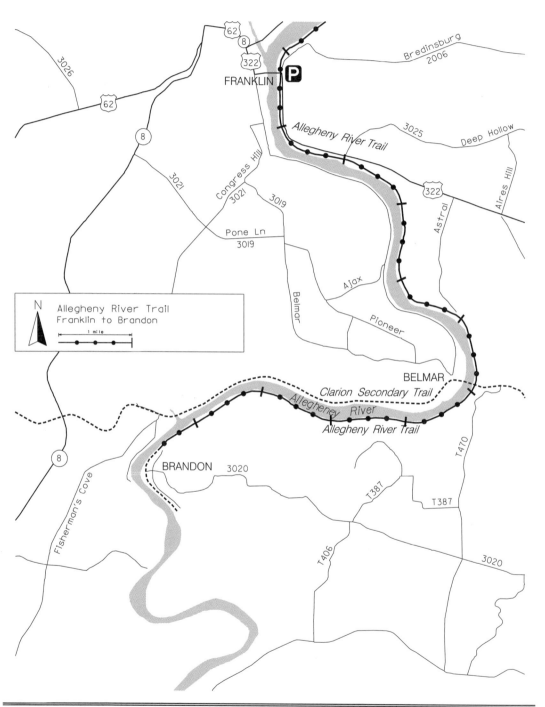

N
Allegheny River Trail
Franklin to Brandon
1 mile

3026
62
8
322
FRANKLIN
62
8
3021
Congress Hill
3027
3019
Pone Ln
3019
Belmar
Ajax
Pioneer
P
Bredinsburg
2006
Allegheny River Trail
3025
Deep Hollow
322
Astral
Aires Hill
BELMAR
Clarion Secondary Trail
Allegheny River
Allegheny River Trail
8
BRANDON
3020
Fisherman's Cove
T470
T387
T387
T406
3020

Amenities

Rest rooms, water: No water; chemical toilets at Franklin trailhead.

Bike shop, rentals: Country Pedalers bike shop with rentals at Franklin trailhead, (814) 432-8055; Ken and Lynn Cochran are active in the Allegheny Valley Trails Association and will provide information on trails or volunteer opportunities.

Restaurant, groceries: Minimal snacks at the bike shop. Restaurants and groceries in Franklin.

Camping, simple lodging: Motels and B&Bs in Franklin.

Swimming, fishing: In Allegheny River. Be careful of current if it's high. Good fishing for bass and walleye.

Winter sports: Cross-country skiing.

Wheelchair access: Narrow gates near Belmar Bridge (26″) and Brandon (28.5″).

Trail organization

Allegheny Valley Trails Association
Franklin Area Chamber of Commerce
1256 Liberty St, Suite 2
Franklin PA 16323
Membership: $20/year individual, $25/year family

Maps, guides, other references

Trail brochure, "Bicycle Trails of Venango County"

Walking tours of Historic Franklin, America's Victorian City, Franklin Rotary Club, 1990.

USGS Topographic Maps: Franklin, Kennerdell.

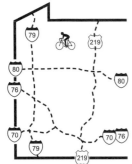

Tidioute Riverside Rec Trek Trail

Along Allegheny River from Tidioute to (near) Trunkeyville in Warren County

This trail, like the Kellettville to Nebraska Trace, is included here chiefly because it appears on lists of rail-trails in Pennsylvania. Both are lovely hiking trails, but most readers of this guide will find them unrewarding as bicycle trails.

The Tidioute Riverside Rec Trek Trail runs alongside the Allegheny River along the railbed of the former Oil City Secondary RR, 20-30 feet above the river. US62 is on the opposite shore of the Allegheny, but the traffic noise is not intrusive. The trail itself is double-track grass and ballast, ranging from reasonably smooth to quite rough in spots.

From the trailhead at the water treatment plant on the west side of Tidioute, you plunge into the forest. An 8' mowed swath and a few signs and mileposts are the only signs of development. The trail here is double-track grass over small ballast or coarse cinders. A third of a mile from the trailhead, you reach Lower Eddy, a small rest area with a bench. Milepost 1 appears at 0.3 miles. You get periodic views through the shrubbery to the Allegheny River. After three-quarters of a mile, the trail begins getting rougher, with larger stones, some wet spots, and some small humps. Not far after milepost 2, a sign marks the waterfall on Grove Run. The falls, really a 10-12' cascade, are 150 feet back from the trail. There's a bench at the falls. Former roads run up both sides of Grove Run. As we did not follow either of them, we have no idea where they lead. Another half-mile brings you to a spring along the trail. There are several short sections on original ballast in this area. The cliffs here have small caves going back 5-10'.

Near milepost 3, a sign identifies "Beaver Flat", but there's no sign of beaver, nor is there enough space for either a town or a beaver pond. Soon after Beaver Flat, the trail crosses a creek, and the amount of raw ballast on the trail increases. After about milepost 4, there's little sign of trail improvement other than tracks left by ATVs. From here south, the trail gets rougher and rougher, with some ties remaining and with tree roots and overhanging branches. After half a mile of this, things get even worse: The trail is blocked by fallen trees and underbrush, not far before a small stream comes around the end of the ridge and about half a mile before Trunkeyville.

Although the trail is sometimes described as running from Tidioute to Trunkeyville, you should be aware that about half a mile before Trunkeyville the trail is blocked by numerous downed trees and is nearly impassable. Getting off the trail without working your way through the blockage requires you to pass through private land on trails established (probably informally) by ATVs. So, although the trailhead in Trunkeyville is there (though unmarked), we must regard this, at least as of fall 1998, as an out-and-back trip from Tidioute.

Development plans

The trail is supposed to reach Trunkeyville, but the last half-mile hasn't been developed.

Tidioute Riverside Rec Trek Trail	
Location	Tidioute to near Trunkeyville in Triumph Township, Warren County and Harmony Township, Forest County
Trailheads	Tidioute
Length, Surface	5 miles planned, 3.5 miles complete, dirt to single-track
Character	Uncrowded, rural, shady, level
Usage restrictions	No motorized vehicles
Amenities	None
Driving time from Pittsburgh	2 hours 30 minutes northeast

Access points

Vicinity: Directions begin across the Allegheny River from Tidioute, at the intersection of PA127 and US62. To reach this point from Pittsburgh, follow I79 to I80, turn north on PA8 to US62, then continue on US62.

Tidioute trailhead: From the intersection of PA127 and US62, turn on PA127 to cross the Allegheny River. After 0.3 mile, turn left at the "T" to remain on PA127, following the sign for the trail. The trailhead is 0.4 mile farther, just before PA127 swings right and starts climbing.

Amenities

Rest rooms, water: None

Bike shop, rentals: None

Restaurant, groceries: Along US62

Camping, simple lodging: Along US62; dispersed camping in Allegheny National Forest

Swimming, fishing: None

Winter sports: Cross-country skiing

Wheelchair access: No gates, but some sections of trail are rough.

Trail organization

Allegheny National Forest
Sheffield Ranger District
Route 6
Sheffield PA 16347
(814) 968-3232
e-mail: anf/r9_allegheny@fs.fed.us
web: www.fs.fed.us/r9/allegheny/

Maps, guides, other references

USGS Topographic Maps: Tidioute.

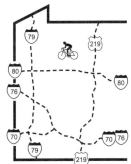

Kellettville to Nebraska Trace

Along Tionesta Ck from Kellettville to Nebraska Bridge in Forest County

This trail, like the Tidioute Riverside Rec Trek Trail, is included here chiefly because it appears on lists of rail-trails in Pennsylvania. Both are lovely hiking trails, but most readers of this guide will find them unrewarding as bicycle trails.

The main portion of the Kellettville to Nebraska Trace is alongside the Tionesta Ck and Lake on the railbed of the former Sheffield and Tionesta RR. The trail is sparsely blazed with plastic signs about 4" square. Little has been done to improve the trail surface, however. We walked in from each end to the first creek crossing.

The trail starts at the end of the Corps of Engineers' Kellettville campground, which runs along the south side of Tionesta Ck just downstream from the Kellettville bridge. A short footpath from the end of the campground crosses a field and joins the railroad embankment shortly before the railroad grade reaches Salmon Ck. This is 0.5 miles downstream from the bridge. The trestle is missing, and the only way across the creek is to jump along a series of rocks and logs.

We haven't checked the trail from Salmon Ck to Coon Ck, a distance of around 10 miles. The ranger advises us that it is unimproved throughout, with surface ranging from single-track to asphalt. The trail crosses four main perennial streams and several minor ones—all without bridges. It also has a few washouts and occasional trees down. The trees are easy to get around and the creek crossings have stepping stones, at least at low water. So this is, as far as we have seen it, a pleasant hike. The environment is riverine, and the plentiful wildlife includes deer, beaver, waterfowl, and raptors.

The railbed ends at the edge of Tionesta Lake about half a mile above Nebraska Bridge. At this point, the trail becomes a footpath through the woods, swinging up Coon Ck for over a mile to find a crossing (unbridged) above the high-water level of the lake. The path then comes down the other side of Coon Ck and over the last point of land to emerge at the upper end of the parking area on the south side of Nebraska Bridge.

Access points

Vicinity: Directions begin in Tionesta, where US62 crosses the Allegheny River. To reach this point from Pittsburgh, take I79 to I80, turn north on PA8 to US62, and follow US62.

Kellettville trailhead: From the Allegheny River crossing in Tionesta, turn right on PA36 and go 0.5 miles to German Hill Rd (also called Dutch Hill Rd). Turn left on German

Hill Rd and go 11.4 miles to the T intersection with PA666. Turn right on PA666 and go 2.6 miles to a Y with Forest Rd 127. Bear right and down to cross Tionesta Ck. Park on the left near the bridge. To get to the trail, cross the road into the campground and go out the far end of the campground.

Nebraska Bridge trailhead: From the Allegheny River crossing in Tionesta, turn right on PA36 and go 7.4 miles to Weaver's Country Market, where PA36 turns right. At this point turn left on Nebraska Rd, following the "bridge out" signs. Continue for 3.7 miles and park in the upper parking lot not far before the closed bridge.

Kellettville to Nebraska Trace	
Location	Kellettville to Nebraska Bridge in Green and Kingsley Townships, Forest County
Trailheads	Kellettville, Nebraska Bridge
Length, Surface	12.2 miles reported, dirt with much single-track
Character	Uncrowded, forest, shady, mostly level with missing bridges
Usage restrictions	No motorized vehicles
Amenities	Rest rooms, camping
Driving time from Pittsburgh	2 hours 30 minutes northeast

You can also reach Nebraska Bridge from the north side (German Hill Rd, then south on Nebraska Rd). This makes a much easier shuttle than the south approach. However, the bridge over Tionesta Lake is closed to vehicles and may be underwater if the lake is high. So unless you're sure what you'll find at the bottom, it's safer to enter from the south.

Amenities

Rest rooms, water: Pit toilet at Kellettville, chemical toilet at Nebraska

Bike shop, rentals: None

Restaurant, groceries: In Tionesta

Camping, simple lodging: Corps of Engineers Campground at Kellettville, and dispersed camping in Allegheny National Forest

Swimming, fishing: In Tionesta Ck and Lake. Swim at your own risk

Winter sports: Cross-country skiing; Allegheny National Forest snowmobile routes from Kellettville

Wheelchair access: Not suitable

Trail organization

US Army Corps of Engineers
One Tionesta Lake
Tionesta PA 16353
(814) 755-3512
web: www.lrp.usace.army.mil/rec/lakes/tionesta.htm

Maps, guides, other references

USGS Topographic Maps: Kellettville, Tylersburg, Tionesta.

Buzzard Swamp features meadows and fishing lakes

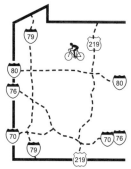

Buzzard Swamp

Southeast of Marienville in Forest County

Allegheny National Forest offers many opportunities for bicycling. They are more rugged than most of the trails in this guide. The Buzzard Swamp area offers a 9.6-mile network of rolling grassy trails with good opportunities to see wildlife. It offers an easy transition from developed rail-trails to off-road cycling.

In the early 1960's the US Forest Service and the PA Game Commission created a chain of 15 ponds for wildlife habitat. Now the dams and meadows around these ponds offer hiking and mountain biking. For the most part, the trail surface is wide and smooth. About half of the trails are small gravel and dirt; the other half are firm base with grass. If you're there soon after a trail is mowed, it's like riding on the lawn. If the grass is high, it's a meadow experience you won't forget. The southern loop, around the propagation area and the largest lakes, is a 10' wide gravel road (double-track), a bit firmer than most. However, the east edge of the interpretive trail and north from there is tricky single-track with stream crossings, logs, rocks, and soft spots that can be muddy after a rain. The interpretive trail is single-track; we recommend against riding this on a bike because of possible interference with walkers.

Most of the trails are on closed roads. These aren't blazed except at points of possible confusion, but they're easy to follow. Trail signs that formerly named the trails have disappeared, but most intersections have copies of the trail map with a you-are-here indicator. The National Forest brochure will help you stay oriented.

Buzzard Swamp	
Location	Southeast of Marienville, Jenks Township, Forest County
Trailheads	East and south of Marienville
Length, Surface	9.6-mile network; dirt to gravel
Character	Little-used, forest, sunny, rolling
Usage restrictions	No motorized vehicles; no snowmobiles; no horses
Amenities	Rest rooms, fishing
Driving time from Pittsburgh	2 hours 45 minutes northeast

The area is a special management area that balances wildlife management and recreational opportunities. Fishing in the ponds is encouraged. Entry to the small (40 acre) wildlife propagation area is strictly prohibited, but you may peer in from the bordering trails. This is an important link in the Atlantic flyway, so it's a great place to see birds during seasonal migrations. Spring migration brings 20-25 species of waterfowl. You may also see nonmigratory birds, mammals, and reptiles.

Buzzard Swamp itself lies on the southern edge of the area. The higher ground is not swampy, and we found most of the trails firm. However, mosquitoes thrive here, and they get denser as you approach the swamp. Combined with the lack of tree cover to provide shade, that makes this a better spring or fall trip than a summer trip.

Extensions of the ride

Allegheny National Forest has an extensive network of forest service roads. For the most part, they're gravel, and they carry little traffic. Get the National Forest map from the ranger and pick out your own routes. These roads can be very hilly.

A number of traffic-free trails in Allegheny National Forest are open to bicycles. Several of them incorporate sections of former railroad grades, but many of them are more rugged. They are dispersed through the forest. The closest is the 7.1-mile trail system at Beaver Meadows, about 4 miles north of Marienville on FR128 (N Forest St). Get more detailed information from the Forest Service or Rails to Trails.

Access points

Vicinity: Directions begin at the 7-way junction in Marienville, where PA66 (Chestnut St) intersects forest service route FR130 and several other streets. To reach this point from Pittsburgh, go north on I79, then east on I80, then northeast on PA66 near Clarion. Marienville is around 20 miles northeast of I80.

North trailhead: At the 7-way junction in Marienville, go east on FR130 (Spruce St) for 2.5 miles. Turn right (south) on FR376, a short dirt road that soon ends in a parking lot.

West trailhead: At the 7-way junction in Marienville, go south on the road to Loleta (S Forest St, also labeled SR2005) for 1.3 mile. Turn left (east) on FR157 at the sign for Buzzard Swamp and go 2.3 miles to parking at the trailhead.

Amenities

Rest rooms, water: Rest room at west trailhead

Bike shop, rentals: None

Restaurant, groceries: In Marienville

Camping, simple lodging: Allegheny National Forest campgrounds at Loleta, Kelly Pines, Beaver Meadows. Check with the ranger about dispersed camping in Allegheny National Forest. Commercial campground south of Marienville.

Swimming, fishing: No swimming. All the ponds in the area have small and largemouth bass, perch, catfish, crappie, and bluegill.

Winter sports: Cross-country skiing encouraged. Snowmobiles prohibited.

Wheelchair access: Dams are level but mostly grass-covered. Best surfaces are near west trailhead. Paths around gates permit wheelchair passage.

Trail organization

Allegheny National Forest
Marienville Ranger District
Star Route #2, Box 130
Marienville PA 16239
(814) 927-6628
e-mail: anf/r9_allegheny@fs.fed.us
web: www.fs.fed.us/r9/allegheny/

Maps, guides, other references

Buzzard Swamp Wildlife Viewing & Hiking Area. Trail brochure from Allegheny National Forest.

USGS Topographic Maps: Marienville East.

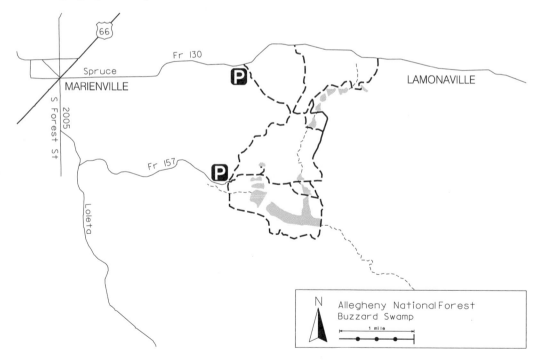

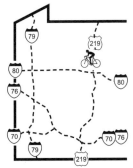

Clarion-Little Toby Bike and Hike Trail

Along Clarion River and Little Toby Ck from Ridgway to Brockway in Elk and Jefferson Counties

Way up in the headwaters of the Clarion River, where the Clarion is still a creek and the mountains tower 700 feet over the water, two railroads once ran south from Ridgway along the Clarion River and Little Toby Ck to Brockway. Now only one remains, and the other, the former Ridgway and Clearfield Branch of the Pennsylvania RR is becoming a trail. The route runs for 18 miles, largely through woods, and punctuated by homes, camps, ghost towns, and industrial relics. Currently 5.8 miles near Ridgway and 4.3 miles near Brockway are completed. An additional 5.2 miles from the Civilian Conservation Corps camp at Croyland to the ghost town at Carrier are semi-finished in coarse cinders. For the 2.7 miles from Dog Hollow Run to Croyland, you must choose between low-traffic PA949 and large loose ballast along the remaining railroad; we strongly recommend the former.

The trail starts in Ridgway on the south side of the Clarion River, a block west of Main St. It leaves town passing a few stores and the water treatment plant, then breaks away into a lovely creekside trail with rhododendron towering on the shore side. The Clarion was recently selected as a Wild and Scenic River. A home sits across the railbed at mile 2.7, and the trail detours briefly to the road to avoid this house. At mile 4.1 you can see the remnants of Mill Haven Dam, which was destroyed in the flooding of 1936. At mile 5 the active railroad, which has been on the opposite side of the Clarion River, crosses and runs parallel to the trail, though a little distance away. Now the railroad grade, the trail, and PA949 are pinned between the cliff and the river, but the railroad and road have little traffic, and the road is high enough to keep traffic noise away from the trail.

At mile 5.8, the finished trail ends at a short crossover to PA949. If this isn't your destination, cross out to the road, go 1.8 miles, and turn left at the first opportunity. This is the town of Carman, though there's no sign of it on this side of the creek. The turn will put you on a dirt road just before the road crosses Little Toby Ck; a sign for the trail marks the turn. You'll encounter relatively little traffic along PA949 and virtually none on the dirt road. You can descend to the trail at the Carman trailhead a tenth of a mile after the turn, but the connecting trail is narrow and steep. We recommend following the dirt road for 0.7 mile to the former CCC camp at Croyland, which provided jobs for 250 men during the Great Depression. A sign in the parking area directs you to the trail.

From Croyland (mile 8.5) to a little past Little Vineyard Run (mile 13.7), the trail surface is loose cinders. You're wholly isolated from roads and houses and most other signs of civilization, except for some industrial remains and signs marking the location of ghost towns. You'll pass the ghost towns of Grove (mile 9.8), Shorts Mill (mile 10.1), Blue

---

Rock (mile 12.2), Vineyard (mile 13.3), and Carrier (mile 14.5). Be sure to stop at Blue Rock ghost town and walk down to the creek to check out the suspension footbridge. The trail here runs through central Pennsylvania woods, with small to medium trees and lots of ferns in the understory. Be alert for the bridge at Coward Run near mile 10.1; the northern abutment has eroded seriously (summer 1998; repairs expected spring 1999), and you'll need to walk your bike onto the bridge. You're likely to see wildlife anywhere along the trail, but especially near the streams. Expect birds, deer, rabbits, and chipmunks; rejoice at rarer species.

At Carrier, the crushed limestone surface resumes for the remainder of the trip into Brockway. The woods and ferns are now punctuated by homes and camps, and you occasionally see the road paralleling the trail. The trail emerges in Brockway at Taylor Park, with pond, playground, swimming pool, ballfields and (you guessed it) parking.

Clarion-Little Toby Bike & Hike Trail	
Location	Along Clarion River from Ridgway to Carman and along Little Toby Ck to Brockway in Ridgway and Spring Ck Townships in Elk County and Snyder Township, Jefferson County
Trailheads	Brockway, Carman, Ridgway
Length, Surface	18 miles planned, currently 10.1 miles packed crushed stone, 5.2 miles dirt, 2.7 miles ballast
Character	Uncrowded, forest, shady, flat
Usage restrictions	No motorized vehicles; no snowmobiles; no horses
Amenities	Rest rooms, water, bike rental, food, fishing
Driving time from Pittsburgh	2 hours northeast

Extensions of the ride

For the truly hard-core, there's a possible extension via a CCC road that goes over the mountain from Carman to Brockway. We haven't ridden this, so we don't know the actual conditions. The topo maps and reports from long-time local residents indicate that you can continue riding through the CCC camp near Carman, climb along Laurel Run and a small tributary nearly 700' to the top of the ridge (500' of it in a single mile) and descend along Vineyard Run to rejoin the trail at Jenkins Run. The road runs through PA State Game Lands. It's gated 0.4 miles south of the CCC camp and 4.8 miles north of Brockway. The 7 miles or so between gates should be traffic-free. Most of the road is dirt, and some sections are rutted and bumpy. Take the topo maps so you don't get lost, and let us know how it is. The gradients look less brutal if you ride it south to north.

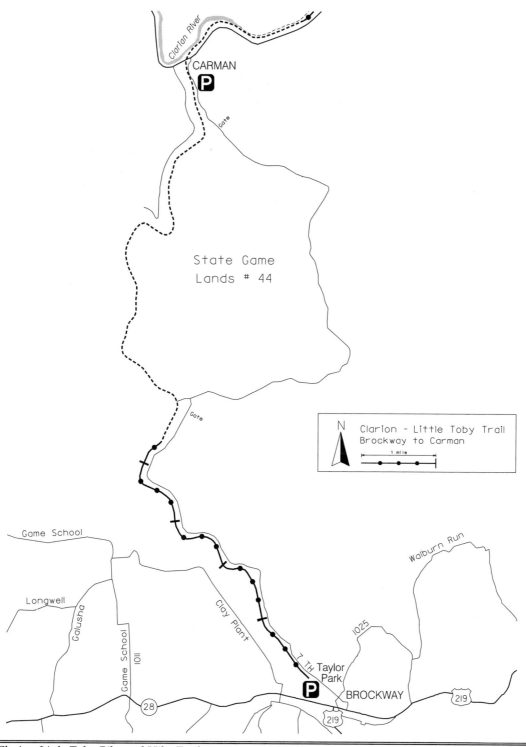

Clarion River

CARMAN

🅿

Gate

State Game
Lands # 44

Gate

N Clarion - Little Toby Trail
   Brockway to Carman
   1 mile

Game School

Walburn Run

Longwell

Galusha

Game School

1011

Clay Plant

7 TH

1025

Taylor
Park

🅿

BROCKWAY

28

219

219

Clarion-Little Toby Bike and Hike Trail   183

Development plans

Completion of the central section depends on funding. The trail council is planning an extension from Brockway to Falls Creek (9 miles) and studying the feasibility of continuing from Brockway to Brookville (17 miles)

Bridge over Little Toby Creek

Access points

Vicinity: Directions begin at the intersection of I80 and US219 (I80 exit 16). To reach this point from Pittsburgh, go northeast on PA28 to I80, then east on I80.

Brockway trailhead: From I80, go north on US219 for 7 miles to Brockway and turn west (left) on PA28. After 5 blocks turn north (right) on Seventh St. Go a few blocks, through Taylor Park and past several ball fields to parking across 7th St from a small lake.

Ridgway trailhead: From I80, go north on US219 24.5 miles to Ridgway and go straight on PA948 (Main St) when US219 turns right. Go 0.2 miles on PA948 and turn left on Water St, across the street from Love's Canoe and Bike Rental shop. The trailhead is a block down Water St, with parking just before the trailhead

Carman trailhead: From I80, go north on US219 24.5 miles to Ridgway and follow the signs for PA949. Go 7.5 miles on PA949. Just before crossing the bridge over Little Toby Ck, turn left on a dirt road marked by a sign for the Clarion-Little Toby Bike and Hike Trail. In 0.7 miles you pass through the old stone gates of a former CCC camp. Park here and follow signs a few yards to the trail.

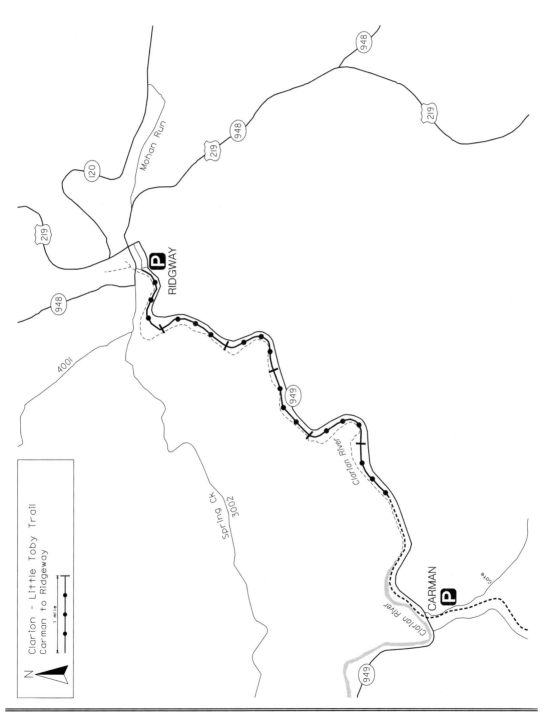

Amenities

Rest rooms, water: At the park in Brockway and at Love's in Ridgway

Bike shop, rentals: Love's canoe and bike rental in Ridgway

Restaurant, groceries: In Brockway and Ridgway

Camping, simple lodging: Hotels and B&Bs in Ridgway and Brockway

Swimming, fishing: Swimming in Clarion River (exercise caution, and don't cross the RR tracks) and at pool in Taylor Park in Brockway (fee, check hours). Fishing in the Clarion.

Winter sports Cross-country skiing. Snowmobiles prohibited.

Wheelchair access: Trailheads are accessible, but major portions of trail are rough

Trail organizations

Rails to Trails
PO Box 115
Ridgway PA 15853

Elk County Chamber of Commerce
231 Main St

(814) 776-1424
web: www.ncentral.com/~dlove/lrail.htm

Maps, guides, other references

Trail brochure

USGS Topographic Maps: Brandy Camp, Carman, Portland Mills, Ridgway.

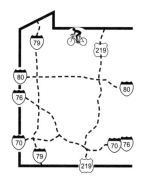

Warren/North Warren Trail

Along Conewango River from Warren to North Warren in Warren County

The Warren/North Warren Trail, also called the Black Walnut Trail, provides an off-road access path between the northern edge of Warren and the commercial area of North Warren. Following the path of the former Allegheny RR, the trail's southern half is rural, and the northern half is urban.

The trail begins at the northern edge of Warren, between US62 and the western shore of Conewango Ck. It is paved, 8'4" wide, with wide shoulders. Near the trailhead, the highway and railroad grade is squeezed between the end of the ridge and the river. The highway here is 30-40' above the trail, so the road noise is not intrusive. The creek is close at hand, and you can enjoy the riffles, the islands, and the ducks. After a quarter-mile the highway swings away, and houses appear beside the trail. After three-quarters of a mile of relative isolation, the trail emerges in the commercial area of North Warren. A trailside restaurant, followed quickly by a road crossing, marks the change. The trail soon parallels US62, separated by a few feet of grass. Stores along the highway include grocery stores and restaurants. Wetmore Cemetery, with headstones dating back to the 1830's, provides a brief change of scenery. Stone benches offer resting spots. Just past another trailside restaurant, the trail ends at PA69 (Jackson Run Rd).

Warren/North Warren Trail	
Location	Warren to North Warren in Warren City and Conewango Township, Warren County
Trailheads	Warren, North Warren
Length, Surface	3 miles planned, 1.7 miles complete, paved
Character	Busy, urban, sunny and shady, level
Usage restrictions	No motorized vehicles
Amenities	Food, lodging
Driving time from Pittsburgh	2 hours 30 minutes northeast

Development plans

Plans for 1999 include a 0.7 mile extension past Warren State Hospital and the forestry service arboretum to N State St. The trail may someday reach the Chataqua trail and wildlife area in New York state.

Access points

Vicinity: Directions begin in Warren at the intersection where US62 goes north and US6 goes east. To reach this point from Pittsburgh, follow I79 to I80, turn north on PA8 to US62, then continue on US62 to Warren.

Warren trailhead: From the intersection of US62 and US6, go 2 miles north on US62. Turn east (right) on 7th St for a block to the "T", then left on East St for 0.1 mile to the trailhead.

North Warren trailhead: From the intersection of US62 and US6, go 3-4 miles north on US62. There isn't a trailhead as such, but the trail runs alongside the road for about a mile from Big Joe's to PA69 (Jackson Run Rd). Park anywhere legal.

Amenities

Rest rooms, water: None

Bike shop, rentals: None

Restaurant, groceries: Along US62 in North Warren. Two restaurants (0.8 and 1.6 miles from the Warren trailhead) have trailside tables.

Camping, simple lodging: In Warren

Swimming, fishing: None

Winter sports: Cross-country skiing

Wheelchair access: Gates all measure 44" or wider. Ramps all good except for a few curbs.

Trail organization

> Warren County Planning and Zoning Commission
> 207 W Fifth Av
> Warren PA 16365
> (814) 726-3861

Maps, guides, other references

USGS Topographic Maps: Warren, Russell.

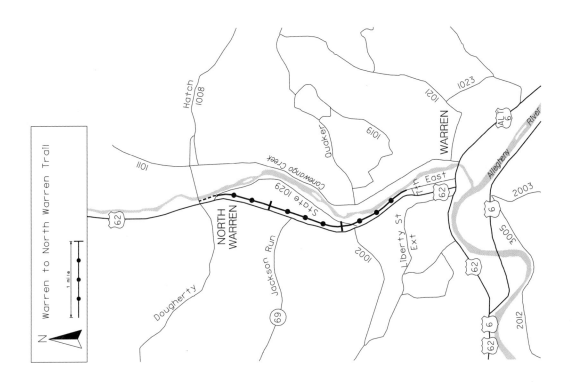

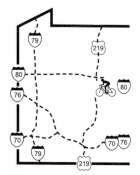

Clearfield to Grampian Trail

Along West Branch Susquehanna River and Kratzer Run from Clearfield to Grampian in Clearfield County

This trail connects Clearfield, Curwensville, Grampian, and several small towns between them, affording a convenient near-to-town recreational opportunity to residents and visitors. The trail follows the former Grampian Industrial Track along the West Branch Susquehanna River and Kratzer Run for 10.5 miles. The surface is fine cinders, not quite as firm as many other rail-trails, but certainly firm enough for a hybrid bike.

You'll encounter a variety of scenery and settings. The first mile is beside a busy road. The middle third is largely wooded through farmland. The next mile is again beside the road, and the last mile runs between buildings in town.

The trail begins in Clearfield behind a hardware store and remains in the commercial area for a half-mile before the stores give way to residences and farms. It runs alongside busy PA879 for a while, then retreats into the woods for some respite from the sun. Watch for waterfowl on the adjacent ponds. The trail comes out of the woods long enough to cross the West Branch of the Susquehanna R on a long trestle with a fine view up the river, then ducks into a deep cut. After the cut it's tucked between the road and the river to the outskirts of Curwensville. Here it leaves the West Branch and crosses a busy intersection. A block later it crosses PA453 and joins Kratzer Run for the climb to Grampian. The developed portion of the trail narrows as it crosses PA453. When we rode the trail in summer 1998, the developed portion ended where SR3030 crosses the Louis R Donahue Memorial Bridge. Since then the trail has been completed to Grampian.

Access points

Vicinity: Directions begin entering Clearfield on US322/PA153. To reach this point from Pittsburgh, go northeast on PA28, east on I80, and southeast on PA153 at Exit 18.

Clearfield trailhead: Follow US322/PA153 until it crosses the West Branch of the Susquehanna River. Here US322 goes straight and PA153 turns right. Turn right to stay on PA153 south. Follow PA153 along the river (Front St) until it rejoins the northbound lanes on 2nd St. Stay on 2nd St (toward Curwensville) when PA153 turns away from the river. About 1.4 miles from the bridge, the residential area ends. Turn left into the True Value Hardware parking lot, just before Riverside Quality Food Market. Go back about 2 blocks to the rear of the True Value Hardware store. Trailhead parking is here.

Curwensville trailhead: Follow instructions to the Clearfield trailhead, but don't turn into the True Value parking lot. Continue on Second St for another 0.6 mile to the stoplight and go straight on PA879. Continue for 4.6 miles to the junction with PA453. Turn left on PA453 for 1 block to the trail crossing.

Grampian trailhead: Follow instructions to the Clearfield trailhead, but don't turn into the True Value parking lot. Continue on Second St for another 0.6 mile to the stoplight and go straight on PA879. Continue for 9.8 miles to the junction with PA729 and US219. Turn left on PA729 to trailhead parking just across the creek. Alternate route: Go northeast on US219 to Grampian and turn right on PA729 to trailhead parking.

Clearfield to Grampian Trail	
Location	Clearfield to Grampian in Lawrence, Pike, and Penn Townships, Clearfield County
Trailheads	Clearfield, Curwensville
Length, Surface	10.5 miles, crushed cinders
Character	Uncrowded, rural, sunny and shady, level
Usage restrictions	No motorized vehicles; no snowmobiles; no horses
Amenities	Bike shop, food, fishing
Driving time from Pittsburgh	2 hours 45 minutes northeast

Amenities

Rest rooms, water: None

Bike shop, rentals: In Clearfield

Restaurant, groceries: In Clearfield, Curwensville, and Grampian

Camping, simple lodging: At Curwensville Lake, 2 miles south of Curwensville on PA453

Swimming, fishing: No swimming. Fishing in river

Winter sports: Cross-country skiing encouraged. Snowmobiles prohibited.

Wheelchair access: OK

Trail organization

Clearfield County Rails-to-Trails Association
310 East Cherry St
Clearfield PA 16830
814-765-1701

Maps, guides, other references

USGS Topographic Maps: Clearfield, Curwensville.

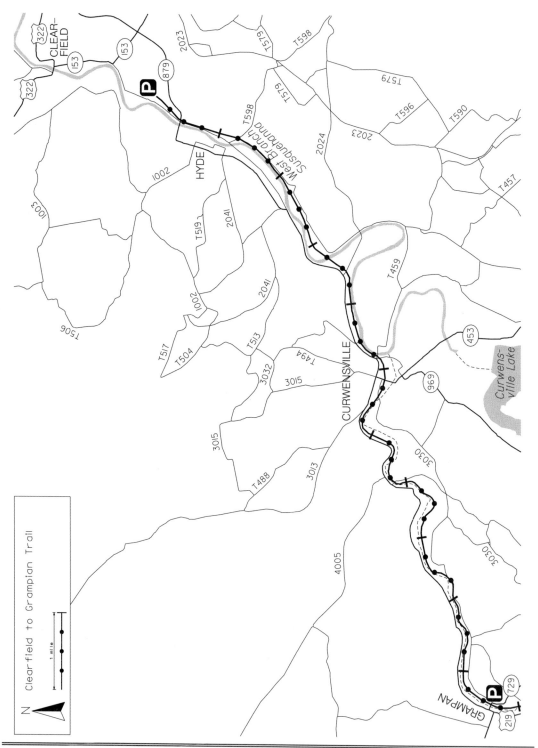

Clearfield to Grampian Trail

Trials North & West: Lake Erie and the Western Border

In this section we present several trails on the north and west edges of Pennsylvania outside the Allegheny River watershed plus a few in northeastern Ohio. Four are on or near the PA/OH state line; one is on a peninsula in Lake Erie; three are near Cleveland, in northeastern Ohio.

Eastern Ohio isn't western Pennsylvania, but these trails are close at hand, and they're too good to pass up. From Pittsburgh, the Akron-Cleveland area is about as convenient as the Franklin-Oil City area and much closer than Presque Isle. From northwestern Pennsylvania, these trails are closer than the Youghiogheny-Allegheny Highlands system. So we decided that opportunity and convenience are more important than details of geography, and here they are.

All but one of these trails are developed and maintained by public organizations—state or regional park districts or the National Park Service. Stavich Trail is maintained privately. Ernst Trail is technically in the Allegheny watershed, but geographically it's closer to the trails in this section, so we include it here.

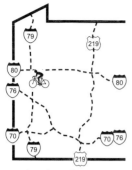

Moraine State Park (Lake Arthur)

Bicycle concession at North Shore Drive to Marina Restaurant, Moraine State Park in Butler County

The designated bicycle trail runs on the north side of Lake Arthur, generally between North Shore Drive and the lake. It winds in and out of trees, up and down gentle hills, past picnic areas and other park activities and facilities. The trail passes several boat launching areas and provides views of the sailing and other boating activities on the lake. The swimming area for this side of the lake is near the trail (miles 3.6-3.8). The east end (mile 7.2) is at the Marina Restaurant. The park is very popular, so you'll have plenty of company any time during the season.

The route of the trail is lovely. Unfortunately, the surface itself is very narrow (only 8') and the asphalt is often rough. Sharp curves and short steep dips make the trail interesting. However, sight lines are quite short, and it's usually busy. If this trail had a smooth 12' path, it would be a gem.

Moraine State Park Bike Trail	
Location	Moraine State Park, Worth Township, Butler County
Trailheads	Bicycle concession, Lakeview Beach area, Marina restaurant
Length, Surface	7.2 miles; paved
Character	Busy, park setting, mostly sunny, gentle hills, sharp curves, steep dips
Usage restrictions	Snowmobiles ok; no motorized vehicles; no horses
Amenities	Rest rooms, water, bike rental, food, fishing
Driving time from Pittsburgh	1 hour north

Local history, attractions

During the ice age 14,000 years ago, the Wisconsin Ice Sheet came just this far south, where it dammed Muddy Ck to create a large glacial lake. When the glacier receded the lake burst, and the water it liberated carved the deep gorge a few miles west on Slippery Rock Ck, making major changes to the regional drainage patterns. Geological remnants of glaciation, including the moraine and an esker can still be found in the area. Present-day Lake Arthur is in approximately the same location as the glacial lake.

More recently, this area has been exploited for its minerals: first oil in the late 19th century, then coal. Deep mines predominated in the early 20th century, and the area was strip-mined in the 1940s and 1950s.

A park was proposed in 1951 when a geological survey revealed traces of the glacial lake. Extensive restoration was required to reclaim the land that is now the park. Deep mines were sealed, hundreds of oil and gas wells were plugged, and strip mines were re-contoured. The park opened in 1970.

Extensions of the ride

A 7.2-mile mountain bike trail lies east of the Davis Hollow Marina. It has very steep rocky sections and is definitely not a novice trail. It's not our kind of riding, and it's noted here only because it's handy. You can reach the trailhead by taking Mt Union Rd north from North Shore Drive where the road to Nealy's Point goes south. The trailhead is about a third of a mile up Mt Union, just past the Glacier Ridge Hiking Trail.

Access points

Vicinity: Directions begin on either US422 or I79 headed toward Moraine State Park. Details depend on where you're coming from.

Lake Arthur Trailhead (bicycle rental concession):

> *From the east:* You'll approach the park headed west on US422. About a mile after you cross the lake (and just before the I79 intersection), take the "North Shore" exit from US422. Go a quarter-mile to the stop/yield signs. Turn right and follow signs for 0.8 mile to the bicycle concession and trailhead parking.

> *From the south:* You'll approach the park headed north on I79. Take the PA488 exit (Portersville, Exit 28) and go west 0.6 miles to US19 in Portersville. Turn north (right) on US19, go 0.5 miles, and turn right on SR4007 (West Park Rd, also numbered TR890). Follow signs for "North Shore Moraine State Park". Go 2.8 miles on SR4007, crossing I79, US422, and Muddy Ck. Just after crossing the creek, turn right and follow signs 0.8 mile to the bicycle concession and parking.

> *From the west:* You'll approach the park headed east on US422. Turn south (right) on US19, go a bit over half a mile to Burnside Rd and turn left. Follow Burnside Rd just over a mile to SR4007 (West Park Rd) and turn left. Go 0.5 mile on SR4007, crossing US422 and a creek. Just after the creek crossing, turn right and follow signs 0.8 mile to the bicycle concession and trailhead parking.

> *From the north:* You'll approach the park headed south on I79. Take the US422 exit (Exit 29). Go west 1.2 miles to US19, turn south (left) on US19, then proceed as if you were coming from the west.

Marina trailhead (eastern): Instead of turning into West trailhead (bicycle concession) parking, continue on the access road, which becomes North Shore Dr. Follow signs to the Marina Restaurant. This trailhead is closed from Oct 31 to Apr 15.

Other access: Since the trail lies between North Shore Drive and the lake, practically any parking lot along North Shore drive provides access, especially the ones at lakeside.

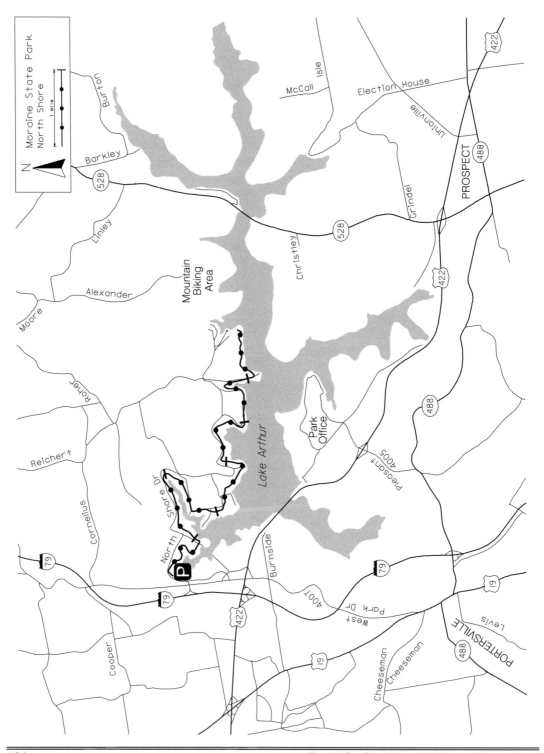

Moraine State Park
North Shore

1 mile

N

McCall Isle
Election House
Unionville

Burton

Barkley

528

Linley

Alexander

Moore

Rother

Reichert

Cornelius

Cooper

79

422

79

Mountain Biking Area

North Shore Dr

P

Lake Arthur

Christley

528

Grindel

PROSPECT

488

422

488

Park Office

Pleasant 4005

Burnside

West Park Dr 4007

79

19

422

19

19

Cheeseman

Cheeseman

Levis

PORTERSVILLE

488

Free-Wheeling Easy in Western Pennsylvania

Amenities

Rest rooms, water: Water and rest rooms are available at both trailheads and at the Lakeview Picnic area and the Watts Bay Marina in between. There are also water fountains at intervals.

Bike shop, rentals: No bike shop, but a rental concession operates at the west trailhead daily from Memorial Day to Labor Day and warm weekends in April, May, September, and October.

Restaurant, groceries: The Marina Restaurant serves full meals during the season. There's a snack bar at Lakeview Beach, near milepost 3.7. The bike rental concession has vending machines, as does Watts Bay.

Camping, simple lodging: No camping in the park. The park office can give you a list of private campgrounds and hotels in the area.

Swimming, fishing: Swimming in the state park is permitted only at official swimming areas; they issue citations to swimmers at other locations. The north shore swimming area is at Lakeview, near milepost 3.7. It has lifeguards 11am to 7pm Memorial Day to Labor Day. Fishing in the lake features muskellunge, northern pike, striper, largemouth bass, walleye, channel catfish, black crappie, and bluegill.

Winter sports: The cross-country skiing area is quite short and on the south side of the lake. Jennings Nature Reserve, not far northeast, has a more extensive trail system suitable for cross-country skiing. The bike trail becomes part of the snowmobile trail in the winter. There's also ice fishing, ice boating, ice skating, and sledding.

Wheelchair access: A few short steep hills where trail dips to cross creeks.

Trail organization

DCNR - Moraine State Park
 225 Pleasant Valley Rd
Portersville PA 16051
(724) 368-8811
e-mail: moraine.sp@a1.dcnr.state.pa.us
web: www.dcnr.state.pa.us/stateparks/parks/morain.htm

Maps, guides, other references

The map in the park's information brochure shows the bike route. Trail maps for the mountain bike area are available at the Park office and the bike rental concession.

USGS Topographic Maps: Prospect.

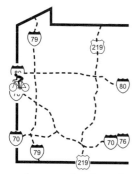

Stavich Bicycle Trail

New Castle PA to Struthers OH in Lawrence County PA and Mahoning County OH

An excellent asphalt surface carries you through farmland and woods along the Mahoning River. The trail corridor originally served as railbed for the Penn-Ohio interurban trolley line rather than a railroad. Trolleys are more forgiving about gradients than railroads, so you'll find noticeable (but still slight) slopes. The only scenic drawback is the existing trackage of the Pennsylvania and Lake Erie railroad, especially the switch yard near Struthers. Much of this track is now being salvaged, though two tracks are still in use.

Most of the trail runs through woods and farms with occasional houses near the trail. Just past mile 2 (we use westbound mileposts here), a beaver dam between the trail and the railroad has created a lake and marsh on the opposite side of the trail. At mile 6.9 the trail crosses into Ohio. Ducks sometimes occupy the pond at mile 7.1.

From miles 7.5 to 8.0, the trail is on Liberty St in Lowellville, affording an opportunity for lunch in the parklet on the opposite side of the railroad, across from City Hall. You can buy subs at Ross' Market on Liberty St, a block west of the parklet. Although this short stretch is on roads, traffic is very light and slow.

Stavich Bicycle Trail	
Location	New Castle PA to Struthers OH, Union and Mahoning Townships in Lawrence County PA; Lowellville and Poland Townships in Mahoning County OH
Trailheads	New Castle PA, Edinburg PA, Lowellville OH, Struthers OH
Length, Surface	12 miles reported, 9.8 measured; paved
Character	Busy, rural, sunny, flat
Usage restrictions	No motorized vehicles; no horses
Amenities	Water, food
Driving time from Pittsburgh	1 hour 10 minutes northwest

The trail is largely exposed to the sun, making it a good bet for early and late in the season, but a real oven in the summer. Wildflower displays in season are very fine, especially where the edges of the trail have not been mowed. You'll probably meet several others, but the trail is not crowded. A dozen and a half benches and picnic tables have been installed between New Castle and Lowellville, mostly in the four miles nearest New Castle.

Local history, attractions

The trail runs on the path of the former interurban streetcar line that joined Youngstown and New Castle. The John and George Stavich families, together with other local individuals, have taken full responsibility for its development and maintenance. It is one of the earliest rail-trails, having been dedicated in June 1983 and improved over time.

The Pennsylvania and Ohio Canal, also known as the "Cross-Cut" Canal, connected the Beaver and Erie Division of the Pennsylvania Main Line Canal with the Ohio and Erie Canal in Ohio. It started at New Castle and ran west on the Mahoning River to Youngstown, Warren, and Akron. Operating from 1840 to 1872, it carried primarily pig iron, iron ore, and passengers.

The trail follows also follows the route of the even earlier Mahoning Path, an Indian path that connected Beaver to Cayahaga (now Akron). The Delaware word mahoni means "deer lick". Adding the "-ing" ending makes Mahoning mean "at the deer lick".

Outskirts of Lowellville

Extensions of the ride

A 1.9-mile loop between the trail and the Mahoning River offers a variation on the route. This road is named East River Rd where it crosses the trail at westbound mile 4.2 and Hillsville Rd where it crosses the trail at mile 5.7. You can turn toward the river at either of these crossings; the road name changes where a side road crosses the river (to make the loop, do not cross the river).

It's possible to loop from the west end of the trail back to Lowellville on the south side of the Mahoning River. From the west end of the trail, go west 1.1 miles on OH289

(Broad St) and turn left on OH616 (Bridge St) and cross the bridge. Go straight at two lights; a short block after the second light take the left fork on Lowellville Rd, continue along the river to Lowellville, and cross the bridge back into Lowellville. Of this 4.7 miles on roads, two miles have moderate traffic and none has good shoulder.

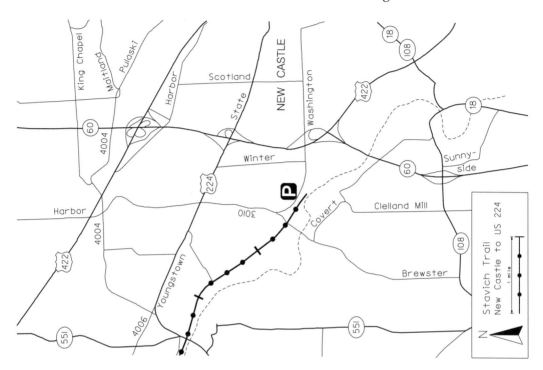

The ride also can be extended to the west with an excursion to the Bike Nashbar outlet store, about 5 miles away on the south side of Youngstown. From the west trailhead, go west 1.1 miles on OH289 (Broad St), turn left on OH616 (Bridge St), and cross the bridge. Go straight at the first traffic light, then right on State St at the second light. Take the first left (Poland St), then the first right (Terrace St), then the next left (diagonally onto Elm). Go up Elm St about 0.5 miles and turn right on Garfield. Garfield emerges from the residential district as Midlothian Blvd. You could continue in heavy traffic on Midlothian, but a better plan is to shift right one block to the parallel road, Mt Vernon. Follow Mt Vernon until it ends, go around the barricade, turn right on Loveland, and take the next left on South Heights, again paralleling Midlothian in a residential area. When South Heights ends, go diagonally left through the park, rejoining Midlothian just before it goes under I680. Tough it out on Midlothian for 0.6 miles under I680 and through three stoplights. Just past the third traffic light (and Schwebel's bakery) turn left on Simon. Nashbar is a long block down on the left. (To get there by car, take Exit 9B from I680, go west on Midlothian and proceed as above).

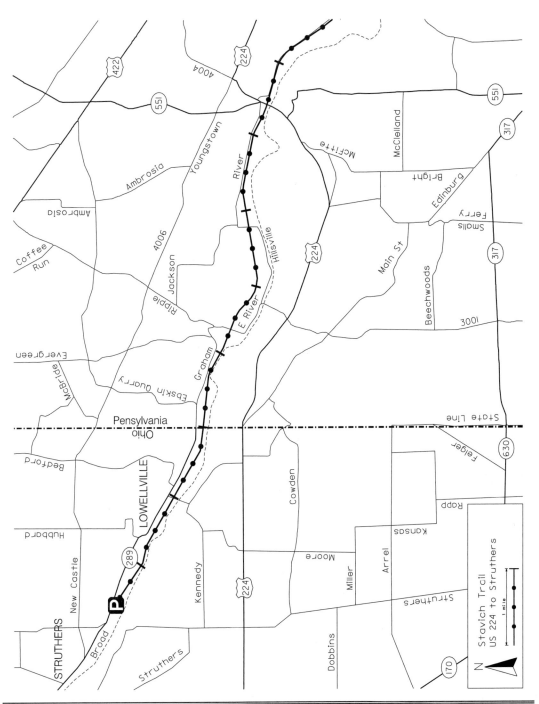

Access points

Vicinity: Directions begin on US224 westbound from its intersection with PA60/US422 in New Castle. To reach this point from Pittsburgh, follow the Parkway West past Pittsburgh International Airport, continuing north on PA60 and paying toll when it becomes PA Toll 60 (the Turnpike extension). 4.7 miles after the exit toll booth, take the US224 west exit (Sampson St) and follow the sign for US224 to Poland.

New Castle trailhead (eastern): 0.7 miles after turning onto US224, turn left on Covert Rd (SR3010) at Riley's and a ballfield. Follow this road 1.4 miles to trailhead parking. *Alternate route:* A shorter but trickier way to get to the New Castle trailhead is to take the PA108 (Mt Jackson, Exit 19) exit from PA Toll 60, go left toward Mt Jackson for 0.5 mile, turn right on Clelland Mill Rd at the crossroads just past Thompson's Alternator/Starter Service (beware — the street sign is hiding in a tree), go 1.4 miles on Clelland Mill Rd, turn left at the fork/triangle onto unmarked Coverts Rd, go 0.8 mile on Coverts Rd, turn right at the "T" intersection of Coverts Rd and Brewster Rd, follow this road for 0.7 mile across a railroad, the Mahoning River, another railroad, and the trail, then at the stop sign turn slightly right onto an unmarked road (West Washington St extension) to the trailhead parking about 0.1 mile ahead.

Struthers trailhead (western): Follow US224 10.5 miles to Poland OH. Turn right (north) on OH616. Follow OH616 across Mahoning River, immediately turn right on OH289 (Broad St), and continue 1.1 miles to trailhead parking.

Amenities

Rest rooms, water: No rest rooms, though you could try Lowellville City Hall, which you pass at Liberty St. Seasonal water fountain in park in Lowellville; Ross' Market will fill your water bottle when you get your sandwich.

Bike shop, rentals: None, but Nashbar Outlet Store 5 miles west, in Youngstown OH.

Restaurant, groceries: Carchedi's in Lowellville, across the tracks from Ross' Market (closed Sundays). Groceries and sub sandwiches at Ross' Market on Liberty St in Lowellville. If you ride the extension to Nashbar, you'll find restaurants at the intersection of Loveland and Midlothian (near the end of Mt Vernon).

Camping, simple lodging: None

Swimming, fishing: In the Mahoning River, in the highly unlikely event that the water quality is up to your (or the fish's) standards.

Winter sports: Cross-country skiing.

Wheelchair access: OK

Trail organization

Falcon Foundry
6th and Water Sts
PO Box 301
Lowellville OH 44436-0301
(216) 536-6221

Maps, guides, other references

Trail brochure. "Two states on two wheels: the Stavich Bicycle Trail"

USGS Topographic Maps: Bessemer, Edinburg, Campbell OH.

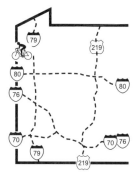

Pymatuning State Park Trail

On the east side of Pymatuning State Park in Crawford County

Pymatuning Lake makes a great crescent in the headwaters of the Shenango River, straddling Crawford County in Pennsylvania and Ashtabula County in Ohio. The Erie & Pittsburgh Branch of the Penn Central RR once cut a smaller arc between the tips of the lake. Much of that railbed has been swallowed by adjacent back yards and other uses, but a few miles at each tip remain open for trail users. Unfortunately, the two sections are about ten miles apart. Both sections are most conveniently accessed from parking areas at their midway points. We'll describe each section end-to-end for simplicity.

The southern section runs from Jamestown on the south to an area of private homes on the eastern shore of Pymatuning Lake. In Jamestown it starts inconspicuously on Main St about half a block north of the Golden Dawn food store. For a few blocks it runs behind residential back yards. After the second road crossing the surface gets rough for a tenth of a mile; you can avoid this by using adjacent Water St. If you re-enter the trail at a "no motor vehicle" sign, you will have a quarter mile of narrow double-track to Headley Field, a baseball field. Alternatively, you can follow Water Street until it ends in the parking lot for Headley Field, and rejoin the trail at the far end of the lot. The trail now becomes packed cinders in young growth woods, but with some depressions that hold water. In another tenth of a mile the trail crosses a road near the Jamestown Area Elementary School and enters an embankment looking down on houses. The ground gradually rises, and after a mile the trail is in a 40' tree-shaded cut. It crosses under the road to Pymatuning Dam with steep trails providing access.

Pymatuning State Park Trail	
Location	One section near Jamestown in South Shenango Township and another section near Linesville in North Shenango Township, Crawford County
Trailheads	near dam at south tip, along causeway at north tip
Length, Surface	5.4 miles in two separate sections of 2.8 (south) and 2.6 (north) miles, dirt
Character	Uncrowded, rural, sunny and shady, level
Usage restrictions	No motorized vehicles; snowmobiles in season; no horses
Amenities	Rest rooms, water, bike shop, food, camping
Driving time from Pittsburgh	2 hours northwest

After the underpass, the ground quickly drops away again, and a quarter-mile later you emerge at the lake itself for a complete change of scenery. The trail is now on a small embankment, with lake to the west and wetlands to the east. You have a good chance of seeing lake birds here, especially ducks and gulls with perhaps a heron. This continues for three-quarters of a mile, interrupted briefly by a stretch with woods on the lake side and back yards on the land side. Too soon, the lake shore swings away from the trail and the tread disappears into residential back yards, a total of about two and three quarters miles from Jamestown.

Pymatuning Lake

The northern section of the trail runs from Fries Rd to the fish hatchery at the north end of the causeway. On the south side of Fries Rd the rail grade is posted against entry. To the north of Fries Rd the trail begins in open woods and quickly emerges on an embankment that separates a small pond at the mouth of Bennett Run from the main lake. The trail surface is grass growing through coarse cinders and small gravel. Aside from some shrubbery on both sides, you get great views across the lake and the pond. You're likely to see feeding birds, especially ducks, gulls, and herons, on the pond and sailboats on the lake. Some of the best views are half a mile from the road, where a bridge crosses the inlet connecting the pond and the lake. Three quarters of a mile from Fries road the trail passes the parking lot for boat access. Here the trail starts to parallel the road on the causeway, separated from the road only by a drainage ditch. The trail continues across the causeway as grass and cinders. It effectively ends at the fish hatchery at the end of the causeway, a total of 2.6 miles. The rail grade continues toward Linesville, but there doesn't appear to be good trail access in Linesville.

Midway on the causeway you can stop at the spillway to see one of western Pennsylvania's most peculiar tourist attractions, the fish feeding area at the spillway. People feed the fish and ducks so regularly that the fish are jammed in gill-to-gill and the ducks walk on the backs of the fish to compete for the food

Extensions of the ride

At the southern tip of the lake, you can cross the dam to an extensive network of paved and gravel roads between West Lake Rd and the lake. Although these roads are open to traffic, the speed limit is 25 mph. These roads reach rest rooms, picnic areas, the swimming beach, and the park restaurant.

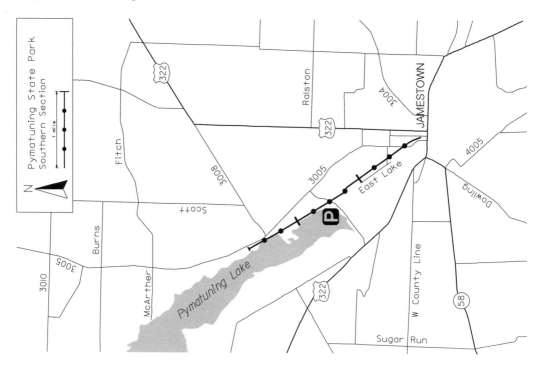

Local history, attractions

At the end of the 19th century, the state of Pennsylvania began looking into ways to reclaim the Pymatuning area swamplands. The Pymatuning Act of 1913 enabled the project, and the state acquired land for the lake in the 1920's. Pymatuning Dam was completed in 1934. The dam's primary purpose is conservation of waters entering Pymatuning Swamp, and it also regulates water flow for the Shenango and Beaver Rivers. As a secondary purpose, it also provides flood control and recreation.

Pymatuning Lake is a vacation destination featuring fishing, sailing, camping, and sightseeing. The Linesville causeway features fish feeding at the spillway, a wildlife museum at the visitor center, and a live fish viewing tank at the PA Fish and Boat Commission visitor center. Nearby Conneaut Outlet Swamp attracts migratory birds.

Access points

Vicinity: Directions begin entering Jamestown from the east on PA58. To reach this point from Pittsburgh, go north on I79, then west one exit on I80, north to Mercer on US19, and northwest on PA58 through Greenville to Jamestown.

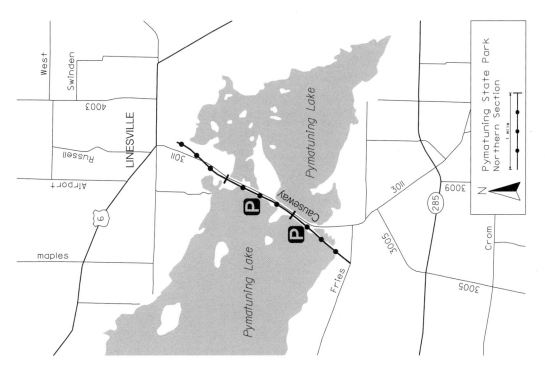

Pymatuning Dam (southern) trailhead: In Jamestown, follow signs for East Side, Pymatuning State Park. These will lead you north (right) on East Lake Rd. In about 2 miles, turn left toward the dam. In 0.3 miles, just after crossing the bridge over the trail, turn right into a large parking lot. To reach the trail from this lot, go back out to the road, cross the road, and look for the moderately steep trail down to the trail; there's one of these on each side of the bridge. This point is near the middle of the trail, so you can go either direction from here. Jamestown is in the direction away from the parking lot.

Pymatuning Causeway (northern) trailhead: In Jamestown, follow signs for East Side, Pymatuning State Park. These will lead you north (right) on East Lake Rd. In about 11 miles, at a "T" intersection, turn left. Look for a parking lot and boat launch on the left just before starting across the causeway. Park here or at the spillway parking area 0.5 mile later. This lot is near the middle of the trail, so you can go either way from here.

Amenities

Rest rooms, water: Various locations in the park

Bike shop, rentals: Bike shop in Linesville

Restaurant, groceries: Park restaurant near picnic groves (south), restaurant on causeway (north). Groceries and food in Jamestown and Linesville.

Camping, simple lodging: Camping and family cabins at several locations in Pymatuning State Park. Reservations required for the cabins. Campsite reservations available.

Swimming, fishing: It's a state park, so you may swim only at official swimming beaches, which are open from Memorial Day to Labor Day and possibly at other times (check with park office). Official beaches are at Linesville, Tuttle Point, and west of Jamestown, all 2-3 miles west of the trail on lightly trafficked roads. Fishing in lake and from shore for walleye, muskellunge, carp, crappies, bass, and many others.

Winter sports: Snowmobiles and cross-country skiing permitted on trail. Ice fishing, ice skating, sledding, ice boating at various locations in park.

Wheelchair access: Gates wider than 36", but trail somewhat rough. Steep access path at trailhead near dam; gain access at a road crossing.

Trail organization

DCNR - Pymatuning State Park
PO Box 425
Jamestown PA 16134
(724) 932-3141
888-PA-PARKS (reservations)
e-mail: pymatuning.sp@a1.dcnr.state.pa.us
web: www.dcnr.state.pa.us/stateparks/parks/pyma.htm

Maps, guides, other references

USGS Topographic Maps: Greenville West, Hartstown, Linesville.

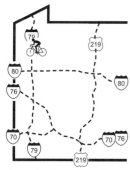

Ernst Bicycle Trail

Along French Ck from Meadville to Watson Run in Crawford County

The Ernst Bicycle Trail offers relative isolation at the edge of Meadville. Following the path of the former Meadville branch of the Bessemer & Lake Erie RR, it runs south for 2 miles on the edge of the French Ck flood plain, then swings west to follow a small tributary. The northern part of the trail is a broad path finished in crushed cinders, with occasional gravel showing through. The western leg is a little rougher and narrower, often going to double-track with grass in the center. The vehicle excluders are vertical posts, with the center post removable to let maintenance vehicles through. At several points, we found the center posts removed, leaving the sockets sticking up a couple of inches in the center of the trail; watch out for these near roads and bridges.

The trail will eventually start near the Park Avenue Plaza on US322 and continue to US19 near Watson Run. For now, however, the 5 miles of developed trail is accessible only from its midpoint on Mercer Pike. This provides out-and-back rides of 5 miles roundtrip in both directions.

Ernst Bicycle Trail	
Location	Meadville to Watson Run in Union Township, Crawford County
Trailheads	Mercer Pike
Length, Surface	5 miles planned, 4 miles complete, crushed cinders
Character	Uncrowded, rural, shady, level
Usage restrictions	No motor vehicles
Amenities	Rest room
Driving time from Pittsburgh	1 hours 45 minutes north

Heading east from the Mercer Pike trailhead toward Meadville, the trail runs for half a mile through woods, then swings left to join the active Conrail track—the former Erie R main line—for a tenth of a mile. The trail soon leaves the railroad through a small cut and enters the rich bottomlands of French Ck for a mile and a quarter. French Ck is one of the most biologically diverse waterways in Pennsylvania, supporting 66 species of fish and 27 species of mollusk. At first the trail is pinned next to the creek by a ridge, but the trail moves away from the creek as you go away from the ridge. To soon I79 looms overhead and you share the trail with traffic noise for half a mile. A few light industrial buildings appear, and you ride past a few farm fields before the trail ends at Van Horne Run. This creek will be bridged in 1999.

If instead you head west from the Mercer Pike trailhead toward Conneaut Lake, you'll pass through marshy woodland for the whole 2.5 miles. The tread here is double-track in cinders and coarse gravel. There's some sign of logging to the south, but the trail is pleasant under a leafy canopy. At 0.6 miles from the trailhead you emerge at a crossing of Mt Pleasant Rd (dirt) followed immediately by the two bridges of I79 overhead and a crossing of Kennedy Hill Rd (paved). Now the trail becomes rather narrower, still double-track on cinders. The woods change to evergreens on the left, and in three-quarters of a mile the developed trail ends at an unbridged creek, 1.5 miles from the trailhead. Don't be surprised if you see deer, turkey, squirrel, hawks, songbirds, or even an eagle or a bear.

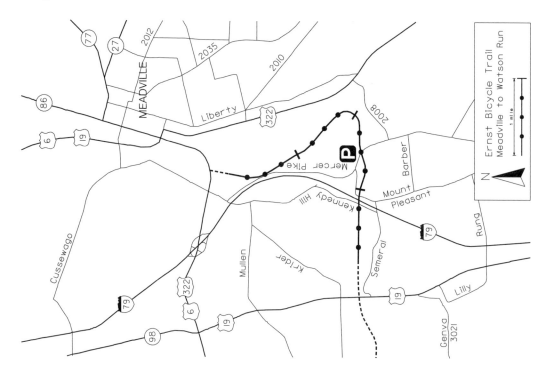

Development plans

Current construction is aimed toward connecting the trail to US322 at the north end and to US19 at the west end. A proposed extension would continue the trail westward from US19 to Conneaut Lake along Conneaut Marsh.

Access points

Vicinity: Directions begin at the junction of I79 and US322. To reach this point from Pittsburgh, go north on I79 and take the US322 exit towards Meadville.

Mercer Pike trailhead: From the intersection of I79 and US322, head east on US322. In about half a mile, at the Sheetz gas station, turn right (south) on Kennedy Hill Rd. In 0.9 mile, just after you pass the Crawford County Humane Society shelter, turn left on Mercer Pike. Follow Mercer Pike for 2.1 miles to the parking area on the right just before the railroad crossing at the bottom of the hill.

Amenities

Rest rooms, water: Chemical toilet at trailhead

Bike shop, rentals: In Meadville

Restaurant, groceries: On US322

Camping, simple lodging: Motels on US322

Swimming, fishing: None

Winter sports: Cross-country skiing

Wheelchair access: Gates near I79 only 34" (east side) and 29" (west side); trail somewhat rough.

Trail organization

French Creek Recreational Trails
c/o Community Health Services
747 Terrace St
Meadville PA 16635
(814) 724-6073
Membership $20/year individual, $30/year family

Maps, guides, other references

USGS Topographic Maps: Geneva.

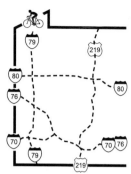

Presque Isle State Park Bikepath

Presque Isle State Park in Erie County

Presque Isle is a 3200-acre, apostrophe-shaped peninsula of glacial sand that juts 7 miles into Lake Erie from the city of Erie. A loop road popular with sightseers extends the length of the peninsula. The State Park recently extended its multipurpose trail from 5.8 to 9.5 miles, mostly as a bike lane along the loop road. The trail forms a loop at the east end of the peninsula, so a trip from the first parking lot around the loop and back will run 12-13 miles. This welcome extension adds variety and versatility to the ride.

The trail begins at the park entrance. The first two miles share the narrow neck of the peninsula with the road and parking lots. Here the trail is often right on the shoreline of the bay, just inches above the water. As the peninsula widens, the trail moves away from the shore, shifting alternately away from the road, then back again. The Park is improving the sight lines on the resulting curves. The pavement is barely two lanes wide, so stay right and exercise caution. The trail can get crowded, especially near the park entrance.

At mile 3.9 the trail crosses to the north side of the main road. This begins the loop portion of the trail. Turn right to ride the loop counterclockwise. The trail remains on the inland side of the road for most of a mile, offering views of the ponds and marsh that form the interior of the peninsula. The trail crosses the road again about half a mile west of Perry's Monument.

At Perry's Monument, 5.7 miles from the park entrance, the trail becomes a designated bike lane 8' wide and follows the road around to the less-protected north shore on the lake. Here woods alternate with beaches that offer the only surf swimming in Pennsylvania. Near Ainsworth Beach (mile 9.3) the bike lane turns left on a side road, then heads off through the woods for 0.3 miles to close the loop (mile 9.6). The trail emerges on the bay side where the outbound trail split. Cross the road to return 3.9 miles to the park entrance.

Development plans

In late 1999, the Park will begin constructing a 3.1-mile extension that will continue along the lake side to the park entrance. This will improve access to the beaches and the views of Lake Erie, and it will provide a 12.6-mile loop.

Local history, attractions

Presque Isle is a geologically unique sand spit of glacial sand. The ponds support a variety of aquatic biological successions. The location is a favorite of migratory birds, with late May and late September the prime seasons. As you move inland you go from sand beaches and wetlands to climax forest within a couple of miles.

This was a strategic location in the War of 1812. Commodore Oliver Hazard Perry's fleet was constructed here between February and June 1813. On September 10, 1813 the US fleet of nine boats engaged six British warships under Captain Robert Barclay in the Battle of Lake Erie. Flying his battle flag, "Don't Give Up the Ship", Perry defeated Barclay and returned to Misery Bay, near the Perry Monument. At the end of the battle he sent his classic message of victory, "We have met the enemy and they are ours." The Flagship Niagara historic site is nearby in Erie.

Presque Isle State Park Bikepath	
Location	Presque Isle State Park, Erie County
Trailheads	Parking lots at intervals along the trail
Length, Surface	9.5 miles open, 12.6 miles planned; paved and bike lane
Character	Busy, state park, mostly shady, flat
Usage restrictions	No motorized vehicles; no horses
Amenities	Rest rooms, water, bike rental, food, lodging
Driving time from Pittsburgh	2 hours 30 minutes north

Extensions of the ride

Within the park, two dead-end roads provide access to fishing piers: West Fisher Dr and Coast Guard Rd. Each is about a mile long and can be used to extend your ride. Coast Guard Rd takes you past Horseshoe Pond, which is dotted with small cottages on pilings in the lake—each one a miniature island.

The Peninsula Drive bike lanes, about 1 mile long with rolling hills, lead from the park entrance toward Erie on the shoulder of PA832. They turn west at Alt PA5 and join the extensive network of bike routes on roads throughout this region. Alternatively, you can turn east on W 6th St and visit the Port of Erie.

Access points

Vicinity: Follow I79 north to its end in Erie (Exit 44B), taking the long curving ramp to the right to join PA5. Go west on PA5 for a mile to PA832, then north (right) on PA832 for 1.2 miles to the park entrance.

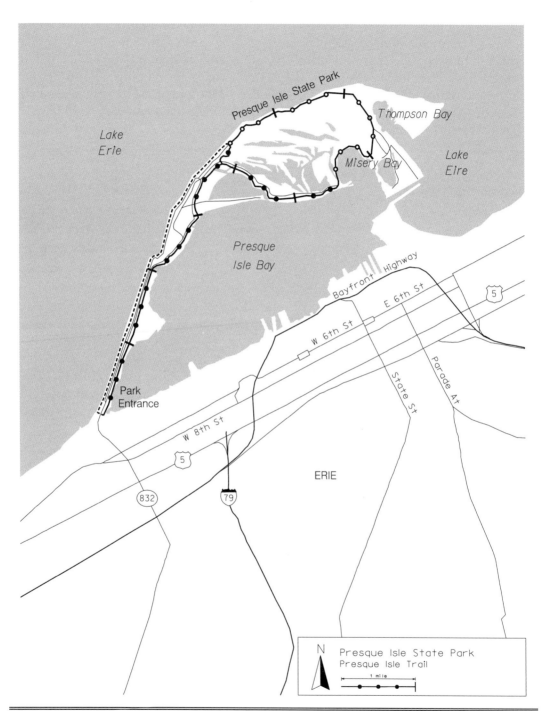

Lake
Erie

Presque Isle State Park

Thompson Bay

Lake
Eire

Misery Bay

Presque
Isle Bay

Bayfront Highway

5

E 6th St

W 6th St

State St

Parade At

Park
Entrance

W 8th St

5

ERIE

832

79

N

Presque Isle State Park
Presque Isle Trail

1 mile

Presque Isle trailheads: Park in lots near the entrance or at any of a variety of other lots along the loop road. You may find the bike path may less busy if you drive to one of the parking areas farther into the park.

Amenities

Rest rooms, water: Comfort stations are located at 14 places along or near the trail.

Bike shop, rentals: Bike rentals are available along PA832 north of PA5, connected by bike lanes to the park.

Restaurant, groceries: Seasonal food and refreshment concessions are located along the trail at Beaches 6, 8, 10, and 11.

Camping, simple lodging: Motels and cottages on PA832 near the park entrance. Other motels and camping in and near Erie.

Swimming, fishing: Swimming only at official beaches, only when lifeguard is on duty. The guarded beaches are open 10 AM to 8 PM from Memorial Day to Labor Day unless posted otherwise. Good fishing. Common catches are perch, coho, smelt, walleye, rainbow trout and bass in Lake Erie, and panfish, perch, bass, muskellunge, walleye, northern pike, crappies, smelt, and coho in Presque Isle Bay. Boating of all kinds.

Winter sports: Cross-country skiing. Ice fishing.

Wheelchair access: Good

Trail organization

DCNR - Presque Isle State Park
PO Box 8510
Erie, PA 16505
(814) 833-7424
e-mail: presqueisle.sp@a1.dcnr.state.pa.us
web: www.dcnr.state.pa.us/stateparks/parks/presqueisle.htm

Maps, guides, other references

Presque Isle State Park brochure

The Western Pennsylvania Conservancy offers a detailed 2-page description of walking trails on the peninsula.

USGS Topographic Maps: Swanville, Erie North.

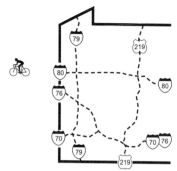

Ohio and Erie Canal Towpath Trail

Along Cuyahoga River in Cuyahoga Valley National Recreation Area

The Cuyahoga River valley has served as a transportation corridor for centuries. At some places along this trail you'll see canal and railroad beside you and modern superhighway overhead. This trail follows the towpath of the Ohio and Erie Canal, which was built between 1825 and 1832 to connect Cleveland, on Lake Erie, with the Ohio River 308 miles away. The route was from Cleveland upstream along the Cuyahoga River to Akron, then down the Tuscarawas River. Until the middle of the 19th century the canal was an economic success. However, like many canals, railroads and floods spelled its end. The final blow for this canal was the flood of 1913.

Parts of the canal and traces of its heritage are now being restored in the corridor from Cleveland to Zoar. Cleveland MetroParks is adding 5.5 miles of the towpath to their Emerald Necklace system as the Ohio & Erie Canal Reservation. The modern-day trail in the Cuyahoga Valley National Recreation Area runs 19.5 miles from Lock 39 in Valley View south to the northern edge of Akron. Mileage markers along the trail are based on historical mileages measured from Lake Erie, so the northern end of the trail is near milepost 11 and the southern end is about half a mile past milepost 30. The modern trail does not follow the towpath exactly, so canal mileposts are not exactly a mile apart on the trail and our intermediate measurements are approximate.

This trail follows the canal towpath from mile 10.75 to mile 30.3, including lock 39 to lock 24. Most of the trail surface is packed crushed stone. In some sections there is a parallel equestrian trail. Where the equestrian trail shares the towpath trail, it is hard surfaced. Other areas can get a little soft when they're wet. Confusingly, the miles are numbered starting from Cleveland, but the locks are numbered starting from Akron (both northbound and southbound). This stretch lies in the Cuyahoga Valley National Recreation Area, an "urban park". As a result, the setting is varied, but never industrial or commercial.

The trail currently starts near Rockside Rd at a trailhead parking lot (mile 10.75). This lot also serves the southern end of the towpath in the Ohio & Erie Canal Reservation of Cleveland's Emerald Necklace. The canal holds water for the first six miles or so in the National Recreation Area, nearly to Station Road Bridge. For the first three and a half miles the canal is squeezed between the river and the road. The road is not intrusive, though, because the towpath is on the river side of the canal. The Canal Visitor Center is in a restored canal-era two-story frame building next to the restored lock at mile 12.5; you can view interpretive exhibits or pick up maps or other information here. To the west, bottomlands separate you from the river; to the east, across the road from the visitor center, is a historic house. Just past mile 13 the trail and canal cross Tinker's Ck on an aqueduct, one of 14 on the entire canal.

At mile 14 the trail passes another lock, this one beside a grist mill. Alexander's Mill, now called Wilson's Mill, was built in 1855 to use water bypassing the lock to power its grinding wheel. It had an interior horizontal turbine rather than the more common overshot wheel. It continued to use water power until 1972, when it was converted to electrical power. Just south of the grist mill, a waste weir provides control over the water level in the canal, both to maintain the working water level and to prevent flooding. The mechanical apparatus is visible and functional; it's not hard to understand how the gates were raised and lowered. In another quarter-mile, the Frazee House appears across the canal. This Federal style house was restored by the National Park Service and serves as a museum of life in the Western Reserve.

Ohio and Erie Canal Towpath Trail	
Location	Along Cuyahoga River in Cuyahoga Valley National Recreation Area, Cuyahoga and Summit Counties OH
Trailheads	Rockside Rd, Canal Visitor Center, Station Rd Bridge, Redlock, Boston, Peninsula, Hunt Farm, Ira, Indian Mound (Bath Rd)
Length, Surface	19.5 miles, mostly packed crushed stone with tar and chips where equestrian trail overlaps
Character	busy; suburban to rural, wooded; shady; flat
Usage restrictions	Horse trail partly overlaps towpath trail; no motorized vehicles; no snowmobiles
Amenities	Rest rooms, water, bike rental, food, lodging, fishing
Driving time from Pittsburgh	2 hours 30 minutes northwest

Just past the Frazee house, the road swings away and the canal, the river, and the railroad all squeeze through a narrow gorge called Piney Narrows that runs to the OH82 bridge. The 2.5-mile section from mile 14.4 to 16.9 is the most isolated and tranquil section of the trail. You're likely to see ducks, geese, deer, and other wildlife here. The end of the Narrows is marked overhead by OH82 and underfoot by the remains of Lock 36 and the feeder dam and canal that supplied water to the lower end of the canal. This is the end of the watered section of the canal. From here south, your imagination will have to put the canal back in its prism.

Just past OH82 (mile 17.1), the historic Station Road Bridge has been restored to connect the trail with the Brecksville Reservation of the Cleveland Metroparks and parking. The bridge is paved in wooden blocks, end-grain up. At mile 18.3 and 18.8, footbridges provide access to the Old Carriage Trail, which meanders for 3.25 miles on the other side of the canal. It also provides a connecting link to the Bike & Hike trail on the plateau at the top of the valley. Bicycles are permitted only on the direct path from the mile 18.8 bridge to the Bike & Hike trail.

The valley around the canal gradually becomes more developed as you go south. Across the river on Highland Rd, for example, is the former Jaite Paper Mill company town. These buildings are now used as National Park Service Headquarters. On the towpath just south of Highland Rd (mile 19.6) you'll see the remains of a corrugated box company; this was the Jaite Mill. A side trail at mile 20.95 takes you to Stanford Farm Youth Hostel and onward to Brandywine Falls. At mile 21.5 the trail reaches Boston Mills Rd. Just across the road an original canal-era building has been restored as a museum; there's a large parking lot and rest room here as well. Between here and mile 22 the trail passes under I271 and I80 far overhead.

Grist mill alongside canal, mile 14

From mile 22.3 to mile 22.6, a boardwalk carries the trail over Stumpy basin. This was originally a turning basin and work area on the canal. The river has reclaimed part of the towpath and turned the basin into a swamp. In any case, this is now a good area for viewing wildlife. At mile 23, the towpath clings to the side of the cliff; here too the river has reclaimed part of the canal. The remains of another feeder canal appear near Lock 30 (mile 23.4). At mile 23.7 you can cross over to the Peninsula parking area or continue on the towpath, crossing the Cuyahoga River on an aqueduct. If you leave the towpath here you can visit the town of Peninsula, the chief source of food or other services in the area. The town, once larger then Cleveland, began as a canal town during the canal's heyday in the mid-19th century. Now it is on the National Register of Historic Places.

Continuing south from Peninsula, the towpath passes Deep Lock quarry, reachable by a side trail, and Deep Lock. Deep Lock is so-called because it has a 17' lift instead of the usual 9'. The Berea Sandstone quarry nearby provided stone for canal structures and was a major source of millstones for the region. The valley here is predominantly rural, with farms and villages dotting the valley. Another visitor center at mile 27 offers information and amenities. At mile 28 the beaver have won out over the canal, and another boardwalk carries the trail over swamp for a tenth of a mile. The Beaver Marsh area was once an auto junkyard; when the cars were removed, it reverted to a natural marsh. From Ira (mile 28.5) the road was constructed between the canal and the river, so close to the canal that parts of the towpath and even of locks 24 and 25 were replaced by roadway. Here the trail is on the west side of the road, not always on the original towpath. Mile 30.5 is the Indian Mound trailhead and the current south end of the trail.

Extensions of the ride

The historic Cuyahoga Valley Scenic Railroad parallels the towpath for the entire length of the trail. Most of the trailheads are also boarding areas for the scenic railroad. It is possible to arrange bike/train options; call (800) 468-4070 for current information.

The northern trailhead, at Rockside, is also the southern terminus of the towpath in the Ohio & Erie Canal Reservation of Cleveland MetroParks.

The Old Carriage Trail offers a 3.25-mile excursion for walkers only.

Part of the Old Carriage Trail can be used to connect with the Bike & Hike Trail on the rim of the valley. At the mile 18.8 bridge that links the towpath to the Old Carriage Road, bikes can start up the hill. The trail emerges at the end of Holzhauer Rd; go north for half a mile to the intersection with the Bike & Hike trail. By following the Bike & Hike trail north, you can also connect with the Bedford Reservation all-purpose trail of Cleveland Metroparks.

At the Station Road Bridge trailhead you're not far from the 4.5 miles of all-purpose trail in Cleveland Metroparks' Brecksville Reservation. Go out Station Rd to Riverview Rd and pick up the all-purpose trail at the end of Chippewa Creek Parkway.

At Deep Lock you can explore the quarry on walking trails (not suitable for bicycles).

Information centers can supply maps for bicycle tours on park roads.

Development plans

Plans call for extending the towpath southward by 2 miles. This extension was not yet accessible in mid-1998.

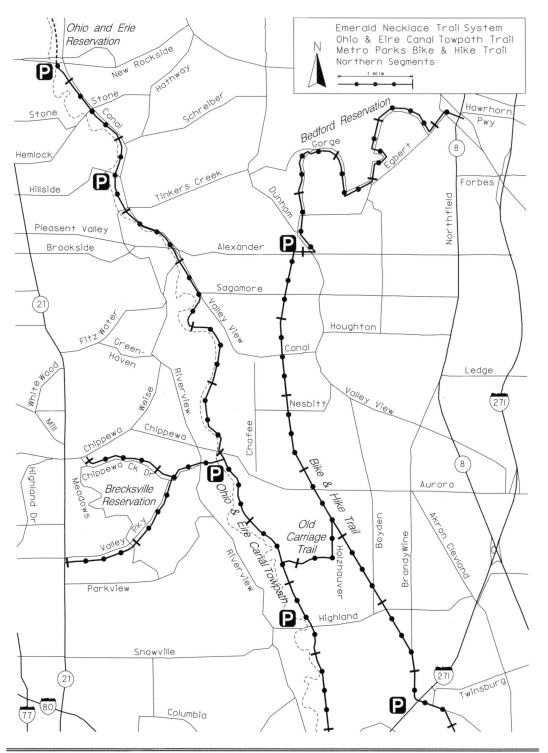

Emerald Necklace Trail System
Ohio & Eire Canal Towpath Trail
Metro Parks Bike & Hike Trail
Northern Segments

N

1 mile

Ohio and Erie Reservation

New Rockside

Hathway

Schreiber

Stone

Stone

Canal

Hemlock

Hillside

Tinkers Creek

Pleasent Valley

Brookside

Alexander

Sagamore

21

Fitz Water

Green-Haven

Valley View

White Wood

Weise

Riverview

Mill

Chippewa

Chippewa

Chafee

Chippewa Ck Dr

Brecksville Reservation

Meadows

Highland Dr

Valley Pky

Parkview

Snowville

21

77

80

Columbia

Bedford Reservation

Gorge

Egbert

Hawrhorn Pwy

8

Forbes

Dunham

Northfield

Houghton

Canal

Nesbitt

Valley View

Ledge

271

Bike & Hike Trail

Old Carriage Trail

Holzhauer

Aurora

8

Boyden

Brandywine

Akron Cleviand

Ohio & Eire Canal Towpath

Riverview

Highland

271

Twinsburg

Access points

Vicinity: Directions begin on Riverview Rd, at Boston Mills Rd. Riverview Rd runs along the Cuyahoga River for much of the length of the National Recreation area. To reach this point from Pittsburgh, go west on the PA Turnpike to the state line and continue 60 miles on the OH Turnpike. Leave the OH Turnpike at Exit 12 (Akron, OH8) headed south on OH8. At the first traffic light, turn right (west) on Boston Mills Rd and go about 5 miles to Riverview Rd, just after you cross the river.

Rockside Rd/Lock 39 (northern) trailhead and Canal Visitor Center: At the intersection of Boston Mills Rd and Riverview Rd, turn right (north) on Riverview Rd and go about 8-9 miles to the intersection with Brookside Rd. Turn right on Brookside and go a short distance to Pleasant Valley Rd. Go east on Pleasant Valley Rd to the Canal Rd exit and then go north. For the Canal Visitor Center, go north about 1.5 miles to Hillside Rd; turn left and cross the canal to the parking lot. For the Lock 39 trailhead, go north about 3 miles to Rockside Rd; turn left and cross the canal. The parking lot will be on the left.

Station Road Bridge trailhead: At the intersection of Boston Mills Rd and Riverview Rd, turn right (north) on Riverview Rd and go about 5 miles to the Station Road Bridge parking area.

Boston trailhead: Instead of following Boston Mills Rd all the way to Riverview Rd, turn left into the trailhead parking lot soon after the road reaches valley level, just past the white building next to the trail and about a block before crossing the river.

Peninsula (Lock 29) trailhead: At the intersection of Boston Mills Rd and Riverview Rd, turn left (south) on Riverview Rd and go about 1.5 miles to OH303 (Streetsboro Rd). Turn left (east) on OH303, cross the Cuyahoga River, and turn left at the traffic light 1 block east of the river. Follow signs to the trailhead.

Hunt Farm visitor center, Ira and Indian Mound (southern) trailheads: At the intersection of Boston Mills Rd and Riverview Rd, turn left (south) on Riverview Rd and go about 5 miles to the Hunt Farm visitor center, 7 miles to the Ira trailhead, or 9 miles to the Indian Mound trailhead.

Amenities

Rest rooms, water: At Canal Visitor Center, Station Road Bridge trailhead, Lock 29 (Peninsula) trailhead, Hunt Farm information center, Indian Mound trailhead.

Bike shop, rental: In Peninsula.

Restaurant, groceries: In Peninsula.

Camping, simple lodging: AYH Stanford Farm Hostel 1.5 miles down a steep rough road from Brandywine Falls or 0.5 miles from Boston on Stanford Rd. The Inn at Brandywine Falls.

Swimming, fishing: Swimming and other water activities at Dover Lake Waterpark (fee). Fishing in Cuyahoga River subject to Ohio fishing regulations.

Winter sports: Cross-country skiing.

Wheelchair access: Fully accessible, though the Old Carriage Road connector is steep.

Trail organization

Cuyahoga Valley National Recreation Area
15610 Vaughn Rd
Brecksville OH 44141
(216) 524-1497
web: www.nps.gov/cuva/ohioerie.htm

Maps, guides, other references

The Ohio & Erie Canal Towpath Trail, trail brochure.

Cuyahoga Valley National Recreation Area, National Park Service brochure.

Ohio & Erie Canal Corridor Guide, Ohio & Erie Canal Corridor Coalition, PO Box 435, Canal Fulton, OH 44614

Trail Guide Handbook, Cuyahoga Valley Trails Council, 1991.

USGS Topographic Maps: Cleveland South, Shaker Heights, Northfield, Peninsula.

Metro Parks Bike and Hike Trail near Boston Ledges

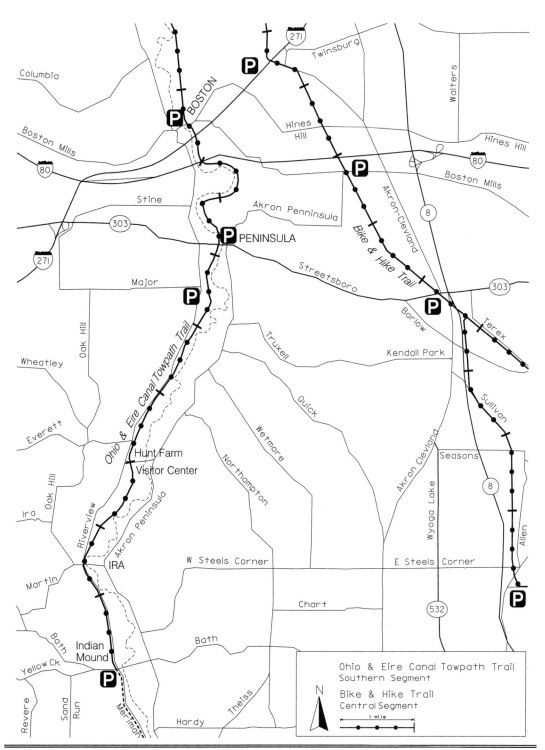

Columbia

Boston Mills

Twinsburg

Walters

Hines Hill

Hines Hill

Boston Mills

BOSTON

Stine

Akron Penninsula

Akron-Cleveland

Bike & Hike Trail

303

271

Major

PENINSULA

Streetsboro

303

Barlow

Terex

Oak Hill

Truxell

Kendall Park

Wheatley

Quick

Sullivan

Ohio & Eire Canal Towpath Trail

Everett

Wetmore

Seasons

Oak Hill

Hunt Farm
Visitor Center

Northampton

Akron Cleveland

8

Ira

Riverview

Akron Peninsula

Wyoga Lake

Allen

Martin

IRA

W Steels Corner

E Steels Corner

Chart

532

Bath

Bath

Indian
Mound

Yellow Ck

Ohio & Eire Canal Towpath Trail
Southern Segment

Revere

Sand Run

Merriman

Bike & Hike Trail
Central Segment

N

1 mile

Hardy

Theiss

Ohio and Erie Canal Towpath Trail   223

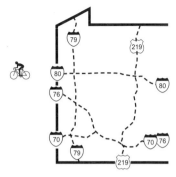

Metro Parks Bike and Hike Trail (to Kent and Stow OH)

From Walton Hills to Kent and Stow, OH

The Bike and Hike Trail follows the routes of a former railroad, the New York Central, and two former interurban trolley lines, the Akron, Bedford, and Cleveland (or "alphabet" railroad) and another branch of the Northern Ohio Traction & Light Company. It features a variety of terrain along the route. The trail runs roughly as a "Y" with the base of the stem near Cleveland and arms reaching to Kent and Stow. The junction, where the arms join the stem, is just east of OH8. Most of the road crossings are at grade level, so watch for traffic.

The northern end of the trail is at Alexander Rd, just west of Dunham Rd, where a parking area serves both the Bike & Hike Trail and the Cleveland Metroparks Bedford all-purpose trail (see Emerald Necklace trail description). The Bike & Hike trail runs south on a crushed limestone surface along the former route of the New York Central Railroad. In half a mile, at Sagamore Rd, a high-voltage electric transmission line joins the trail. For the next 2.5 miles the electric line and the trail coexist, exposed to the summer sun. This segment is somewhat less scenic than the rest of the trail.

At the Highland Rd crossing, the road and power line diverge and the trail becomes more shaded. Mileage signs along the southern part of the trail appear to count from here. At Brandywine Rd, about 5 miles from Alexander Rd, the trail emerges on Brandywine Rd, joining Brandywine Rd for a mile to cross over I271. Just north of the I271 bridge, it passes Brandywine Falls. This area of the Cuyahoga National Recreation area features a 75-foot waterfall and old mill. A boardwalk descends from the parking area to the falls, one of the highest in Ohio. A B&B overlooks the falls from the opposite side. Half a mile past I271, the trail returns to the railroad grade and runs through open woods for 1.5 miles to Boston Mills Rd. After you pass Boston Mills road you'll be reminded that Ohio isn't flat, for the railroad grade runs past fine rock formations in cuts and on fill for most of a mile; this area is called Boston Ledges. After emerging from the cuts and fills, the trail becomes suburban again, crosses under OH303 and over OH8, and arrives at a "Y" junction. Here the trail splits, running separately to Stow and Kent. The north branch, to Stow, runs on the railbed of the Akron, Bedford, and Cleveland, a former interurban trolley line. Early this century, the AB&C merged with other Akron services to form the Northern Ohio Traction & Light Company; service ended in 1932.

At the "Y" junction you can go left for 5.2 miles to Silver Springs Park and Stow or right for 11.4 miles to Munroe Falls and Kent. The sign also says you've come 5.3 miles south from Sagamore Hills and Highland Rd, ignoring the 5 miles to the north of Highland Rd (you're actually 10 miles from the trailhead at Alexander Rd).

If you go left from the "Y" junction toward Stow, the character of the trail remains much the same—open woods, glimpses of suburbia, and occasional road crossings at grade. 4.5 miles from the junction the trail passes the swimming lake at Silver Spring Park, where (for a fee) you can take a dip in the summer. The trail ends at Young Rd 5.2 miles from the junction. At this point you can go right (south) half a mile on the road and pick up the Stow bikeway to the high school on Graham Rd in Stow.

Metro Parks Bike and Hike Trail	
Location	Walton Hills to Kent and Stow, Cuyahoga and Summit Counties OH
Trailheads	Walton Hills, Brandywine Falls, Boston Mills, Streetsboro Rd, Silver Springs Park, Springdale, Munroe Falls
Length, Surface	29 miles, paved and packed crushed stone, 4.3 miles on-street
Character	busy, suburban; sunny; flat in north, hilly in south, with short steep hills at many road crossings
Usage restrictions	No motorized vehicles, no snowmobiles, no horses
Amenities	Rest rooms, water, food, fishing
Driving time from Pittsburgh	2 hours 20 minutes northwest

If you go right from the "Y" junction toward Kent, you'll find a very different kind of riding ahead. At first the trail continues through open woods and rural residences. 2.5 miles past the junction, though, it emerges alongside OH8. The surface changes to asphalt here, but the trail becomes hilly and noisy. After a mile of highway, the trail takes a quick dip for a tenth of a mile through the woods, then emerges at the intersection of busy Hudson Rd and Springdale Rd. There's trailhead parking just ahead on Springdale Rd. The next 3.3 miles are on roads. The intersections are well marked, but there are a few long stretches where it would be nice to have some reassurance that you're still on track. After half a mile on Springdale Rd, the trail turns right into a residential area of Stow reminiscent of an Audubon Society meeting: it rolls up and down Goldfinch, Whippoorwill, Meadowlark, and Hummingbird. Eventually it crosses Graham Rd and enters the upscale community of Silver Lake, still with rolling hills. At Kent Rd (OH59), the trail ducks down a dirt road and enters a park to become a motor-free trail again. Now it follows the Cuyahoga River, winding and still somewhat hilly. This is one of the best sections for wildlife, especially large birds along the river. The Kelsey Bike Trail branches off in this area (it goes south across the river to Waterworks and Galt Parks). After 4.5 miles along the river, the trail finally ends on North River Rd 11.4 miles from the junction near OH8.

Many of the road crossings must once have been on bridges or trestles—at many crossings you must ride up a brisk (though short) hill to the road, then cross and ride right back down again. The former bridges have been converted to fill, and the cost of converting all these crossings back to bridges would be prohibitive.

Extensions of the ride

The northern end of the Bike & Hike Trail connects with the Bedford Reservation segment of the Cleveland Metroparks all-purpose trail. See the Emerald Necklace trail description for information about where this takes you.

Brandywine Falls

You can also connect with the Ohio & Erie Canal towpath via the Old Carriage Trail. When the Bike & Hike Trail crosses Holzhauer Rd (the first road south of OH82), turn south on Holzhauer Rd and follow it half a mile to its end. Bear right on another crushed stone path, which descends steeply to the towpath along part of the Old Carriage Trail. You'll emerge on the towpath just north of milepost 19. Remember that you'll have to get back up somehow.

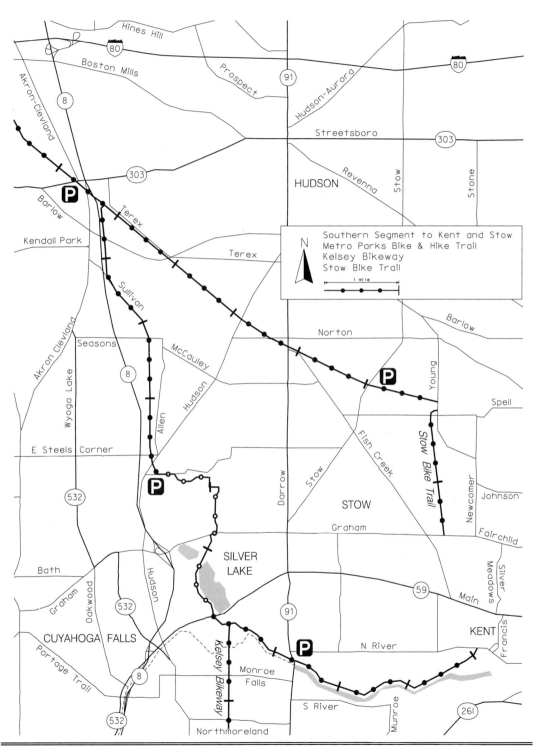

At the end of the Stow branch, you can turn right (south) on Young Rd, go about half a mile on this lightly-traveled road, and turn right (west) onto the Stow Bikeway. This currently runs almost 2 miles to the Stow/Munroe Falls High School on Graham Rd in Stow. Someday it will be extended to connect with the southern branch of the Bike & Hike Trail near Kent, completing the loop.

On the Kent/Munroe Falls branch, shortly after the trail joins the Cuyahoga River at Kent Park, the Kelsey Bikeway branches off to the south. Operated by the City of Cuyahoga Falls, it goes about a mile south across the Cuyahoga River, connecting to Waterworks Park and Galt Park

On the map, this trail looks like a curving "Y", with the open end to the east of southeast. Your immediate reaction is probably that you'd like to close the open end to form a loop—that was certainly ours. The Stow Bike Trail takes you more than halfway across, but it leaves you on busy Graham Rd. Plans call for extending Stow Bike Trail to close the loop. Until then, here's the best route we've found: When the Kent branch of the trail ends at North River Rd, turn right on North River Rd for one block. Turn left on Meadow, go one block, and turn left on Francis St. Follow Francis St for four blocks to Main St and turn left on Main St at the traffic light. There are restaurants here, virtually the only ones we found along the trail. If you're hungry, you can eat Geppetto's barbecued ribs in the shadow of his rib cook-off trophies. After eating or not, as the case may be, go one block west from Francis St on Main St and turn right on Spaulding Dr. Go one block on Spaulding Dr, then turn left on Silver Meadows Blvd and follow it a half-mile or so through a series of apartment buildings until it ends at Fairfield Av. Turn left on Fairfield Av, cross Newcomer Rd, and turn into the Stow/Munroe Falls High School driveway. Pick up the Stow Bike Trail at the far side of the parking lot. Follow the trail 2 miles to Young Rd and turn left. The Bike and Hike trail is almost half a mil later, not far after you cross Call Rd. Total distance on roads is just under 2 miles.

Access points

Vicinity: Directions begin at Exit 12 (Akron, OH8) of the Ohio Turnpike. To reach this point from Pittsburgh, go west on the PA Turnpike to the state line and continue 60 miles on the Ohio Turnpike.

Alexander Rd (northern) trailhead: From Exit 12 of the Ohio Turnpike, go north about 7.5 miles on OH8 to Alexander Rd. Turn left on Alexander Rd and go about 2 miles to trailhead parking, just past Dunham Rd.

Brandywine Falls trailhead: From Exit 12 of the Ohio Turnpike, go north to the first traffic light, Hines Rd. Turn left on Hines Rd and go about half a mile to Cleveland Rd. Turn right, then immediately take the left fork, Brandywine Rd. Follow Brandywine Rd a little over a mile until it crosses over I271. (At this point the trail will be sharing the shoulder of the road.) Just as you come off the bridge, turn left into the Brandywine Falls parking area.

Boston Mills trailhead: From Exit 12 of the Ohio Turnpike, go south on OH8 to the first traffic light. At this light, turn right (west) on Boston Mills Rd and go 1 mile to trailhead parking.

Streetsboro Rd trailhead: From Exit 12 of the Ohio Turnpike, go south on OH8 just over 1.5 miles to Streetsboro Rd (OH303). Turn right (west) on Streetsboro Rd. Follow Streetsboro Rd about half a mile to parking on the right, just after crossing the trail.

Silver Springs Park trailhead: From Exit 12 of the Ohio Turnpike, go south on OH8 just over 2 miles to Barlow Rd. Turn left (east) on Barlow Rd. Follow Barlow Rd about 4 miles to Stow Rd. Turn right (south) on Stow Rd, then turn left to park at Silver Springs Park.

Springdale Rd trailhead: From Exit 12 of the Ohio Turnpike, go south on OH8 just over 2 miles to Barlow Rd. Turn left (east) on Barlow Rd. Follow Barlow Rd just over 2 miles to Darrow Rd. Turn right (south) on Darrow Rd make the first right turn, on Hudson Dr. Go about 3.5 miles on Hudson Dr to Springdale Rd (the trail crosses here). Turn left (east) on Springdale Rd and go half a block to trailhead parking.

Munroe Falls (Darrow Rd) trailhead: From Exit 12 of the Ohio Turnpike, go south on OH8 just over 2 miles to Barlow Rd. Turn left (east) on Barlow Rd. Follow Barlow Rd just over 2 miles to Darrow Rd. Turn right (south) on Darrow Rd and go just over 5 miles to trailhead parking, just before you cross the Cuyahoga River.

Amenities

Rest rooms, water: Rest rooms at Brandywine Falls area of Cuyahoga Valley National Recreation Area, the Darrow Rd trailhead in Munroe Falls, and (in season) the Silver Springs swimming area near the end of the Stow branch. Chemical toilets at the Silver Lake recreation area where the trail leaves the road near Kent Rd and at Silver Springs park. Water at Silver Springs park. The Wagon Wheel lounge 0.1 mile north of the trail junction will fill your water bottle for $.50.

Bike shop, rental: In town of Peninsula in Cuyahoga National Recreation Area.

Restaurant, groceries: Wagon Wheel lounge 0.1 mile north of the trail junction. Several restaurants near the intersection of Francis Rd and Main St 0.7 mile from the end of the Kent branch, along the extension on roads that connects Kent to Stow.

Camping, simple lodging: AYH Stanford Farm Hostel 1.5 miles down a steep rough road from Brandywine Falls or 0.5 miles from Boston on Stanford Rd. The Inn at Brandywine Falls. Budget Inn 0.1 mile north of trail junction near OH8.

Swimming, fishing: Swimming at swim lake, Silver Springs Park (fee); there's an entry from the trail. Swimming at Munroe Falls Metro Park (fee in season); from Munroe Falls parking lot on Darrow Rd, go south 1 mile on Darrow Rd and left (east) 1 more mile on South River Rd to park entrance. Fishing in Cuyahoga River at various points along last 4 miles of Kent Branch. Favorite fishing spots are the section of the trail between Silver Lake Village and Darrow Rd and the area just upstream from the dam and trailhead parking in Munroe Falls. Primary catches are large- and smallmouth bass, northern pike, and channel catfish. The extremely attractive park alongside the trail as it runs through Silver Lake Estates is private.

Winter sports: Cross-country skiing. Naturalists from Metro Parks, Serving Summit County offer organized ski excursions. Snowmobiling is not permitted.

Wheelchair access: In Summit County, several bridges across the rail line were removed and replaced with earthen fill. At these locations, the trail goes up and down steep hills to cross the road at grade. Gates have been widened to 36".

Trail organization

Metro Parks, Serving Summit County Section

Metro Parks, Serving Summit County
975 Treaty Line Rd
Akron OH 44313-5898
(330) 867-5511
web:
www.neo.lrun.com/MetroParks/bh_main.html

Cleveland Metroparks Section

Cleveland Metroparks
4101 Fulton Parkway
Cleveland OH 44144-1923
(216) 351-6300
web: www.clemetparks.com/

Maps, guides, other references

Trail brochure from Metro Parks, Serving Summit County

Trail Guide Handbook, Cuyahoga Valley Trails Council, 1991.

USGS Topographic Maps: Northfield, Peninsula, Hudson.

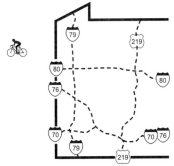

Emerald Necklace

Cleveland Metroparks surrounding Cleveland OH

The Cleveland Metroparks system includes 19,000 acres of public land including 100 miles of parkways and 15 "reservations" for recreational activities. The system is called the Emerald Necklace because the lands nearly encircle Cleveland. Most of the reservations have paved all-purpose trails for cycling, walking, jogging, in-line skating, and other activities.

All of these trails are park trails, running past picnic areas and recreational areas such as ballfields. They also visit nature centers, geologic features, and historic sites. Trail access is not an issue, as the trails are near, often in sight of, roads and parking is abundant near picnic areas.

Seven of the all-purpose trails can be combined with each other and with three nearby trails (Bike & Hike Trail, Old Carriage Trail, and Ohio & Erie Canal Towpath) for longer rides. Two gaps, of 2 and 9 miles, prevent this from being a fully-connected system. However, those gaps are covered by Metroparks parkway roads, which are not too bad for cycling—and the 2-mile gap is scheduled to get a trail.

The portion of the necklace to the west of the 9-mile gap includes 29 miles of all-purpose trail:

Mill Stream Run Reservation all-purpose trail	4.0 miles
West end meets Rocky River Reservation	
Big Creek Reservation all-purpose trail	7.5 miles
South end meets Rocky River Reservation	
Rocky River Reservation all-purpose trail	17.5 miles
East end meets Mill Stream Run Reservation	
Branch near east end meets Big Creek Reservation	

The east end of the Mill Stream Run reservation trail connects to a road, the Royalton-Brecksville Parkway. This leads, in about 9 miles, to the west end of the southern branch of the Brecksville Reservation.

The portion of the necklace to the east of the 9-mile gap includes 24.5 miles of all-purpose trail, 12.6 miles of connections on other trails, and 2 miles of road.

South Chagrin Reservation all-purpose trail	8.5 miles
West end meets Bedford-Chagrin Parkway	
Bedford-Chagrin Parkway (road)	2.0 miles
East end meets South Chagrin Reservation	
West end meets Bedford Reservation	

Bedford Reservation all-purpose trail   5.3 miles
    East end meets Bedford-Chagrin Parkway
    South end meets Bike & Hike trail
Bike & Hike Trail to Holzhauer Rd   4.0 miles
    North end meets Bedford Reservation
    Old Carriage Trail connector on Holzhauer Rd
Old Carriage Trail   0.6 miles
    East end meets Bike & Hike Trail at Holzhauer Rd
    West end meets Ohio & Erie Towpath in NRA at mile 18.8
Ohio & Erie Canal Towpath in MRA from
          Old Carriage Trail to Station Rd Bridge   8.0 miles
    Meets Old Carriage Trail at mile 18.8
    Meets Brecksville Reservation across river from mile 17.1
    Meets Ohio & Erie Canal Reservation at mile 10.75
Ohio & Erie Canal Reservation all-purpose trail   6.2 miles
    South end meets Ohio & Erie Towpath in NRA
Brecksville Reservation all-purpose trail   4.5 miles
    East end meets Ohio & Erie Canal

Emerald Necklace	
Location	An arc around Cleveland, in Cuyahoga County OH
Trailheads	Many picnic areas in the Cleveland Metroparks system
Length, Surface	47 miles of all-purpose trails, paved
Character	crowded; urban; shady; hilly
Usage restrictions	No horses, no motor vehicles
Amenities	Rest rooms, water, bike rental, food, lodging, fishing
Driving time from Pittsburgh (to Bedford)	2 hours 40 minutes northwest

The north end of the Ohio and Erie Reservation, the zoo/Brookside Reservations, and the north end of Big Creek Reservation are not far apart. The geography is tantalizing, but we don't know good routes on the connecting roads.

Cleveland continues to expand their trail system. A bikeway along the Erie lakefront is emerging, and numerous short bike paths dot the city.

Access points

Any good city map of Cleveland will show the locations of the Metroparks reservations. There is no shortage of access to the trails. To get you started, we provide access points to the eastern and western segments.

Vicinity: Directions begin headed west on the Ohio Turnpike approaching Exit 12. To reach this point from Pittsburgh, go west on the PA Turnpike to the state line and continue 60 miles on the Ohio Turnpike.

Alexander Rd trailhead (Bedford Reservation): Take Exit 12 of the Ohio Turnpike headed north on OH8. Go north about 7.5 miles on OH8 to Alexander Rd. Turn left on Alexander Rd and go about 2 miles to trailhead parking, just past Dunham Rd.

Albion Rd trailhead (Mill Stream Run and Rocky River Reservations): Take Exit 10 of the Ohio Turnpike headed south on US42. Go south on US22 about half a mile to Albion Rd. Turn left on Albion Rd and stop at the first convenient picnic area.

Amenities

Rest rooms, water: At many picnic areas throughout the reservations.

Bike shop, rental: Many in and around Cleveland.

Restaurant, groceries: Refreshment stands in the park. Many other stores near the park.

Camping, simple lodging: Nearby in numerous places.

Swimming, fishing: Swimming at Wallace/Baldwin Lake area in Rocky River Reservation (South). Fishing at Shadow Lake in South Chagrin Reservation, Ranger Lake and Bonnie Park picnic area in Mill Stream Run Reservation, the entire length of Rocky River, Wallace/Baldwin Lake area and Lagoon picnic area in Rocky River Reservation (South), Scenic Park marina and Rockcliff Springs in Rocky River Reservation (North).

Winter sports: Cross-country skiing.

Wheelchair access: Trail are asphalt, but some hills are steep.

Trail organization

> Cleveland Metroparks System
> 4101 Fulton Parkway
> Cleveland OH 44144-1923
> (216) 351-6300
> web: www.clemetparks.com/

Maps, guides, other references

A Guide to the Cleveland Metroparks System. Folded map, Cleveland Metroparks System.

Trail Guide Handbook, Cuyahoga Valley Trails Council, 1991.

USGS Topographic Maps: Chagrin Falls, Shaker Heights, Northfield, Broadview Heights, Berea, Lakewood, North Olmstead, Cleveland South.

Trails South & West: The Monongahela Valley and Upper West Virginia

This section presents several trails the Mon Valley of Pennsylvania in nearby parts of West Virginia.

There has not yet been much trail-building in Greene County and the southern part of Washington County in Pennsylvania. The first development will be the Greene County Trail, on the west side of the Monongahela River. Development will start at Greene Cove Marina at the mouth of Ten Mile Ck, near the Greene/Washington County line. The trail will eventually run south to the town of Nemacolin on a former Pennsylvania RR right of way. The first mile should be finished by summer 1999. For current information, call Greene County at (724) 852-5222.

West Virginia has an extensive system of rail-trails, most of which is beyond the scope of this guide. However, a few trails are close enough to western Pennsylvania to be of interest to our readers. Wheeling, for example, is practically in Pennsylvania, Morgantown is reasonably close, and even Clarksburg is within range for a weekend.

We include a trail in Wheeling that may gradually grow along the Ohio River and an extensive trail network that will connect with Pennsylvania's Sheepskin Trail at the PA/WV state line and with the Ohio River near Parkersburg.

Connecting Trails in West Virginia

The Sheepskin Trail will connect the Yough River Trail at Connellsville with Pt Marion on the Monongahela River near the state line. From here a series of trails will run south down the Monongahela River to Fairmont, then upstream on the North Fork River to Clarksburg. From there it will roughly parallel US50 to Parkersburg. Information on these trails us updated on the West Virginia Rails to Trails Council's web site, http://www.wvrtc.org/

The trails in this system are

- *Monongahela River Trail,* called the Gasper Caperton Trail in Morgantown, 52 miles from Pt Marion to Morgantown with one branch along the Mon to near Fairmont and another up Deckers Ck to Masontown. Some trail development has been done in Morgantown, and 3.5 miles from Masontown to Greer are complete. Most of the trail along the Mon is still rough ballast. For information, call the Monongahela River Tails Conservancy at (888) 530-7661.
- *McTrail,* the Marion County Trail, 2.5 miles from Prickett's Fort State Park to Fairmont. It's open but rough. For information, call Marion County at (304) 363-7037.

- *Cross-town connection on roads,* 3-4 miles in Fairmont. The city plans to mark a bike route to bridge the trail gap. We've been unable to find this route, though.
- *West Fork River Trail,* 16 miles from Fairmont to Shinnston. Most of it is finished; see description in this section.
- *Gap between Shinnston and Spelter,* 7-8 miles. We don't know the plans for closing this gap.
- *Harrison County Trail,* 7 miles from Spelter to Clarksburg. The trail parallels the West Fork River. The Spelter end is currently closed for industrial cleanup. In Clarksburg the trail starts on 19th St behind an abandoned glass factory. For information, contact Harrison County at (304) 624-8619.
- *North Bend Rail-Trail,* from Clarksburg to Parkersburg. Most of it is open; see description in this section.

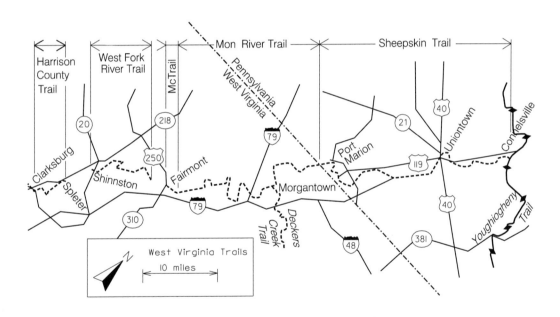

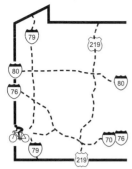

Wheeling Heritage Trails

Along Ohio River from Pike Island Dam to South Wheeling with spur along Wheeling Ck from Wheeling to Elm Grove in Ohio County WV

Located in the northern panhandle of West Virginia, this trail is almost in western Pennsylvania. It's a Y-shaped asphalt-paved trail with a main stem of 8.5 miles along the Ohio River and a partly-finished 4.7-mile spur eastward along Wheeling Ck to Elm Grove. The core of the trail lies in urban Wheeling, and its three legs reach out into the suburbs and beyond. We're used to meeting friendly people along trails, and the folks here were particularly congenial.

The main stem of the trail runs from Pike Island Lock and Dam, 6 miles north of Wheeling, to 48th St in South Wheeling. The setting varies from open countryside to downtown park. All along, you have superb views of the Ohio River. Pike Island Lock and Dam provides an observation deck from which you can watch boat traffic on the Ohio River pass through the locks. The trail starts here in open countryside within sight of WV2. Soon you enter the residential community of Warwood, where many of the yards beside the trail are attractively landscaped. The residential setting gives way to light industry, then the trail returns to parallel WV2. There are a few restaurants here; the one 4.7 miles from Pike Island has tables beside the trail for you to eat pizza and subs. Several side roads cross the trail in this area. In contrast to the practice on many trails, the trail traffic has the right of way; vehicle traffic must stop. There are two 10' hills where the trail jogs from the former railroad grade to highway level to go around obstacles.

You soon enter North Wheeling and cross under I70, 5.7 miles from Pike Island. Immediately afterward, you go under the historic Wheeling Suspension Bridge. This was the longest bridge in the world when it was constructed in 1849. It was also the first bridge across the Ohio River, serving as "gateway to the west"; when it opened, the toll was 10 cents for a man and a horse. It is now a National Civil Engineering Landmark, a National Historic Landmark, and the most significant pre-Civil war engineering structure in the country. The trail here is below street level, with the Ohio River on one side and a stone wall on the other. Frequent stairs and ramps provide access to local businesses. After the suspension bridge, you go through a small park beside the waterfront amphitheater, pass the parking garage at 12th St that serves as the Wheeling trailhead, and enter the park in front of the Civic Center. The downtown section is lighted for night use. Leaving the park, the trail leads between the Civic Center and the Ohio River to the mouth of Wheeling Ck, 6.2 miles from Pike Island. Eventually the spur trail up Wheeling Ck will connect here.

The main trail crosses Wheeling Ck on a wood-decked bridge and continues down the Ohio River through Center Wheeling. At first you're in a former railroad yard with some light industry, then you pass a wastewater treatment plant (a standard feature of rail-trails), and then you go under the I470 bridge. South of I470 you're in South Wheeling. Here the trail is mostly residential—you even ride through far right field of the local ball field. The trail ends in a small parking lot at 48th St, next to Captain Ed's Floating Lounge.

Wheeling Heritage Trails

Location	Along Ohio River and Wheeling Ck in Richland, Triadelphia, and Ritchie Townships and cities of Wheeling and Bethlehem, WV
Trailheads	Elm Grove, Wheeling, Pike Island Dam
Length, Surface	8.5 miles along Ohio River, plus segments of 1.3 and 2.1 miles along Wheeling Ck, paved
Character	busy, urban, sunny, flat
Usage restrictions	No motorized vehicles, no horses
Amenities	Rest rooms, water, bike rental, food, lodging, fishing
Driving time from Pittsburgh	1 hour 20 minutes southwest

The spur trail up Wheeling Ck is known as East Wheeling Trail. It will eventually connect with the main trail at the mouth of Wheeling Ck. For now, there's a 0.65-mile gap on city streets. To connect with the finished parts of the trail, go through the parking lot between the Civic Center and Wheeling Ck, then pick your way through streets and parking lots parallel to Wheeling Ck (directly away from main trail). Try to stay between 16th St (which is pretty busy) and the creek, aiming for the intersection of 17th St and Wood St. The finished trail begins here, running on a bench above limited-access US250. After a block behind residences, the trail crosses a trestle and shares a short gorge with the creek and the highway. Soon the trail swings over the highway and creek and enters a tunnel—one of the few lighted tunnels in this area. You emerge from the tunnel alongside the creek and I70. After 1.3 miles, the trail ends on Rock Point Rd. To reach the other finished segment, follow Rock Point Rd for 0.35 miles, turn right at the "T" with Mt De Chantel Rd, and follow Mt De Chantel Rd for 0.3 miles to its intersection with Washington Av just before it crosses I70. There's not much traffic on this connection except at the last intersection. The finished trail resumes at this intersection (don't cross I70) and continues for 2.1 miles to Elm Grove. The highway crosses to the other side of the creek and exercise stations of a Parcourse appear beside the trail. The highway becomes unobtrusive, though you don't escape its billboards. For now, the trail ends at a dead end street at the edge of Elm Grove.

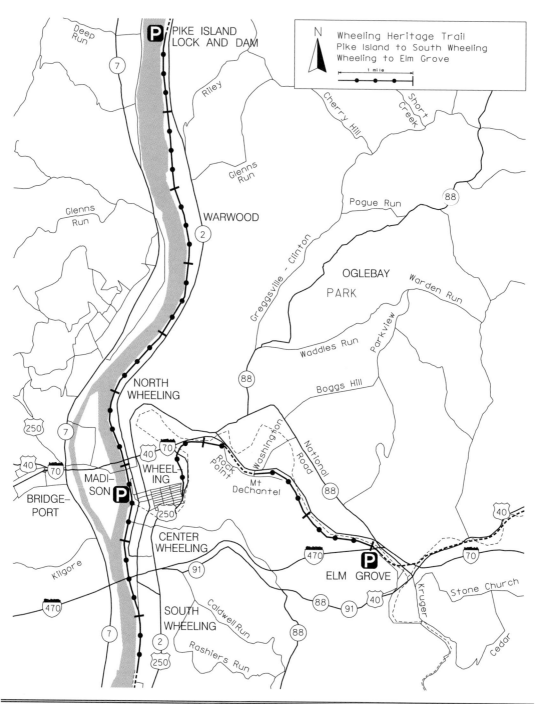

Wheeling Heritage Trail
Pike Island to South Wheeling
Wheeling to Elm Grove

1 mile

Development plans

Active development of this trail continues. Plans call for filling in the gaps on the East Wheeling Trail and possibly extending it 34 miles to Washington PA as the National Pike Trail. On the main stem along the Ohio, the Conrail abandonment includes another 14.2 miles, allowing for eventual extension to connect Benwood (south of Wheeling) to Wellsburg (north of Pike Island).

Access points

Vicinity: Directions begin headed westbound on I70 at the PA-WV state line. To reach this point from Pittsburgh, go south on I79 to Washington PA, then west on I70.

Elm Grove trailhead (eastern): From the PA-WV state line, continue west on I70 for 9 miles to Exit 5, Elm Grove, and exit southbound on WV 88/91. Go about half a mile on WV88/91 to Junior Av, across from the Elm Terrace shopping center. Turn right on Junior Av. Go 0.2 miles on Junior Av and turn left on Lava Av. This is the third left, just as you reach a school. Continue 0.4 miles on Lava Av and cross over to the unfinished trail to park.

Wheeling (downtown): From the PA-WV state line, continue west on I70 for 13.5 miles to Exit 1A, WV2, and exit southbound on WV 2. To make this exit gracefully, be in the right lane as you enter the tunnel and take the exit at the west end of the tunnel. Follow signs to Downtown; you'll be on Main St. Continue to 12th St. Turn right on 12th St. You'll see a parking garage straight ahead. You cross the trail just before entering the parking garage.

Pike Island Lock & Dam trailhead (northern): From the PA-WV state line, continue west on I70 for 13.5 miles to Exit 1A, WV2, and exit northbound on WV 2. To make this exit gracefully, be in the right lane as you enter the tunnel and take the exit at the west end of the tunnel. Follow signs for Pike Island; you'll wind up northbound on WV2. Follow WV2 for 6 miles to Pike Island Lock and Dam; turn left into the parking lot. The dam is easy to spot from a distance because of the overhead structure.

Amenities

Rest rooms, water: Rest rooms and water at the Pike Island Lock and Dam overlook. Chemical toilets at several ball fields within sight of the trail.

Bike shop, rental: Rentals beside the trail in a shop near 11th St and sometimes in the park near 14th St in downtown Wheeling.

Restaurant, groceries: This is, for the most part, an urban trail. There are many places to get food within a few blocks of the trail. The most convenient is Bartoli's, a pizza/sub shop with tables beside the trail 1.3 miles north of the amphitheater in downtown Wheeling.

Camping, simple lodging: Many motels near Wheeling.

Swimming, fishing: Fishing in Ohio River and Wheeling Ck. We have no information on water quality in Wheeling Ck.

Wheelchair access: Trailheads OK. A few short steep grades where trail deviates from railroad grade.

Trail organization

Heritage Trail Partners
Department of Development
1500 Chapline St, Room 305
Wheeling WV 26003
(304) 234-3701

Maps, guides, other references

Trail brochure

Adventure Guide to WV Rail Trails, from the WV Rails-to-Trails Council, PO Box 8889, South Charleston, WV 25303-0889, (304) 722-6558.

USGS Topographic Maps: Tiltonsville OH-WV, Wheeling WV-OH.

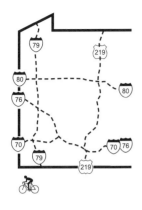

West Fork River Trail

Along West Fork River from Shinnston to Fairmont in Harrison and Marion Counties, WV

In the busy I79-US19 corridor between Fairmont and Clarksburg West Virginia, the trail along the West Fork River provides both moderate isolation and easy access. The river keeps US19 at a distance, and the interstate is over in the next valley. South of Fairmont, US19 runs through a series of small towns. You see these across the river, and occasionally pass through the fringes of the towns that spill across the river.

The surface is packed crushed stone, the trail offers great river views, and the Worthington Park provides recreation and river access. The overall gradient is as gentle as you'd expect from a rail-trail, but local dips provide gentle undulations that will keep you shifting gears. Unfortunately, the gates block the entire finished trail surface, so you must drop onto the rough surface to get through the gate openings. Also, parts of the trail surface in Harrison County near Enterprise have been damaged by horses.

Don't confuse this trail with the other West Fork trail in West Virginia, which runs the West Fork of Glady Fork and Greenbrier River from Glady to Durbin. The other one is much wilder and less developed.

This trail leaves Shinnston in an industrial area, crosses under the US19 bridge, and soon comes out on a bench blasted into the hillside, squeezed between a sheer rock face on the east and the river on the west. After three miles the cliff ends and the trail alternates between woods and the streets of small towns: Enterprise, Hutchinson, Worthington, Everson, and Monongah. Along the way you'll see an old mill at Worthington, not far from the town park. You'll also see remnants of the railroad, most notably small octagonal buildings, and of mining operations.

The finished trail ends at the north end of the 510-ft curved trestle across West Fork River. After the end of the trestle the trail is rougher but still manageable for 0.3 miles. It dead-ends at a chain-link fence. Here you can jog left to a gravel road that soon gets steep. After 0.1 mile it emerges on Edgeway Dr. If you turn left here, you'll reach Country Club Rd in 0.3 mile.

Extensions of the ride

There is supposed to be a 3.6-mile marked road route connecting the Fairmont end of this trail with the south end of a trail that leads north to Pricketts Fort State Park. However, we can't find all the markings, and the markings we can find put us on a route with hills and traffic.

Development plans

Plans call for this to be a segment of a trail system that connects the Youghiogheny River Trail in Pennsylvania with Morgantown, Clarksburg, and Parkersburg WV. This system will incorporate the existing McTrail, Harrison County, and North Bend trails plus the Caperton Trail now under development and connections between these.

West Fork River Trail

Location	Fairmont and Grant Township, Harrison County and Northern Township, Marion County
Trailheads	Shinnston, Worthington, Monongah, Norway, Fairmont
Length, Surface	16 miles planned, 13.3 miles complete, packed crushed stone
Character	Uncrowded, rural, sunny and shady, level
Usage restrictions	No motorized vehicles; horses stay beside the trail, off finished surface
Amenities	Rest rooms, water, bike rental, food
Driving time from Pittsburgh	1 hours 50 minutes south

Access points

Vicinity: Directions begin headed south on I79 to Fairmont WV. To reach this point from Pittsburgh, go south on I79 into West Virginia.

Shinnston trailhead: Leave I79 at Exit 125 westbound. Go about a quarter-mile and turn left on Saltwell Rd (WV131). Follow Saltwell Rd about 7 miles to US19 in Shinnston. Turn left and follow US19 about 6 blocks. Turn left just past the yellow brick Catholic church and just before US19 swings left and climbs to cross the river. The trailhead is near the river under the US19 bridge.

Monongah trailhead: Leave I79 at Exit 137 headed north on WV310. Follow WV310 for 1.8 miles. Just after crossing the Monongahela River, turn south (left) on US250. Follow US250 for 1 mile and turn right on Country Club Rd. Follow Country Club Rd for 1.0 mile and turn south (left) on US19 at the Country Club Motel. Follow US19 for 3.4 miles and turn left just before Monongah Middle School. This isn't well marked, but US19 makes a sharp right just past your turn. Go down the hill for 0.1 mile and turn left at the stop sign. Cross the West Fork River 0.2 miles later. Parking is on the left of the road just past the trail.

Norway trailhead: Leave I79 at Exit 137 headed north on WV310. Follow WV310 for 1.8 miles. Just after crossing the Monongahela River, turn south (left) on US250. Follow US250 for 1.1 mile and turn right just after crossing the West Fork River, following signs to Mary Lou Retton Park. Park there, and ride down the hill on the road for 0.8

miles. Small signs for "Rail Trail Link" give you occasional hints. There's essentially no parking at the trailhead.

Fairmont (north) trailhead: Leave I79 at Exit 137 headed north on WV310. Follow WV310 for 1.8 miles. Just after crossing the Monongahela River, turn south (left) on US250. Follow US250 for 1 mile and turn right on Country Club Rd. Follow Country Club Rd for 0.9 miles to the shopping center for Shop-and-Save, Big Lots, and 84 Lumber on the left side of the road. Find inoffensive parking. Leave the shopping center on Edgeway Dr, to the right of the drive-through bank as you face the shopping center from the road. Follow Edgeway Dr for 0.3 mile, looking for a gate on the right. Go around the gate and down a steep gravel path for 0.1 mile. At the bottom of the hill, jog left to pick up the trail where it dead-ends at a chain link fence.

Amenities

Rest rooms, water: At Mary Lou Retton Park and Worthington Park, in season

Bike shop, rentals: Along trail in Monongah and in Fairmont

Restaurant, groceries: Along trail at Monongah, in Fairmont and Shinnston

Camping, simple lodging: Motels in Fairmont

Swimming, fishing: Fishing access and beach at Worthington Park

Winter sports: Cross-country skiing.

Wheelchair access: Wide gates, but trail surface does not extend through gates. Trail has dips and rises.

Trail organization

Marion County Parks and Recreation Commission
PO Box 1258
316 Monroe St
Fairmont WV 26554
(304) 363-7037
mcparc@access.mountain.net

Maps, guides, other references

USGS Topographic Maps: Shinnston, Fairmont West.

North Bend Rail-Trail

Parallel to US50 in Harrison, Doddridge, Ritchie, and Wood Counties, WV

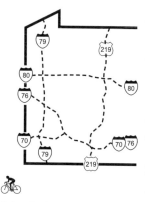

West Virginia is well known for its rugged terrain. The great thing about this trail is that you can ride for 60 miles in West Virginia, going *through* the mountains instead of *over* them! Ten tunnels and over two dozen bridges carry you on gentle grades alternately above the creeks and through the hills. Three more abandoned tunnels await exploration beside the trail, and deep cuts mark places where former tunnels were "daylighted". The trail offers considerable variety in terrain, in scenery, and—unfortunately—in trail surface. The trail is often remote and rough. Except near towns, you won't encounter very many other people. This is part of the trail's attraction—but if you plan to ride long distances, be ready to be self-sufficient.

Built by the Northwestern Virginia Railroad between 1853 and 1857 and later incorporated in the Baltimore and Ohio Railroad, the line served as the main line between Baltimore and St Louis.

The trail is planned to start at Wilsonburg, but the trail currently starts about a mile east of Wolf Summit. The trail is rough but passable to Wolf Summit, which is the easternmost public access and the point from which trail mileage is measured. Westward from Wolf Summit, the trail is finished in packed crushed stone for 7.3 miles to just west of Salem. The first three of these miles are wooded but in the shadow of US50. The trail's first tunnel, Tunnel #2 (mile 3.0), marks a change to more development, and the trail runs through the small towns of Bristol (mile 4), Salem (mile 5.4), and Industrial (8.1). The largest town is Salem, with its beautifully restored railroad depot. Salem is also the best place on the eastern third of the trail to find food. In Industrial, the finished surface ends at mile 7.3, and the trail surface gets rough.

From mile 7.3 to mile 15.5 the large ballast has been removed, but the trail has seen little other development. The surface is variable, but mostly coarse gravel. Fortunately, paved Long Run Rd roughly parallels the trail from mile 7.3 to 13.6. There isn't much traffic on this road, and the few drivers are careful and courteous to bicyclists. The railroad here is on the side of the hill, passing through it via Tunnel #4 at mile 13.4. The road is generally lower than the trail and closer to the creek, running past farms and homes.

The second finished section starts 2 miles east (mile 15.5) of Smithburg. In Smithburg you can inspect the restored Smithton Depot at Spencer Park (mile 17.4). The finished trail continues through woods with several crossings of Middle Island Ck to the town of West Union (mile 20.3). Here the surface reverts to coarse gravel and heads for 2297-

foot Tunnel #6, the longest and still the wettest of the tunnels on this trail (mile 22.1). You will definitely want a light for this one. After the tunnel the trail emerges to pass through farmland and the small towns of Central Station (mile 23.5), Greenwood (mile 27.8), and Tollgate (mile 29.4). The surface remains rough to Tunnel #7 (mile 32.0).

Good surface resumes near the west end of Tunnel #7 and carries you into Pennsboro (mile 32.9), where the old B&O Depot is being restored. Soon after leaving Pennsboro, Tunnel #8 (mile 33.8) takes you to a more developed area. If you're lucky, you'll be able to peek in at the artisans blowing glass marbles at a glass factory a bit east of Ellenboro. Ellenboro (mile 37.5) features a glass outlet and a modern bridge carrying the trail across WV16. You can find food within sight of the trail in both Pennsboro and Ellenboro. The trail soon leaves the small towns and becomes quite remote, with a few farms punctuating the woods. It passes through three dry tunnels (#10, #12, #13) and reaches a side trail to North Bend State Park (mile 42.9). Takes special note of the first of these tunnels (#10, at mile 39.8). Unlike the others, which are lined with brick, Tunnel #10 is blasted from solid rock and unlined.

North Bend Rail-Trail	
Location	Wolf Summit to Happy Valley in Harrison, Doddridge, Ritchie, and Wood Counties WV
Trailheads	Wolf Summit, Salem, Smithburg, Pennsboro, Ellenboro, North Bend State Park, Cairo, Petroleum, Walker
Length, Surface	70.1 miles planned, 60.1 miles open; surface varies from packed crushed limestone to heavy ballast
Character	Uncrowded, rural, sunny and shady, level
Usage restrictions	No motorized vehicles
Amenities	Bike rental, food, lodging
Driving time from Pittsburgh	2 hours south

After the side trail to the park, civilization gradually returns, with more farms and towns. After Cornwallis (mile 43.5), which is just a crossroad, the trail weaves back and forth across the N Fork Hughes River to the town of Cairo (mile 45.1) with its bike shop, restaurant, and a few other shops. About a mile west of Cairo the finished trail surface ends again, about half a mile before Tunnel #19 (mile 49.2). West of this tunnel, the trail plays tag with Goose Ck, crossing it 9 times in 2.5 miles. You'll be so busy crossing Goose Ck that you might miss the hamlet of Petroleum (mile 53.2). A mile and a half after parting company with Goose Ck, the trail goes through Tunnel #21 (mile 57.0), the second-longest on the trail at 1840'.

Good trail surface resumes after Tunnel #21 and continues to Walker (mile 60.1), which was the end of the trail until 1998. The trail bed from Walker to Happy Valley (mile

70.1) was under construction when 1998 flooding caused considerable damage west of Cairo. The trail should be open again in 1999, but it would be a good idea to check.

Development plans

Flooding in early summer of 1998 caused serious damage to the western end of the trail. At the end of 1998, the western end of the trail, about 5 miles in Wood County, was still closed pending repairs. In other areas, land slips are marked with orange mesh fencing and some sections of finished trail have been eroded, leaving the surface rough again.

In 1996, the state acquired an additional 11 miles of railbed west of Walker. This will allow the trail to extend nearly to I77 near Parkersburg. When this section is developed, the west end of the trail will be much more accessible.

North Bend Trail features ten tunnels

Access points

Vicinity: Directions begin in Clarksburg WV at the intersection of I79 and US50. To reach this point from Pittsburgh, go south on I79.

Wolf Summit (eastern) trailhead: From the intersection of I79 and US50, go 9.6 miles west on US50. Turn north (right) on Wolf Summit Rd. Follow Wolf Summit Rd for 0.4 miles until it crosses the trail. Just after crossing the trail, turn right and go another 0.1 mile to park at the end of the finished section. Alternatively, just after crossing the trail, turn sharp left and go 0.1 mile to park just past the church (this is probably not a good choice on Sunday mornings).

Salem trailhead: From the intersection of I79 and US50, go 13.7 miles west on US50. Take the exit marked "Downtown Salem" and follow the road 1.5 miles. You should see the renovated railroad depot on your left. Unfortunately, the parking at the depot is all reserved for permit holders and there don't seem to be any good parking alternatives.

Smithburg trailhead: From the intersection of I79 and US50, go 24.9 miles west on US50 and take the exit for Smithburg. Turn right at the bottom of the ramp. You'll almost immediately cross under US50; this is the edge of Smithburg. Park at the restored depot a quarter-mile ahead on the left.

Pennsboro trailhead: From the intersection of I79 and US50, go 39 miles west on US50 and take the Pennsboro exit from US50. In 0.4 miles, turn left at the stop sign. Follow WV74 by turning right, then left, then right. Trail parking is just before crossing the trail at a railroad depot being restored, 0.9 mile from the stop sign.

Ellenboro trailhead: From the intersection of I79 and US50, go about 45 miles west on US50 to WV16. Go north on WV16. The trail is on the small bridge that crosses the road at the bottom of the hill. Turn right just after this bridge for trailhead parking.

North Bend State Park trailhead: From the intersection of I79 and US50, go about 45 miles west on US50 to WV16. Go south on WV16 for nearly 5 miles to Harrisville. In Harrisville, go straight on CR5 when WV16 and WV31 turn off. Follow CR5 for about 3 miles into the park, then follow signs in the park to descend as far as you can to the picnic area closest to the connecting trail.

Cairo trailhead: From the intersection of I79 and US50, go about 55 miles west on US50 to WV31. Go south on WV31 for a little more than 4 miles. The trail runs through the center of town, and there's plenty of parking in front of the bike shop.

Amenities

Rest rooms, water: None for trail proper. Facilities in North Bend State Park and Salem RR Depot (if it's open).

Bike shop, rentals: In Clarksburg, Salem, Ellenboro, Cairo, Parkersburg

Restaurant, groceries: In Clarksburg, Salem, West Union, Pennsboro, Harrisville, Ellenboro, Cairo, Parkersburg

Camping, simple lodging: In North Bend State Park

Swimming, fishing: None

Winter sports: Cross-country skiing

Wheelchair access: Some narrow (e.g., 35") gates. Trail often gravel or ballast. Even where trail is finished, gates block finished surface, forcing you to skirt the end of the gate on rough surface

Trail organization

North Bend Rail-Trail
Route 1, Box 220
Cairo WV 26337
(304) 643-2931
web:

North Bend Rails to Trails Foundation
PO Box 206
Cairo WV 26337
(800) 899-NBRT

www.wvweb.com/www/travel_recreation/state_parks/north_bend_rail/north_bend_rail.html

Maps, guides, other references

USGS Topographic Maps: Wolf Summit, Salem, Smithburg, West Union, Pennsboro, Ellenboro, Harrisville, Cario, Petroleum, Kanawha, South Parkersburg.

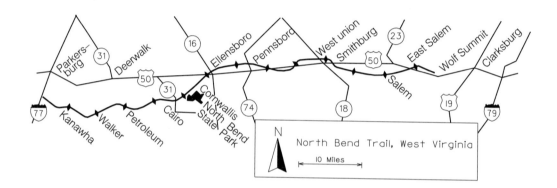

Rails-to-Trails Conservancy

Most of the trails described here started life as railroads. As the US rail system has shrunk, many of the abandoned rights-of-way are gaining new life as recreational trails. A national nonprofit organization, the Rails-to-Trails Conservancy, coordinates these conversion efforts. The 14-year-old RTC has over 62,000 members nationally, 7,000 in Pennsylvania. Support for trail development includes

- Notifying trail advocates and local governments of upcoming abandonments
- Assisting public and private groups with legal details about trail acquisition
- Providing technical help to private citizens and trail developers
- Publicizing rail-to-trail issues throughout the country

In Pennsylvania, over 79 rail-trails are open, under active development, or in some stage of planning. 26 of those are represented in this guide. To add your support to this organization, contact either the state chapter or the national office. They do take Mastercard and Visa.

PA Chapter, Rails-to-Trails Conservancy
105 Locust St
Harrisburg PA 17101
(717) 238-1717

Rails-to-Trails Conservancy
1400 16th St NW, Suite 300
Washington DC 20036
(202) 797-5400

Annual membership: $18 individual, $25 family, $50 organization, $100 benefactor

About this Guidebook

We created this guidebook to support development of the trail systems. First, by making more people aware of the trails, we help to build the community of users. Second, we will contribute part of the proceeds from sales to trail development, and we will provide discounted copies of the book to trail councils for their use in fund-raising.

For additional copies of this guidebook, check with your favorite trail council, local bicycle shop, outfitter, or bookstore. If they don't have any, ask them to order some. If you'd rather order directly from us, send a check for $14.97 per copy (that's $12.95 + $.90 tax + $1.13 shipping and handling) with your name and address to

Shaw-Weil Associates
414 South Craig St, #307
Pittsburgh PA 15213

Ask for *FreeWheeling Easy in Western Pennsylvania*. Sorry—no cash, credit cards, or COD. You can also let us know if you want to be notified when the next edition is published.

Maps

Trailhead Locations

Pelipetz
40° 17' 08.67"N
80° 05' 57.68"W 46

Peninsula
41° 14' 32.97"N
81° 33' 14.58"W 221

Pennsboro
39° 17' 08.31"N
80° 58' 09.38"W 247

Petroleum Centre
41° 31' 00.94"N
79° 40' 54.87"W 160

Pike Island Lock & Dam
40° 08' 59.51"N
80° 42' 03.13"W 239

Piney Fork
40° 17' 03.30"N
79° 59' 16.65"W 50

Pittsburgh 40th Street
40° 28' 15.49"N
79° 57' 54.02"W 54

Pittsburgh Downtown
40° 26' 08.36"N
79° 59' 49.80"W 26

Pittsburgh Southside
40° 25' 54.96"N
79° 58' 23.67"W 20

Presque Isle
42° 07' 47.97"N
80° 08' 33.45"W 215

Pymatuning Causeway
41° 37' 09.21"N
80° 27' 10.13"W 207

Pymatuning Dam
41° 30' 14.24"N
80° 27' 18.70"W 207

Quicksilver
40° 23' 39.49"N
80° 17' 03.96"W 38

Ramcat Hollow
39° 49' 35.81"N
79° 22' 45.09"W 80

Rexis
40° 29' 05.70"N
78° 55' 25.15"W 128

Ridgway
41° 25' 08.70"N
78° 44' 06.14"W 184

Riverview Avenue
40° 28' 58.11"N
80° 01' 06.43"W 55

Rockside Road/Lock 39
41° 23' 34.85"N
81° 37' 47.88"W 221

Rockwood
39° 54' 42.80"N
79° 09' 40.32"W 91

Rosston
40° 44' 59.28"N
79° 33' 13.62"W 145

Salem
39° 16' 59.40"N
80° 33' 33.26"W 246

Sarver
40° 43' 45.31"N
79° 44' 50.01"W 155

Schenley
40° 41' 18.73"N
79° 39' 40.09"W 143

Shinnston
39° 23' 50.03"N
80° 18' 06.45"W 242

Silver Springs Park
41° 11' 40.69"N
81° 25' 01.95"W 229

Smithburg
39° 17' 20.96"N
80° 44' 02.14"W 247

Smithton
40° 09' 25.36"N
79° 44' 46.47"W 70

Springdale Road
41° 10' 34.60"N
81° 28' 30.67"W 229

Station Road Bridge
41° 19' 05.17"N
81° 35' 27.22"W 221

Streetsboro Road
41° 13' 56.39"N
81° 29' 47.13"W 229

Struthers
41° 02' 57.42"N
80° 33' 54.01"W 202

Sutersville
40° 14' 28.29"N
79° 48' 23.12"W 70

Swinburne
40° 25' 33.99"N
79° 57' 09.21"W 26

Tidioute
41° 40' 46.66"N
79° 25' 18.05"W 173

Triphammer Road
40° 16' 54.83"N
79° 59' 10.12"W 51

Twin Rocks
40° 29' 23.75"N
78° 51' 43.13"W 128

Vintondale
40° 28' 53.66"N
78° 55' 07.37"W 128

Warren
41° 51' 15.60"N
79° 08' 46.32"W 188

Wehrum
40° 28' 16.48"N
78° 57' 00.98"W 126

West Newton
40° 12' 38.95"N
79° 46' 15.42"W 70

Wheeling
40° 04' 07.48"N
80° 43' 29.78"W 239

White Mill
40° 31' 40.04"N
78° 53' 17.70"W 128

Whitsett
40° 06' 25.30"N
79° 45' 23.72"W 70

Williamsburg
40° 27' 48.72"N
78° 11' 55.95"W 132

Williamsport
39° 35' 57.79"N
77° 49' 33.98"W 96

Wolf Summit
39° 16' 53.78"N
80° 27' 40.80"W 246

Yatesboro
40° 47' 53.28"N
79° 20' 04.89"W 150

Index of Places

Roy Weil and Mary Shaw have canoed, biked, hiked, and XC-skied in Western Pennsylvania for the past 30 years. Many people have introduced us to trails, and we return the favor by writing guidebooks.

Logbook

Date	Distance	Time	Weather	Companions	Comments

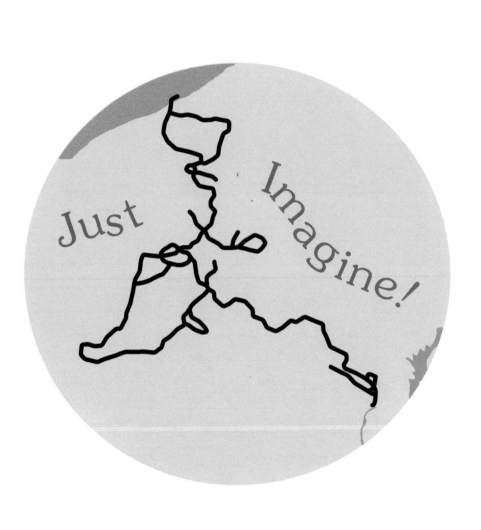